MODERN NOVELISTS

General Editor: Norman Page

MODERN NOVELISTS

Published titles

MARGARET ATWOOD   Coral Ann Howells
SAUL BELLOW   Peter Hyland
ALBERT CAMUS   Philip Thody
FYODOR DOSTOEVSKY   Peter Conradi
GEORGE ELIOT   Alan W. Bellringer
WILLIAM FAULKNER   David Dowling
GUSTAVE FLAUBERT   David Roe
E. M. FORSTER   Norman Page
ANDRÉ GIDE   David Walker
WILLIAM GOLDING   James Gindin
GRAHAM GREENE   Neil McEwan
ERNEST HEMINGWAY   Peter Messent
CHRISTOPHER ISHERWOOD   Stephen Wade
HENRY JAMES   Alan W. Bellringer
JAMES JOYCE   Richard Brown
FRANZ KAFKA   Ronald Speirs and Beatrice Sandberg
D. H. LAWRENCE   G. M. Hyde
ROSAMOND LEHMANN   Judy Simons
DORIS LESSING   Ruth Whittaker
MALCOLM LOWRY   Tony Bareham
NORMAN MAILER   Michael K. Glenday
THOMAS MANN   Martin Travers
GABRIEL GARCÍA MÁRQUEZ   Michael Bell
TONI MORRISON   Linden Peach
IRIS MURDOCH   Hilda D. Spear
VLADIMIR NABOKOV   David Rampton
V. S. NAIPAUL   Bruce King
GEORGE ORWELL   Valerie Meyers
ANTHONY POWELL   Neil McEwan
MARCEL PROUST   Philip Thody
BARBARA PYM   Michael Costell
JEAN-PAUL SARTRE   Philip Thody
MURIEL SPARK   Norman Page
MARK TWAIN   Peter Messent
JOHN UPDIKE   Judie Newman
EVELYN WAUGH   Jacqueline McDonnell
H. G. WELLS   Michael Draper
PATRICK WHITE   Mark Williams
VIRGINIA WOOLF   Edward Bishop
SIX WOMEN NOVELISTS   Merryn Williams

Forthcoming titles

IVY COMPTON-BURNETT   Janet Godden
JOSEPH CONRAD   Owen Knowles
JOHN FOWLES   James Acheson
SALMAN RUSHDIE   D. C. R. A. Goonetilleke
ALICE WALKER   Maria Lauret

MODERN NOVELISTS

FRANZ KAFKA

Ronald Speirs and Beatrice Sandberg

St. Martin's Press
New York

FRANZ KAFKA

St. Martin's Press, Scholarly and Reference Division,
175 Fifth Avenue, New York, N.Y. 10010

First published in the United States of America in 1997

This book is printed on paper suitable for recycling and
made from fully managed and sustained forest sources.

Printed in Hong Kong

ISBN 0–312–17377–6

Library of Congress Cataloging-in-Publication Data
Speirs, Ronald
Franz Kafka / Ronald Speirs and Beatrice Sandberg.
p.   cm. — (Modern novelists series)
Includes bibliographical references and index.
ISBN 0–312–17377–6 (cloth)
1. Kafka, Franz, 1883–1924—Criticism and interpretation.
I. Sandberg, Beatrice, 1942–   . II. Title.   III. Series.
PT2621.A26Z878 1997
833'.912—dc21   96–6514
                                                        CIP

Contents

General Editor's Preface

The death of the novel has often been announced, and part of the secret of its obstinate vitality must be its capacity for growth, adaptation, self-renewal and self-transformation: like some vigorous organism in a speeded-up Darwinian ecosystem, it adapts itself quickly to a changing world. War and revolution, economic crisis and social change, radically new ideologies such as Marxism and Freudianism, have made this century unprecedented in human history in the speed and extent of change, but the novel has shown an extraordinary capacity to find new forms and techniques and to accommodate new ideas and conceptions of human nature and human experience, and even to take up new positions on the nature of fiction itself.

In the generations immediately preceding and following 1914, the novel underwent a radical redefinition of its nature and possibilities. The present series of monographs is devoted to the novelists who created the modern novel and to those who, in their turn, either continued and extended, or reacted against and rejected, the traditions established during that period of intense exploration and experiment. It includes a number of those who lived and wrote in the nineteenth century but whose innovative contribution to the art of fiction makes it impossible to ignore them in any account of the origins of the modern novel; it also includes the so-called 'modernists' and those who in the mid- and late twentieth century have emerged as outstanding practitioners of this genre. The scope is, inevitably, international; not only, in the migratory and exile-haunted world of our century, do writers refuse to heed national frontiers – 'English' literature lays laim to Conrad the Pole, Henry James the American, and Joyce the Irishman – but geniuses such as Flaubert, Dostoevsky and Kafka have had an influence on the fiction of many nations.

Each volume in the series is intended to provide an introduction to the fiction of the writer concerned, both for those approaching him or her for the first time and for those who are already familiar with some parts of the achievement in question and now wish to place it in the context of the total *œuvre*. Although essential information relating to the writer's life and times is given, usually in an opening chapter, the approach is primarily critical and the emphasis is not upon 'background' or generalisations but open close examination of important texts. Where an author is notably prolific, major texts have been made to convey, more summarily, a sense of the nature and quality of the author's work as a whole. Those who want to read further will find suggestions in the select bibliography included in each volume. Many novelists are, of course, not only novelists but also poets, essayists, biographers, dramatists, travel writers and so forth; many have practised shorter forms of fiction; and many have written letters or kept diaries that constitute a significant part of their literary output. A brief study cannot hope to deal with all these in detail, but where the shorter fiction and the non-fictional writings, public and private, have an important relationship to the novels, some space has been devoted to them.

NORMAN PAGE

Acknowledgements

The authors would like to express their thanks for the generous support given by the British Academy, the German Academic Exchange Service, the Norwegian Research Council, and the Meltzer Foundation.

Note on the Text

This book is addressed mainly to two groups of readers: students of German and general readers with an interest in modern literature. For the sake of the latter all quotations have been translated into English, while the Bibliography gives preference to items in English. The Notes and the more specialized German items in the Bibliography are intended to help students with a knowledge of German who wish to explore matters in greater detail and complexity. The quotations of Kafka's works are taken from the new critical edition in paperback (Fischer Verlag), the one most likely to be read by students of German.

1

A Writer's Life

Franz Kafka was born on 3 July 1883 in a house backing on to the old Jewish ghetto in Prague and was buried in the new Jewish graveyard there after his death from tuberculosis on 3 June 1924.[1] He was the oldest child and only surviving son in the family, two younger brothers having died in infancy. Of his three sisters he felt closest to the youngest, Ottla.

His father Hermann Kafka and mother Julie (née Löwy) had both moved to Prague from elsewhere – she from the small town of Podiebrad and he from Wossek in the Czech-speaking countryside of Bohemia – and had opened a haberdashery and accessories shop there when they married in 1882. As the language spoken by the majority in Prague was Czech, Kafka's parents naturally used it alongside German in their business and occasionally (in the case of Hermann) at home, but the language normally spoken at home was German. German was also the language chosen for the children's formal education, which in Franz's case took him from primary school through grammar school to the German University in Prague where he graduated as a Doctor of Laws in 1906. Two years later he joined the partially state-funded Workers' Insurance Institute where his diligence and skill in drafting brought steady promotion to positions of ever greater responsibility before his early, but not unwilling retirement on health grounds in 1922. Only then did he realize a long nurtured ambition to move from Prague to Berlin. In less than a year, however, the spread of tuberculosis to his throat drove him back to the sanatorium at Kierling outside Vienna where he died.

Photographs of Kafka show a slim, smartly dressed youth and man whose conventional demeanour (albeit with an occasional hint of the dandy) seems much what one might expect from any well-placed official in a large insurance firm. His life begins to appear a little less conventional if one adds certain details to this outline, such as the fact that he had three unsuccessful engagements, two of them to the same woman, Felice Bauer.

1

Yet, however closely one studies his life for clues to account for his extraordinary writing, there always remains a gulf separating the unique products of his imagination from the circumstances he shared with other Jews, German-speakers in Prague, insurance officials, tuberculosis sufferers or unhappy sons and lovers. Were it not for his writings, the details of his biography would most likely have remained as little recorded or examined as those of millions of his readers. He himself referred to his periods of creativity as sojourns on Robinson Crusoe's island, and once even likened the relationship between an author's biographical person and his role as a narrator within a work of fiction to the establishment of a 'home on the moon' which has been shaken off by the earth:

> It therefore seems to me that all criticism which operates with the concepts of authentic and inauthentic and looks in the work for the will and feeling of the author who is absent from it, is meaningless and can only be explained by the fact that criticism too has lost its home.[2]

A study of Kafka's life can reveal some of the experiences on which his work almost certainly drew, as well as the effects on his personal and social existence of having such peculiar imaginative gifts, but the workings of his imagination can be studied only through the imagery and structures of the works it produced – by surveying the moon, as it were. Nevertheless these works were not created in a historical, social or intellectual vacuum, so it is useful to know something about the contexts which provided at least some of the points of reference or departure for them.

First, however, an outline is needed of what he wrote and when. None of the stories Kafka wrote while still at school have survived (nor, unfortunately, has a good deal of what he wrote in later years) but we know from anecdotal evidence that he started young. His first extant pieces of fiction are some fragments of the story 'Description of a Struggle' from 1904–5, followed by the fragment of a novel *Wedding Preparations in the Country* (1907). Both stories concern the difficulties experienced by a bachelor in relating to the physical and social world around him. As such they are the first examples of Kafka attempting to grapple imaginatively with problems which were later to cause him pain in real life.[3] The first is a fantasy of jealousy in which the lonely narrator's romantically exalted 'acquaintance' (or *alter ego*) finally stabs himself in the arm, while the second describes the anxieties of Eduard Raban (whose name contains a hidden, punning allusion to Kafka's own) as he sets out, apparently with the greatest reluctance, to join his bride-to-be in the countryside. Although it remained a fragment, this novel contains the germ of what is probably Kafka's best-known story, 'The Metamorphosis', as Eduard Raban recalls that his childhood tactic of dealing with stressful situations was to withdraw in fantasy into an inner or real self, which could assume the form of a vast beetle safely ensconced in bed, while his insubstantial social persona would be sent out, hapless and helpless, to face the hazards of the world. Here the world is already conceived as a threatening place over which the anxious individual vainly dreams of acquiring immense power. In 'The Metamorphosis', as in most of Kafka's mature work, that fantastical power has been transferred to some hidden agency which directs it against the protagonist.

Kafka first discovered that he had the ability to complete a coherent and complex piece of fiction, as opposed to the very short pieces which made up his first published volume entitled *Betrachtung (Contemplation)*, when he composed his 'breakthrough' story, 'The Judgement', at a single sitting during the night of 22–3 September 1912. In this story the hero is again a man on the threshold of marriage. Unlike Eduard Raban, however, Georg Bendemann will not even admit to any conflict between his social roles and his innermost self. The consequence of this repression is a dramatic action which moves rapidly to an astonishing and shocking ending when Georg drops from a bridge in obedience to a death sentence from his own father. In this compelling fusion of psychological and social realism with empirically implausible or even impossible events Kafka had at last found a way of putting on paper what he called 'the uncanny and monstrous world I have in my head' (DW, 137). The exhilarating experience of being able to write 'in such a connected way, with such complete opening of body and soul' (DW, 19) restored Kafka's self-confidence after he had started, abandoned and destroyed a second novel in the preceding summer. He then started work on the idea afresh, producing the long fragment now known as *Der Verschollene* (*The Missing Person*, first published by his friend Max Brod under the title *America*), the first of the three novels discussed in this book. Kafka was sufficiently satisfied with the first chapter to publish it separately under the title of 'The Stoker' in 1913. Despite stubborn efforts, however, he was again defeated by the challenge of sustaining throughout a novel the connectedness, inner truth[4] and immediacy of writing that he had achieved in 'The Judgement'. Such defeats for his writing came from the same source as his victories, in that Kafka was an extraordinarily inspirational author, quite dependent on creative states of mind which would come and go without his appearing to have any control over them, either presenting him with vivid images or 'inner figures'[5] which he longed to 'hunt' through the nights (his favoured time for writing) or withdrawing again for long periods, leaving him with feelings of emptiness, 'nothingness' and thoughts of suicide. Repeatedly he referred to the process of writing in images of movement – as a cart, for example, onto which he would try to swing the weight of a story and drive off (DW, 38) or as the experience of being 'fortgerissen' ('seized and carried off') (DW, 133) into an imagined world. The linear composition of his manuscripts, which he seldom subjected to extensive rewriting, although he would change many minor details of punctuation, spelling or grammar, confirms the aptness of such imagery.

When Kafka embarked on his next novel, *The Trial*, in 1914 he tried to ensure that it would be completed by departing from his usual linear method of composition and writing the last chapter immediately after the first.[6] In the end even this tactic failed to outwit the intermittent nature of his inspiration. In the midst of his fluctuating work on the novel, however, he did manage to complete the story 'In the Penal Colony' which shares the theme of punishment not only with *The Trial* but also with 'The Judgement', *The Missing Person* and 'The Metamorphosis'. At one point he considered publishing 'The Judgement', 'The Metamorphosis' and 'In the Penal Colony' in a single volume entitled 'Punishments', but this plan was not realized.

Kafka's next major bout of creativity fell in the winter of 1916 when he wrote the first stories of the collection published in 1920 under the title of *A Country Doctor* which he dedicated to his father. In the summer of the following year his tuberculosis first manifested itself in the form of bleeding from the lung. This led to a prolonged period of sick leave, much of which was spent in the countryside, at Ottla's smallholding in Zürau. Here he wrote mainly reflective pieces rather than fiction, including the aphorisms to which Max Brod gave the title 'Reflections on Sin, Suffering, Hope and the True Way'. A further, shorter set of aphorisms, centred on an anonymous 'He', was written in 1920. The main piece of writing he produced in 1919 was neither fictional nor philosophical but autobiographical, a long 'Letter to Father' which was never in fact delivered to the addressee. At the beginning of 1922, while staying in the village of Spindlermühle, he began his last and longest novel, *The Castle*, which, like its predecessors, remained unfinished. In his last two years he wrote the stories 'A Hunger Artist', 'The Burrow' and 'Josephine the Singer or the Mouse People'. He was still correcting the proofs of his last published collection of stories on his death bed.

Although outwardly a quiet, controlled, polite and considerate person, Kafka's life was full of tensions and contradictions. He was ambivalent, for example, about Prague, planning repeatedly to leave it but in fact remaining there, apart from increasingly frequent and extended periods of leave from the insurance office, until his brief move to Berlin just before his death. The contradictions are evident in his comment on the city: 'This little mother has claws.'[7] If one of the factors underlying this ambivalence was, as he believed, his 'bureaucratic' timidity about giving up a secure and increasingly well-paid position in Prague, an older and deeper source of inner division lay in his experience of family life there, particularly his relationship with his father. In physique, background and behaviour Hermann Kafka was very different from his son. The hardships of his early years in the countryside, where he had made his living as a pedlar, had combined with his strength of body and mind to produce a man determined to work himself up and out of such conditions. He therefore moved to the city and took the path of 'assimilation', which meant understating rather than stressing his Jewishness.[8] In taking this course Hermann Kafka behaved no differently from many other Jews with similar backgrounds. When it was time for Franz's bar mitzvah, for example, his father followed the practice amongst assimilated Jews of announcing it as a 'confirmation'.

Although the normal fluctuations of business life were aggravated in Prague after 1900 by an anti-Jewish boycott organized by Czech nationalists, the modest family business eventually prospered sufficiently to give Hermann Kafka's life a degree of security which it had notably lacked in childhood. (Kafka's German–Jewish mother, by contrast, had grown up in relatively comfortable circumstances.) The decision to educate the children at German schools enabled them (if they so chose) to participate in the culture of the ruling German-speaking minority in Prague, one of the regional seats of Habsburg rule over the Austro-Hungarian empire. In public life, at any rate, Jews were more readily accepted by the German-speaking community than by the Czech one, particularly once the growing movement of Czech nationalism had begun to harness anti-Semitic sentiments for its own purposes. On the other hand, Hermann Kafka was careful not to dissociate himself from the Czechs among whom he lived and worked. The business stationery bore the emblem of a jackdaw, which, by a pun, linked the family name with the Czech word for this bird ('kavka'). It has been pointed out that the twig on which the jackdaw perched ceased at one point to be identifiable as a German oak, and that after the First World War, when the Czech Republic had come into being, the name over the entrance to the business was spelled in the Czech rather than German manner.[9] Franz Kafka would later make use of the same emblem for his own, non-commercial purposes by scattering throughout his writings jackdaws, ravens, crows, names which allude to this bird family (Raban, Gracchus) and even figures (such as Klamm in *The Castle*) dressed in black, long-tailed coats. This may be a symptom of Kafka's ambivalence towards his paternal inheritance, since some of these images seem to refer to himself whereas others resemble his father, for whom Kafka felt a complex mixture of resentment, admiration, guilt and fascination. Although Kafka felt that his own personality owed much to the Löwy (maternal) side of the family, these symbols probably acknowledge, however reluctantly, the importance of the Kafka strain within him. The presence of such private ciphers in his fiction does not, of course, mean that it is simply and 'really' disguised autobiography.

In addition to the shop Hermann Kafka developed a wholesale business supplying smaller traders. In an effort to live up to his family's financial expectations Franz became co-founder with his brother-in-law, Karl Hermann, of an asbestos factory in 1911. As a trained lawyer he not only contributed to the setting up of the company (of which he was formally a 'sleeping partner'), but also helped out in the factory in the afternoons when he would have preferred to rest and prepare himself for his literary work in the evenings and at night. Thus Kafka bent to family pressure initially, despite having already done six hours of uninterrupted work in the insurance office, but for a while he hated the family intensely for imposing these extra strains on him after his choice of profession had shown that he had no intention of following his father into a business career.

Whereas children often disappoint their parents by neglecting their religion or severing their ties with it, Franz Kafka clashed with his father by associating himself deliberately with areas of Jewishness from which Hermann apparently wanted to distance himself. Thus Franz became very enthusiastic in 1911 about a visiting Yiddish theatre troupe and made friends with the actor Jizchak Löwy from whom he learned as much as he could about the culture of the Hasidic Jews of Eastern Europe. He even gave a talk on the 'Jargon' or Yiddish language by way of an introduction to Löwy's recitation of Yiddish poems. Later (in 1919) Kafka provoked his father's anger yet again by becoming engaged to Julie Wohryzek, a girl from a poor country background whose father was a servant in the local synagogue, thereby seeming to want to reverse the direction of Hermann's own career. Two years previously, during his stay at Zürau with Ottla (who had also opposed her father, more successfully, by marrying a Czech and moving to the countryside), Kafka had studied the biblical story of

Adam and Eve's expulsion from Eden minutely and reflected on it long. He had also begun to study Hebrew with renewed interest. This, too, only served to anger Hermann Kafka who preferred to treat religion as a formality to be performed with as little intellectual or emotional intensity as possible, his attendance at synagogue being that of a so-called 'four-day Jew', three being the high festivals and the fourth the birthday of the Austrian emperor, Franz Joseph. In all of this Kafka appears to have been filled not so much with a strong sense of Jewish identity as with a feeling of not being fully at home in any culture or language (since even the German word 'Mutter', he felt, did not convey what was associated with a Jewish mother)[10] and hence with a wistful longing for the kind of rootedness in community and tradition that he knew to lie out of his reach as one of 'the most western Jewish' of western Jews.[11] When he once asked himself how much he had in common with the Jews Kafka confessed wrily that he had hardly anything in common with himself (GW 10, 225). On the other hand, he clearly felt this to be a lack which demanded compensation. In recent years a renewal of scholarly interest in Kafka's Jewishness has yielded valuable pointers to new possible sources, allusions or points of reference for his work.[12]

The clash between Franz and his father on the occasion of his engagement to Julie Wohryzek gave rise to the 'Letter to Father',[13] in which he attempted to describe, with as little recrimination as possible, the incompatibility of their two natures. The objectivity and accuracy of the account has been questioned, with Kafka himself warning Milena Jesenská about the 'tricks of the advocate'[14] that it contained, but there can be little doubt that it captures central features of the relationship as Kafka experienced it. From early childhood his father had seemed to the slightly built Franz to be both impressively and menacingly powerful, always convinced of the rightness of his own views, however contradictory, capable of imposing rules of conduct on others which he did not observe himself, and unreasoning in the exercise of his power. As a child Franz had been quite unable to understand, for example, why his crying for water in the night should lead to his father putting him out on the balcony. His father's talk of his employees as 'paid enemies' (GW 7, 32) suggested a link between the exercise of power in the family and in the workplace, something later confirmed in his son's eyes by visits to the hated asbestos factory where he noted the submissiveness expected of the female workers toward their superiors.[15] Kafka felt that he never got over his early treatment by his father and he retained a profound, life-long distrust of all parents' ability to educate their children. Their failures were rooted in the fact that the child was flesh of their flesh and thus seen as an extension of themselves rather than being allowed to develop its own, possibly idiosyncratic potential.[16] In the undelivered letter Kafka confessed to the disabling effect of the double-bind of obsession and resentment in his relationship to his father: 'My writing was concerned with you, I only complained there about things I could not complain about at your breast' (GW 7, 47). Towards the end of his life Kafka observed that his writing had amounted to no more than a proud refusal to leave the battlefield after being defeated by him in childhood (GW 11, 196). Whether the defeat really was so complete is open to question. After all, Hermann Kafka, the self-confident family 'tyrant' (as Franz experienced him), had unwittingly helped to educate 'the greatest expert on power'[17] whose writings frequently retain the startled, incomprehending and hurt gaze of the child faced with a world pervaded by power. In these stories power only rarely makes those who exercise it any happier than its victims.[18]

A point on which Kafka was insistent in his 'Letter to Father' was that his own nature or 'organism' was just as responsible for the difficulties in their relationship as his father's. Had Hermann been educating a son as robust as himself, Kafka acknowledged, the effects might have been very different. Many children have endured similar treatment from an over-bearing 'head of the household' without feeling broken by the experience. Kafka's sister Ottla, for example, seems not to have been weakened by it, although of course her situation as youngest daughter was probably different in important respects from Franz's as eldest child and only son. He seems to have responded as he did not simply because of his unusual sensitivity, but because his artistic sensibility perceived in the relationship something more than just a clash between two individuals of unequal strength competing for the same goal. Latterly Kafka even asked himself whether he ought not to be grateful to his father for driving him out of 'his' (i.e the father's) patriarchal world of marriage and business into the 'desert' of loneliness since this was perhaps the only condition in which Kafka's particular form of writing, with its momentary flashes of illumination and elevation, was possible (GW 11, 211). In the midst of their humiliation Georg Bendemann and Gregor Samsa also catch a glimpse, in death or in the strains of music, of a mysterious 'nourishment' for which they have hungered unknowingly. Are they experiencing release or snatching at some comforting illusion in the midst of defeat? Such questions are left characteristically open in the stories, but the fact that they arise at all suggests that there may be something in their lives other than the brute struggle of wills for dominance, and that the presence of this 'something else' may explain why some individuals are less able or willing to seek victory in the battle of wills.

Neither at home nor in school, Kafka felt, had his education taken account of his 'Eigentümlichkeit' (GW 6, 143), that peculiarity of character which gave him such a sense of separateness from others that he is reported to have remarked, 'I am lonely – like Franz Kafka.'[19] This feeling of inexplicable otherness may underlie several of his stories describing creatures or events which defy causal explanation, such as the strange hybrid (GW 6, 92–3) that is half cat, half lamb, or the overnight transformation of Gregor Samsa into some form of enormous vermin, or the 'hunger artist' who continues to starve himself long beyond the plausible limits of physical survival. Imagery like this, so plainly at odds with the conditions of empirical existence, implicitly challenges any attempt at a reductive explanation of the mind that engendered such beings: if its creatures are not to be derived from the laws governing the natural world, then neither is that strangest of phenomena, the human imagination, from which they sprang.

Kafka's sense of being set apart from others emerged at an early age; indeed one anecdote indicates that social experience merely confirmed what he had already grasped intuitively about his situation in the world. In it he describes how, as a boy, he had been seated at a family event, holding, and perhaps thereby drawing attention to, a sheet of paper on which he had composed part of a planned novel about two hostile brothers. The passage in question described a prison corridor, particularly its coldness and silence. A teasing uncle then took the paper out of his hand, read it briefly and handed it back, remarking to the others in the company that it was just 'The usual stuff' (DW, 119). With this judgement ringing in his ears, the young writer felt that he had been thrust outside society 'as with a push', having acquired even within the family circle an insight into the 'cold space of this world' which he would have to warm with a fire that he first had to find. On this and other occasions it seemed not that Kafka's art imitated life, but rather that life imitated, and confirmed, his art.

Kafka felt that there was a peculiar coldness not only in the world around him but also in his own responses to others. He had been 'a cold-fantastical child' (GW 7, 48) who remained equally unfeeling as an adult. Initially he hoped to find the warmth he lacked in the fire of poetic inspiration. Paradoxically, however, he believed that this was only to be found in the kind of cell-like isolation he had evoked in his early prison story. In one of his many warnings to Felice that his writing was incompatible with married life Kafka wrote that the best form of life for him would be to have his writing implements and a lamp, 'in the innermost room of an extensive, closed-off cellar' (DW, 134). He felt happiest in 'the fire of connected hours' (DW, 54) and correspondingly frustrated by the 'so often experienced misfortune of the consuming fire that may not burst into flame' (DW, 148).[20] His description of successful writing suggests alchemy or the purifying fire of purgatory: 'How everything can be dared, how a great fire is prepared for all impressions [*Einfälle*], even the strangest ones, in which they pass away and are resurrected' (GW 10, 101).[21] The 'inner truth' attainable through writing was, he believed, recognized in an experience of unconditional surrender, not to another human being but to the act of imagining:

> Writing means opening oneself up to an excessive degree; the most extreme openness of heart and giving of oneself, in which a human being believes he is about to lose himself in his intercourse with other human beings – for everyone wants to live as long as he is alive – this openness of heart and giving of oneself is much too inadequate for writing. (DW, 134)[22]

If truth lay in intensity for Kafka, failure to achieve intensity was taken to be an indictment of his commitment to the task: 'What I have written was written in a lukewarm bath, I have never experienced the eternal Hell of true writers' (DW, 128). From early on, however, Kafka had scruples not just about his abilities but also on account of the 'hellish' or 'devilish', narcissistic element in writing. On the other hand, he had an equally powerful if intermittent conviction that writing was what he was there for, that it could be a 'heavenly dissolution and a real coming to life' (DW, 122) for him, that it was truly his 'good being' (DW, 138), that it was the way to 'self-knowledge' (DW, 136), the struggle for 'self-preservation' (DW, 144), his 'only inner possibility of existence' (DW, 137), that the 'firmness' which even the most meagre piece of writing gave him was 'doubtless and wonderful' (DW, 45), and that the debilitating effects of writing were merely 'the earthly reflection of a higher necessity' (DW, 142).

Towards the end of his life Kafka came to denounce writing ever more vehemently, scorning it for 'flying around the truth, but with the firm intention of not getting burnt' (DW, 150), and even declaring it to be the sweet reward of service to the devil:

> This descent to the dark powers, this unchaining of spirits which by nature are constrained [...] the devilish element in it seems plain to

me. It is vanity and lust for pleasure which constantly flutters around its own or another figure – the movement then multiplies, it becomes a solar system of vanity – and enjoys it. (DW, 160)

Whereas the inspired intensity of his good hours had once convinced him that writing was the form in which he could be most fully alive, Kafka now charged himself with not having lived at all, with having decorated the house of life and abandoned it to evil powers instead of actually occupying it. There could be no afterlife for him, he wrote despairingly to Max Brod, because his deluded soul had become a mere, insubstantial writer and had abandoned his real self to a living death (rather as Eduard Raban had fantasized about sending his hapless body out into the world without a soul). In this long, self-castigatory letter the imagery of fire is applied not to writing but to the real life he had neglected for its sake: 'I have remained clay, I have not made the spark become fire but merely used it to illuminate my corpse' (DW, 161). In his last will and testament Kafka even revoked his earlier claims on the creative fire of the spirit by asking Brod to burn, in an act of bitter poetic justice, all that remained of his manuscripts. Brod did not in fact do so, having previously warned Kafka that he would not carry out his wishes and thereby giving him the chance to find someone other than the greatest admirer of his art to destroy his papers. Brod's refusal to co-operate can be regarded as a betrayal of friendship or as an attempt to save from the black side of Kafka's nature work which, when this mood was not on him, had filled him throughout his life with the:

> Remarkable, mysterious, perhaps dangerous, perhaps redeeming comfort of writing: the leap out of the murderous sequence action – observation, action – observation, whereby a higher form of observation is created, a higher form, not a sharper one, and the higher it is, the further out of reach from the 'sequence', the more independent it becomes, the more it follows its own laws of movement, the more unpredictable, joyous, ascending is its path. (DW, 158)[23]

Brod acted as he did because he believed that Kafka's work was both great literature and religious in its inspiration. Kafka himself was not always so convinced, tending sometimes to the opposite view that his writing was nothing more than the masochistic consequence of his early defeat at the hands of his father. Uncertainty on this crucial point is one likely source of the ambiguity, ambivalence and contradictoriness which pervade his fiction. The 'country doctor', for example, is left driving aimlessly and end-lessly through the snow on an 'earthly' waggon pulled by 'unearthly horses'.

The interaction of Kafka's writing with other areas of his life, particu-larly his relationships with women, was complex and difficult. His relation-ship with Felice Bauer, for example, was marked by the same strange anticipation of life by art as we have already noted in his early description of a prison corridor. They met as guests of Max Brod in August 1912. Just over a month later he wrote to her in Berlin what was to be the first of a voluminous series of love letters. Immediately thereafter he wrote 'The Judgement', later dedicated to Felice. The story begins with Georg Bend-emann's decision to write a letter to a friend about his recent engagement to a certain Frieda Brandenfeld (F.B.), which sets in train a series of events that culminate in his death by drowning. Two years later, on 1 June 1914, Kafka's official engagement to Felice took place, followed by its dissolution just six weeks later. Before his courtship of Felice Bauer had properly begun, in other words, Kafka had already foreseen the catastrophic con-sequences of a betrothal in fiction, thereby hinting at the undertow of fear and reluctance already present in his own passionate wooing of Felice. In the case of Kafka (as distinct from his fictional hero) marriage was to be feared principally because he believed it would prove incompatible with the isolation and self-absorption he considered essential to his writing. Yet, paradoxically, he had at first felt justified in courting Felice precisely because he thought his writing had finally begun to demonstrate his human worth. With her he hoped he could hold together two forms of life – a close attachment to another person, and the peculiar experience of heightened life he derived from successful writing. As the inspiration of 1912–13 ebbed away, Kafka began to see their relationship not as some-thing justified by his ability to write but as a possible escape from his stubborn failures to do so. No sooner had the engagement been broken in July 1914, however, than he experienced a new release of his imagina-tive powers in the shape of *The Trial*, thanks to which he believed his 'regular, empty, crazy bachelor existence' had a 'justification' (DW, 78). Was the *absence* of a relationship the condition of inspired writing, then? Ironically, the renewed drying up of his inspiration before he could complete *The Trial* demonstrated that the conditions of creativity were guaranteed as little by bachelorhood as they had been by the courtship of Felice.

Despite the pain and recriminations of his first failed engagement to Felice, Kafka repeated the attempt in July 1917. This second engagement was dissolved after just six months, on this occasion with the justification that the outbreak of tuberculosis in September had rendered him unfit for marriage. Kafka interpreted the wound in his lungs as no mere physiological event but as the inevitable symbolic consequence of a chronic spiritual conflict deep within his being which his mind had simply passed over to the lungs when it was too exhausted to carry on: 'The physical disease is only a bursting out of its banks by the spiritual [*geistigen*] disease' (B, 242).[24] The opening of the physical wound, he believed, had been anticipated five years previously in his composition of 'The Judgement': 'At that time the wound broke open for the first time in the course of a long night' (DW, 30). In a letter to his friends Max Brod and Felix Weltsch (B, 160) Kafka took the view that the event had also been anticipated more explicitly in his story 'A Country Doctor', written a year before his renewed engagement to Felice, in which the doctor discovers a strange, maggot-filled wound in the hip of a young boy.[25] When Felix Weltsch tried to dispute Kafka's spiritual interpretation of his disease Kafka was unusually forthright in his counter-attack on such 'accursed psychological theories [...] The theories of nature are wrong, and so are their psychological sisters. But that does not affect the solution to the question of whether the world can be cured from a single point' (B, 187). As Kafka understood them, his problems with Felice had admittedly 'inflamed' his inner wound but it was the depth of the wound which signified 'justification'.[26] Presumably he meant by this not simply that the physical wound justified the ending of their relationship but that it symbolized his deep-seated awareness of the incompatibility of writing and marriage and the commitment to normal social existence this entailed. Here, in this wound, cut by the 'harrow'[27] of his writing, he discerned 'a strengthening of the general seed of death' (B, 177)[28] and a sign of that 'Eigentümlichkeit' ('individuality', 'peculiarity') of his being which had inwardly resisted his father's attempts at education and had made him feel alone even in the midst of the family circle. Kafka believed that his irrepressible urge to write had destroyed him systematically:

> The systematic destruction of my self over the years is astonishing, it was like a slowly developing breach in a dam, an action fully intended. The spirit which achieved this must now be celebrating its triumph; why does it not let me share in its triumph? But perhaps it has not finished its work and is therefore unable to think of anything else. (GW 11, 189)

This was no mere fancy, since Kafka's regime of night-long writing followed by demanding work in the office would have destroyed the health of more robust natures than his, but he had accepted from early on that he might have to pay such a price:

> The uncanny and monstrous world I have in my head. But how to liberate myself and liberate it without being torn apart. And yet I would a thousand times rather be torn apart than hold it back within me or bury it. That is what I am here for, after all, about that I am quite clear. (DW, 137)

Given his obsession with writing, it may seem surprising that Kafka allowed himself to become involved with women as often as he did, not just with Felice Bauer and her friend Grete Bloch, but also with Julie Wohryzek (this third engagement was contracted and broken in 1919), with Milena Jesenská (1920), a married woman and translator of his work into Czech, and finally with Dora Diamant, a young Jewess he had met while convalescing in 1923. He moved with her to Berlin and apparently, at last, enjoyed a happy relationship in which he could share his life with someone else and still continue to write. For all his self-accusations of coldness, Kafka clearly had a gift for love and friendship, something that is confirmed by both men and women who were close to him. Yet there were other reasons for seeking relationships: fear of the loneliness and consuming 'fire' of writing, guilty doubts that it might be the work of 'lower' rather than 'higher' powers, and his attraction to the 'truth'[29] and goodness of ordinary family life, something he knew to be preached by the Talmud: 'A man without a woman is no man' (GW 9, 207). On the other hand, he was prey to the suspicion that it was his writing which actually determined whether he would seek or avoid relationships at any given time. Thus, when unable to make further progress with *The Trial* in November 1914, he thought of turning to Felice again as a stop-gap: 'I would like to try to get F. again for the meantime. And I really will try to do so, provided disgust with myself does not prevent me' (DW, 80). Again the ambivalence has parallels in his fiction, where the protagonists frequently approach relationships with the opposite sex in a calculating manner.

Unique though Kafka's fiction is, his contradictory views on writing have their parallels amongst his contemporaries. His sense of being fated or having a mission to write was not uncommon among German poets at the turn of the century for whom Nietzsche's 'Why I am a Fate'[30] had renewed the high Romantic view of art and artists. Kafka's much quoted reference to 'Writing as a form of prayer' (DW, 153) is a variant on the Nietzschean view of art as the last metaphysical activity of man, which was taken up in one form or another by various writers and artists in response to the spiritual void left by the decay of positive religion. The accompanying self-doubt of the artist was also prominent in the experience of the Romantics, particularly later ones like Heine or E.T.A. Hoffmann (initially seen as an important model for Kafka), but this negative view of art had also acquired a new acerbity in Nietzsche's critique of the decadent, deceptive and self-deceiving streak in artists, particularly modern ones. Thanks to the lively press and cultural life in the clubs and salons of 'provincial' Prague, Kafka was well aware of recent and contemporary intellectual, scientific and literary developments. Although he later became increasingly sceptical of psychoanalytic theory and therapy, for example, he was aware of the parallel between Freud's work on the unconscious and his own delving into what he himself often felt to be 'repulsive' areas of his dream-like inner life. In Thomas Mann's *Tonio Kröger* (1903), which he read with an enthusiasm later matched by Mann's response to his own work, there was confirmation of his belief that a writer had to 'die to life' in order to recreate it.[31] In Hugo von Hofmannsthal's so-called 'Lord Chandos Letter' (1902), the best known contemporary document of the 'crisis of language', Kafka could read of 'words which crumbled in the mouth like rotten fungi',[32] an experience which he described in similarly drastic terms: 'Sentences fall apart, as it were, and show me their innards' (DW, 117). Nevertheless, Kafka's recurrent difficulties in expressing himself adequately in writing (which he found more satisfactory than speech) did not lead him to distrust language fundamentally, as some recent critics have maintained, but simply to doubt his own abilities in handling it:

> The false sentences lie in ambush around my pen, wrap themselves around its point and are dragged along into the letters. I do not believe that one can ever lack the strength to express perfectly what one wants to say or write. It is quite wrong to point to the weakness of language and to compare the limited nature of words with the infinity of feeling. The infinite feeling remains in words exactly as infinite as it was in the heart. That which is clear inwardly will also, inevitably, become just as clear in words. For this reason one must never fear for language, rather one should fear for oneself as one contemplates words. (DW, 135)

At other times he was more prepared to concede that writing could be a source of problems by tempting the writer into false definitions: 'Writing itself often seduces one into false fixations. Sentences have a gravitational pull which one cannot escape' (DW, 143). Kafka was also convinced that language was itself too much a product of the world of the senses for it to be able to speak of things beyond that world; at best it could only hint at such things (GW 6, 237). Nevertheless, although it might happen all too rarely, Kafka felt on occasion that it was indeed possible to raise things in language to the level of 'the pure, the true and the unalterable' (DW, 98). In practice, however, the difficulty of meeting his own high standards of authenticity and coherence meant that many of his works remained fragmentary.

In this last respect Kafka's work resembled his life, or rather the view he took of his life at dark, self-recriminatory moments such as this:

> Unease because my life so far has been a marching on the spot, at most a development only in the sense that a tooth undergoes one as it becomes hollow and rots. For my part there was not the slightest leading of my life, none that stood the test. It was as if, like any other human being, I had been given the centre of a circle, and as if, like any other human being, I then had to walk along the decisive radius and then trace a nice circle. Instead of which I constantly started out along a radius but was forced repeatedly to break it off as soon as I had begun. (Examples: piano, violin, languages, German studies, anti-Zionism, Zionism, Hebrew, gardening, carpentry, literature, attempts at marriage, my own flat.) The middle of the imaginary circle is full of jagged beginnings of radii, there is no more room for another attempt, no room means age, weak nerves, and no further attempt means the end. If ever I carried the radius a bit further than usual, in my law studies, for example, or the engagements, everything was that much worse rather than better. (GW 11, 206)

One does not have to accept Kafka's assessment as the whole story. The testimony of his own letters and of those who were close to him speaks of a life which gave much to others, whether as a diligent official or friend or member of the family. Against the extraordinarily high standards of integrity, intensity and completeness he applied to his life and his work, most lives would probably have to be judged at least as fragmentary as his.

2

Reading Kafka

In Kafka's story 'In the Penal Colony' two characters with very different beliefs and values are made to confront one another. One of them, an officer in charge of punishment in the colony, states quite simply: '"The principle on which I base my decisions is: 'Guilt is always beyond doubt'."' (GW 1, 168). The other, an explorer on a brief visit to the colony, having listened to the officer's explanations and watched the preparations for an execution, concludes, equally simply, that, 'The injustice of the proceedings and the inhumanity of the execution was beyond doubt' (GW 1, 175). Two diametrically opposed views, each held to be 'beyond doubt' ('zweifellos') by the person concerned. Kafka's interpreters are similarly fond of using 'formulae of persuasion' or phrases which claim indubitability for their views.[1] As in the case of his fictional characters, however, the very words critics use to claim that something is beyond doubt can often indicate some uncertainty which the commentator is reluctant to acknowledge. Very little in Kafka's fiction is 'beyond doubt' in the sense of having a demonstrably univocal significance.

This is partly due to the peculiarly eidetic nature of Kafka's imagination. He did not compose according to some rational plan but would 'see' things or figures in his mind's eye and follow them wherever they led – 'even down into the underworld where they are truly at home' (DW, 38). Whenever he had recourse to what he called 'Hilfskonstruktionen' ('scaffolding' or makeshift transitions composed in the head but without genuine emotional engagement), Kafka felt acutely dissatisfied with the resulting 'Machwerk' ('contrived' or 'botched job').[2] When he felt that he had written a satisfyingly 'connected' story, however, one which 'contains its own organisation, already complete, within itself' (DW, 90), as in the case of 'The Judgement', his relationship to the finished work shared at least some of the uncertainty felt by any other reader or interpreter. While correcting the proofs of 'The Judgement', admittedly, he felt that his authorship put him in the privileged position of being able to grasp the 'body' of the story which came out of him 'like a regular birth, covered with dirt and slime' (DW, 22). He therefore sat down immediately to outline the relationships which had 'become clear' to him in the course of writing it. In his letters to Felice Bauer, by contrast, Kafka was much more guarded and self-contradictory about any meaning the story might have, characterizing it clearly enough on one occasion as 'sad and embarrassing' (DW, 21), while claiming on another that it 'cannot be explained' (DW, 25). In one letter he called the story 'a little wild and senseless', but then went on to say that it would be nothing, 'if it did not have inner truth (something which can never be established in general terms but which must be granted or denied on each new occasion by each reader or listener)' (DW, 21). In a later letter he was even more dismissive about the meaning of what he had written: 'Can you find any kind of sense in the "Judgement", I mean any kind of straight, connected sense that one can follow? I cannot find any, nor can I explain anything in it' (DW, 24). This last comment in particular is frequently cited in support of the view that Kafka's fiction conveys no coherent meaning at all. One must be a little wary of taking these remarks to Felice at face value, however, since Kafka would not have found it easy at that point to reveal to her the insight he had confided to his diary, namely that Georg Bendemann's fiancée can be swept aside so easily by his father because she 'lives in the story only through the [i.e. Georg's] relation to the friend' (DW, 22). That Kafka did nevertheless believe that 'The Judgement' contained some kind of subjective and yet communicable meaning is indicated not just by his reference to its 'inner truth' or his request that Felice should give the story to her father to read (in the hope that he would conclude that its author was just as unsuited to marriage as the protagonist), but also by his uncontrolled gestures and the tears which came to his eyes when he read it to friends: 'The indubitability [*Zweifellosigkeit*] of the story was confirmed' (DW, 20). Such elusive, only intuitively graspable and yet indubitable 'truth', rather than some rationally demonstrable 'sense', is what Kafka hoped his fiction, at its best, could achieve. He once described it as the 'music' of his writing, and connected it with fear.[3]

The process leading to this result, admittedly, was an unpredictable, compulsive, often disappointing or even deeply disturbing process of exploration: 'But every day at least one line should be directed at me, like the telescopes people are now directing at the comet' (DW, 116).[4] If one presses the analogy too hard, however, the telescope becomes a rather misleading metaphor for writing, for such instruments capture an image of the object at which they are pointed in a relatively objective way. Language, by contrast, contains multiple possibilities for ambiguity and uncertainty which affect both the sending and the reception of messages. Like other creative writers, Kafka exploited this potential in language so as to preserve the aura of the mysterious and 'uncanny' around the things emerging from his strange inner world, but also to allude to a whole range of shared cultural references. Although he was unable to summon up the creative state by conscious choice, Kafka's use of language reveals complex patterns of anticipation and echo which suggest that he practised consciously the craft ('Handwerk') which he considered indispensable to all art.[5] Thus to read Kafka is to meet not just a dreamer or visionary but also an acute, knowledgeable, ironical, self-aware intelligence.

Difficulties of interpretation are bound to arise from this intermingling of obscurity and precision, mystery and pattern, specificity of event and multiplicity of meaning. Inevitably critics differ markedly in their understanding, with one focusing on this particular set of images while another emphasizes that particular group of associations. Some of these readings are capable of coexisting and augmenting one another while others are mutually exclusive. One can show where a critic has narrowed or widened Kafka's meaning beyond the limits of textual evidence or plausibility, but it will probably never be possible to arrive at a single, demonstrably correct or exhaustive reading of his stories or novels. Critics generally use the language of rational argument to explain and justify a preference for one reading over another, but in Kafka's case they particularly need to keep reminding themselves that they are attempting to understand what Blaise Pascal called the reasons of the heart. Because Kafka's imaginary world differs from our everyday one, we have to be wary of translating its disruptive strangeness into more familiar and less unsettling terms. If the author was engaged in exploration and discovery, his readers cannot expect to do more than join in the quest. Critics must accept that their readings are necessarily tentative and subjective, and that they can learn from each other just as Kafka himself evidently learned from Felice's astute observations on the parable of the doorkeeper in *The Trial* (DW, 81–2). By the same token each new reader may hope to throw fresh light on some aspect of these complex and elusive fictions by attending closely to the details of textual patterning which create particular, often paradoxical meanings from the general store of language.

A type of reading which was once very popular and which has acquired a new lease of life in modified form in recent years is the religious one.[6] Much of the credit or responsibility for popularizing this approach falls to

Max Brod who argued the case in essays, a monograph, a biography and, probably most influentially, in the postscripts to his editions of Kafka's works. Religious interpreters can appeal to evidence of various kinds. The extraordinary events in Kafka's stories, for example, can be seen as the eruption of some hidden, transcendental order through the apparently secure surface of mundane existence. Setting, imagery and vocabulary can all suggest religious meaning, as in the scene from *The Trial* where Josef K. is told a parable about 'the Law' which apparently radiates an inextinguishable light. Similarly, the 'Schuld des Vaters' ('his father's debt') which Gregor Samsa has been slaving for years to repay could be an allusion to the idea of original or inherited sin ('die Erbsünde'). In support of claims that the intended meaning of Kafka's fiction is religious, critics can cite phrases from non-fictional contexts, such as his aphoristic note, 'Writing as a form of prayer' (DW, 153), or his remark in 1922 that, had Zionism not intervened, his writings might have come to form a new Cabbala (GW 11, 199). Critics of this persuasion can also point to Kafka's life-long interest in various forms of religious thought or feeling, ranging from Rudolf Steiner's theosophy to the writings of Buber, Tolstoy and Kierkegaard. Kafka's efforts to keep alive or extend his knowledge of Hebrew and his aphoristic reflections during his stay at Zürau on the first book of Genesis have similarly been cited in support of religious interpretations of his work.

There are difficulties with all these arguments. Some of Kafka's non-literary statements indicate that he lacked ties to either of the main positive religions practised by those around him,[7] while one of the Zürau aphorisms asserts that the belief in a personal god is one of several possible ways of obscuring what is indestructible within us (GW 6, 236). Although there are possible religious overtones in *The Trial*, they seem eclectic to the point of incoherence. Whereas on the one hand the bearded men in the courtroom create some resemblance to an orthodox synagogue and the term 'the Law' suggests an allusion to the core of the Jewish religion, the parable about 'the Law' is told to Josef K. by a 'prison chaplain' in a Christian cathedral. It is difficult to reconcile notions of divine majesty and justice with the dusty, confined premises of the court or the corrupt, vain and lustful individuals who represent it; much the same can be said of the castle and the divine grace it supposedly houses. A determined and ingenious religious interpreter can attempt to resolve such contradictions by drawing an analogy, say, with the fallible human institution of the Church and the divinity it nevertheless serves, or by citing some strand of religious tradition according to which the seeming imperfections of the spiritual courts reflect the imperfections of the soul being tried before them.[8] The difficulties remain nevertheless. If Kafka intended to illustrate some specific esoteric theology, why did he not make this didactic intention plain instead of writing stories which lack any specific and explicit indication that their meaning is divine? Similarly, if the official Sortini's unwanted sexual advances to Amalia are supposed to reflect, say, Jehovah's demand for the sacrifice of Isaac by Abraham, why is there no sign in the novel (as there is in the alleged biblical model) that Sortini acts with divine authority? And why, if Kafka's aim was simply to retell a clear and familiar Bible story in a disguised form, did he bother to write it at all? Even if there were much more persuasive evidence of, say, allusions to the story of Abraham and Isaac in *The Castle*, the interesting question would not concern the similarity but the differences between the ancient religious story and its modern descendant.[9]

Where there is clear evidence of Kafka's interest in the Bible (in the Zürau aphorisms, for example), it is a matter of debate whether his interpretation of the stories in Genesis is religious or not.[10] In either case it cannot be taken for granted that his intention in his philosophical reflections was the same as his practice when writing fiction, for there is often a difference between the views espoused by an author in reality and those adopted for the purpose of telling a story. Further difficulties arise from within the camp of the religious commentators themselves, since they offer such divergent interpretations of the texts, including Zionist and anti-Zionist readings, positive and negative theology, and claims that Kafka was influenced by various competing schools of Jewish and non-Jewish thought.

The two weightiest objections to the religious interpretation of Kafka's fiction, however, concern the relationship of text to meaning and the relationship of fiction to the world at large. Firstly, to equate, say, the castle with divine grace or the court with divine justice is to read the texts allegorically, which is to say that they are taken to be about something other than what they appear to be about. The fiction allegedly makes no sense on its own terms but only as a counterfeit of some other text which lies outside it. But what justifies the interpreters' substitutions of abstract or spiritual concepts for the concrete and seemingly material things described in the stories? When allegory was a widely practised type of writing there also existed widely known and understood 'codes' which enabled the initiated reader to recognize the intended hidden references. Even then writers would often help with the decoding, particularly when the code was being extended or varied in some way. But Kafka was not writing within or for some well-established interpretive community, nor did he provide the reader with an in-built de-coder with which to translate his supposed concrete analogies back into the abstractions they truly signify. How, then, is one to know that the texts are allegorical or what the allegories represent?

Secondly, there is the problem of how Kafka's fictional world relates to the empirical world. When, in the Bible, the waters of the Red Sea are parted, or Lot's wife is transformed into a pillar of salt, or a chariot of fire descends to carry a servant of the Lord to heaven, we know what is happening: God is suspending the normal order of things by a miracle in order to save, punish or bless. Actually, even this contrast between the normal and the miraculous is not quite accurate, since the Bible is full of signs and wonders which are taken to be just as much part of the way God orders the world as routine events are. If Kafka's stories are to be read religiously, is one to assume that they embody the same kind of belief as one finds in the Bible that God can and does intervene miraculously in the course of history, so that He is responsible, say, for transforming a travelling salesman overnight into an insect, or for sending strangely clad emissaries into the life of a bank official to tell him he is 'arrested'? If so, it is surely remarkable that it occurs neither to Gregor Samsa nor to any other character in 'The Metamorphosis' that a miracle has taken place. If no such naive view is to be imputed to Kafka, then how exactly are the events in his stories to be related to the meeting of God and his creatures in history and nature? Where, on a religious view of the world, are the disruptions of the known order of things described in these fictions supposed to take place?

Kafka has also attracted a number of philosophical interpretations. Erich Heller, to take just one example, has argued that the key to Kafka's fiction is to be found in Arthur Schopenhauer's philosophy of the universal Will.[11] According to Schopenhauer, all creatures are doomed to a life of suffering as a result of the so-called 'principium individuationis' which separates them from the universal Will that is the blind and unconscious ground of all being. Their suffering is that of the Will itself which has poured itself out into the myriad, transient forms of material existence in order to assuage its inherently insatiable hunger for life. This, according to Heller, explains why Kafka's characters, like their author, are 'imbued with a sense of guilt that is in "being" rather than "doing"'.[12] Thus Josef K. is supposedly made to suffer by the court not because of any identifiable wrongdoing but simply because he is a human being. This interpretation of Kafka, and a number of others like it, is questionable for a variety of reasons. Firstly, it conflicts with the textual evidence: Josef K.

discovers in the corridors of the court that not everyone is put on trial but only certain individuals, all of them apparently male and mostly from the middle classes like himself. As with theological approaches, the relationship between fiction, philosophy and reality is also problematic. Schopenhauer's philosophy attempted to explain what was hidden behind the solid-seeming surface of shared human experience (which is why it appeals so powerfully to a character like Mann's Thomas Buddenbrook, a man who believes himself to be trapped in a world that seems as inescapably filled with suffering as Schopenhauer alleged). In Schopenhauer's view the undivided nature of the Will and the illusory character of phenomena in time and space can only be intuited *against* the evidence of the world as it appears to the senses, and the determining power of causality can only conceivably be broken if human beings universally and simultaneously renounce the Will. But this is not how the world is described in Kafka's stories, a world of bizarre dislocations of time and space, where giant moles appear, mice sing, dogs conduct research, and apes acquire the level of education of an average European within a few short years. If Kafka had wanted the reader to interpret such events as expressions of how the world might be if only the Will were to start behaving utterly capriciously, then surely he would have had to give some clear indication that this is what he intended. One cannot justify a Schopenhauerian reading simply on the grounds that Schopenhauer was widely read by Kafka's intellectual contemporaries. Contemporary reviewers of the stories, at any rate, did not immediately leap to the conclusion Heller would have us believe was the correct one.[13] This is not to say that the search for Kafka's links with philosophy is a misguided undertaking. A more cautious, detailed and differentiated treatment of Kafka's possible appropriation of Schopenhauerian imagery and thought, for example, has been offered by T.J. Reed,[14] while a number of recent books and articles have examined possible links with the philosophy of Kafka's contemporaries, particularly in the areas of linguistic and perceptional philosophy.[15]

Whereas Heller places the Schopenhauerian Will at the centre of Kafka's work, Wilhelm Emrich has made the same claim for his own concept of the 'true Universal'.[16] Emrich differs from those who explicate Kafka in terms of some other philosopher's system (be it Schopenhauer, Nietzsche, Heidegger or Camus) by attempting to formulate an original system of thought which he finds implicit in Kafka's fictional and non-fictional writings. It is a fascinating and ingenious exercise, but it, too, is fraught with difficulties. Firstly, Emrich does not really treat Kafka's *œuvre* as a self-referential system since he defines it, and thus pre-judges it, with the help of categories drawn from other thinkers. Emrich begins, for example, by outlining Goethe's symbolist aesthetics which, he claims, rested on the belief that spirit pervades the entire material world. To begin thus is to set the terms of an equation, as it were, for Kafka is then seen to invert the Goethean view. He becomes the poet of the modern, alienated world in which no such pre-established harmony of matter and spirit exists. Having posited this general framework, Emrich proceeds to identify Kafka's imagery with abstractions, equating Gregor Samsa's new, insect-like appearance, for example, with his 'true self', a deeper level of his being where he is at one with the obscure harmony and laws of the world which normally remain hidden from us by our alienating and alienated rational mind. Emrich does not explain, however, how Kafka could arrive at such privileged insights into the hidden structure of reality which are denied to the rational minds of others (but capable of rational, systematic explanation by Emrich). The equations required to make the system work often appear forced, arbitrary and unjustifiably exclusive of other suggestions in Kafka's imagery.

The aspect of Kafka's work which is perhaps most noticeable by its omission from Emrich's system is psychology. The physical attributes of the transformed Gregor Samsa, for example, can plausibly be related to features of his previous emotional and social life. Thus his 'armour-like' back points to the same need for protection as is evident in his habit of locking his room at night, not only in hotels but even in the family home, while his many tiny legs at first frustrate his habitual will to control and order life but then open up new, undreamed-of possibilities for pleasure as he learns to crawl on their sticky pads across the walls and ceilings of his 'rather too small human room' (GW 1, 93). Gregor's shrinking in the course of the story from a creature so vast in the beginning that the bedcover perches precariously atop his belly, to something small enough to hide beneath a couch, further suggests an extended symbolic parallel between the physical and the emotional running through the whole story. Taken together with Kafka's definition of his writing as 'the representation of my dream-like inner life' (DW, 144), this kind of symbolism has ensured that the psychological or psychoanalytic approach (Kafka used both terms interchangeably) has become possibly the most widely practised of all methods of interpreting Kafka's fiction. For a time the Freudian psycho-analytic conception of the unconscious supplied the interpretive template, but then it went out of fashion until re-applied in new versions by the followers of Foucault and Lacan.[17] Interpreters of a Freudian persuasion can point to Kafka's remark on the morning after composing 'The Judgement': 'Thoughts of Freud of course' (DW, 19). They are less fond of quoting the later remark, 'For the last time psychology!', and others of similar import.[18]

Any psychological reading which applies an already elaborated system to Kafka's texts runs some of the same dangers as those encountered by his religious and philosophical interpreters. There is the danger of imposing concepts by interpretive 'fiat', as in one notorious study where Freudian concepts of anality, castration fear and neurosis are applied as if they were incontestable truths.[19] There is the danger of stressing details which appear to conform to the system, while ignoring or dismissing other features which do not fit so easily. Thus, an interpretation which takes the 'strong-flanked' horses which wriggle out of the country doctor's pigsty to represent the doctor's repressed sexual desires will have difficulty with the fact that the horses are expressly described as 'unearthly' (GW 1, 206). The reader may reject such interpretations because they are based on an unverifiable theory or, worse still, reject the stories themselves, 'if this is all they amount to'. There is the further difficulty (readily dismissed by interpreters who care little for authorial intention) that Kafka took a very different view of disease from Freud. Whereas Freud located the source of neurosis in a disturbance of bodily needs, believing that a repressed libido sent out coded signals of its inadmissable discontents, Kafka's understanding of psychosomatic illness, at least in later years, gave primacy to the mind or soul rather than the body, arguing that diseases needed to be understood spiritually:

> You say that you do not understand it. Try to understand it by calling it disease. It is one of the many manifestations of disease which psycho-analysis believes it has uncovered. I do not call it disease and see in the therapeutic part of psychoanalysis a helpless error. All these purported diseases, no matter how sad they seem, are facts of belief, anchorages in some maternal ground for human beings in distress. [...] Such anchorages which have a hold in real ground are not the individual possession of a human being, but are pre-formed in his essential being and subsequently re-form his being (including his body) even further in this direction. (GW 7, 161)

In part the difficulty has to do with the term 'psychology' which was so easily associated with one-sided physiological reductionism by Kafka's contemporaries. Under a broader definition of the term, one which includes the 'spirit', Kafka's own understanding of disease is psychological.

In one of the classic studies of Kafka's fiction, Walter Sokel has tried to avoid some of these difficulties by developing his own categories, particularly that of the 'pure self' and its social *alter ego*, to describe the inner struggle he sees running through Kafka's *œuvre*.[20] Although Sokel, too, occasionally makes questionable identifications of Kafka's images with the concepts of Freud and Nietzsche, and has a tendency to force the characters into his antithetical scheme (whereas Kafka disliked antitheses), the result impresses by its close attention to textual detail and the attempt to derive its analytic concepts from recurrent patterns in Kafka's own texts.

The analysis of Kafka's fiction as the representation of an inner world was developed in a different direction by Friedrich Beißner in a series of influential essays.[21] Beißner challenged the philosophical and theological approaches so much in vogue at the time by directing attention to the peculiarities of Kafka's poetic method which, he claimed, runs counter to all attempts to abstract any general view of the world from his fictions. According to Beißner, Kafka's fiction is always strictly 'einsinnig', or 'mono-perspectival', which is to say that the author has no standpoint in the stories or novels distinct from that of the protagonist, whose eyes, ears and mind register everything the author records. To use a technical expression, Kafka's writing is an extended exercise in 'erlebte Rede', or free indirect speech, each word being drawn from the vocabulary of the focal character and simply re-cast in the form of third-person statements by a neutral narrator. As far as the import of the stories is concerned, this means that any valuation or view of the world expressed in them is to be attributed to the protagonist rather than the author.

Beißner's account of Kafka's narrative perspectivism is certainly valuable and has helped other critics to achieve important insights into the fiction.[22] Unfortunately he overstates his case and has to produce contorted arguments to account for textual evidence which patently contradicts it. Gregor Samsa's 'transformation', for example, is declared to be the delusion of a sick mind. Yet Kafka deliberately, it seems, puts obstacles in the path of any interpretation which attempts to explain away the empirically incredible events as mere phantoms of Gregor's deluded imagination. Not only is Gregor himself forced to accept that 'It was no dream' (GW 1, 93), but the perspective shifts away from him, first to other characters, as when he is seen by his mother and sister as a large brown patch against the wall, and later to a conventional impersonal narratorial point of view after the death and removal of Gregor, when the family sets about enjoying life once more. To claim that everything that occurs after his death is actually part of Gregor's delusion is to speculate not just without but against the evidence of the text.

Over the years other critics have accumulated sufficient evidence to establish that Kafka's fictions are not strictly mono-perspectival but are balanced finely between the point of view of the protagonist and that of a narratorial consciousness which makes its presence known subtly but insistently, using the devices of irony to undermine the protagonist's perceptions, interpretations and evaluations of his world.[23] Recently, indeed, the pendulum has swung to the opposite extreme of insisting that the fictions are merely a pretext for playful narratorial self-reflection.[24] Kafka the writer, it is claimed, was obsessed in equal measure with writing and with the lack of fixity in language. A number of interpreters argue that his writing self, with its ability to produce texts full of ambiguities and shifting paradoxes, was cultivated by Kafka in order to escape and defy the constraints and false certitudes of the practical, functional, bourgeois world of his father and indeed of his own daily existence.[25] It is true that there are many allusions to the processes of writing in the fictions and it is important to be aware of the resistance of the language to exhaustive, definitive interpretation, but the critics who insist that the writing is always and *only* about writing do not always escape the danger of narrowing, even closing, the meaning of the texts whose very openness they keep insisting on. It is curious, too, how unanimous so many have become in claiming that the texts are infinitely 'polysemous'. In fact so many have climbed onto this latest bandwagon that it is creaking just as audibly as the one which was once weighed down by the excess baggage of the Freudians. The approach can result in allegorical equations as arbitrary as those made by the philosophical or theological or biographical interpreters. Thus even Stanley Corngold, one of the most sophisticated of the writing-about-writing school, whose malicious glee is palpable as he exposes the weaknesses in one interpretation of 'The Metamorphosis' after another,[26] is equally capable of making questionable allegorical identifications in the pursuit of his preferred way of reading. In one essay, for example, he asserts that the bachelor figure found in the gutter by an undefined 'I' in one of Kafka's early fragments represents an obstacle to the narrator's aim of 'liberating' his writing self.[27] Yet there is nothing in the little story to suggest that the narrator has any such ambition; indeed, the text actually says that the protagonist promises himself everything he lacks by joining the company or society ('Gesellschaft') in an upstairs room (GW 9, 89–94). This first-person narrator seems, if anything, to be a cipher for the social rather than for the isolated literary self. Such difficulties will always arise when critics rely on allegorical equations of Kafka's figures with abstractions drawn from other systems, be they theology, philosophy, psychoanalysis or 'textual self-reflexivity'.

The readings of Kafka's novels offered in the present volume attempt to take them, as far as possible, at face value. Like most novels, after all, they describe forms of human society (albeit of a rather peculiar kind); like most *German* novels, admittedly, they concentrate mainly on the experience of one particular individual in his dealings with others. During his most sustained phase of metaphysical speculation Kafka may have entertained the idea that the true (eternal) life of the human spirit was lived at some deeply hidden level of reality beyond man's cognizance and far distant from the labyrinth of daily existence, but this did not prevent him from observing the latter with great acuity, and producing novels as full of social and psychological insight as any in the mainstream realist tradition. Taking as its starting point the 'description of structures and relations internal to the text' recommended by Günter Heintz,[28] we will argue that Kafka saw the social and psychological sphere – life 'after the Fall', so to speak – as shaped principally by relationships based on power, and that these are illuminated from a new angle in each of his attempts at the genre. These conclusions are offered not as an exhaustive or exclusive interpretation of the novels, but simply as an attempt to understand one of the main strands in Kafka's fictional reflections on life.

3

The Missing Person

As with all his long works of fiction, Kafka found the writing of *The Missing Person* very difficult.[1] A first draft of two hundred pages was felt to be so unsatisfactory that he destroyed it entirely. The comparative ease with which he accomplished his 'breakthrough' story, 'The Judgement', however, encouraged him to resume work on the project from September 1912 until January 1913, with one substantial interruption for the writing of 'The Metamorphosis'. The novel then lay fallow until May 1914, when he took it up again briefly, and then again till August of that year when the success of his work on *The Trial* led him to make another attempt at completing it. The novel was finally left a fragment in October 1914.

The difficulties were partly external and partly internal. Kafka was close to despair at the prospect of having to break off work on the novel for two weeks in October 1912 in order to placate his parents by helping out at the jointly owned asbestos factory. Nevertheless, he tried to reassure Max Brod and himself that he would still be able to withdraw into the imaginary world of the novel even while outwardly occupied with the factory: 'It somehow seemed to me [. . .] that between the beginning of the novel and its continuation in a fortnight I shall move and live within the innermost parts of my novel, particularly in the factory, particularly vis-à-vis my satisfied parents' (DW, 32). In this case the external difficulty may actually have provided material for the novel since this includes descriptions of workplaces where, in the name of speed and efficiency, the employees are not allowed to talk to one another ('das Grüßen war abgeschafft' – V, 55),[2] while Kafka's renewed anger at his own parents' treatment of him may have helped define the long-term effects on Karl Roßmann of his upbringing.

Kafka's difficulties with the novel appear also to have arisen from his inspirational imagination. Editors who have examined the manuscript of *The Missing Person* minutely have shown how closely Kafka identified the progress of his work on the novel with the movement of the hero into an uncertain future. Thus when (in Chapter 3) Kafka was forced to abandon the manuscript for some time (in order to work at the asbestos factory), he has Karl make his way along a seemingly endless dark corridor until his way is barred by an ice-cold marble balustrade, beyond which he can feel only dark emptiness (V, 78). Conversely, Kafka's return to work on the novel after an interruption is signalled in the action of the story by a foreman clapping his hands to tell his men to start work again after their lunch break (V, 219).[3]

This starting and stopping of the novel may also reflect a conflict in the author as to the direction the story should take. In one letter to Felice Bauer, Kafka wrote that the novel ought to give her 'a clearer impression of the good in me' (DW, 33) than a lifetime's letters ever could. In another he stated that his stories were ultimately intended to serve her, which is to say, both love and life:

> If the people in my novel notice your jealousy they will run away from me, for I am only holding on to them by the hem of their clothing anyway. And remember that if they run away from me I would have to run after them, even into the underworld where they are actually at home. The novel is me, my stories are me – where, in that case, I ask you, could there be even the smallest room for jealousy. After all, if everything else is in order, all my characters are running towards you, arm in arm, in order ultimately to serve you. It is certainly true that I would not detach myself from the novel even if you were present; indeed it would be a bad thing if I could, for it is by my writing that I keep a hold on life, keep my hold on that boat on which you, Felice, stand. It is sad enough that I cannot quite succeed in pulling myself up there. But do understand, dearest Felice, that I am bound to lose you and everything, if once I lose my writing. (DW, 37–8)

In a later letter to Milena Jesenská, by contrast, Kafka described the novel as an 'abysmally bad story' in which he could hear 'the all too familiar voice from the old grave' (DW, 47). Eventually Kafka did give Karl's story a kind of half-hearted, ambiguous 'happy ending', which may have been the best he could do by way of making his writing seem to serve Felice, love and life. However, as we shall see, it is an ending which does not flow naturally from the events preceding it. It seems that the figures who led the author down into their 'underworld', where he wandered 'almost endlessly through the subterranean, gloomy, low and ugly passages of the story'

(DW, 48), were reluctant to let him find his way up and out into the light again.

A LITERARY JOURNEY

The Missing Person describes the travels through America of Karl Roßmann, a seventeen-year-old from Prague,[4] who has been sent away from home because he was seduced by the family maid. The city in which he lands is to be thought of as 'the most modern New York' (DW, 43–4) of which Kafka had read recent accounts, with its skyscrapers and ceaseless traffic, immense wealth and harsh exploitation.[5] Yet in his country of exile Karl encounters events and people scarcely less bizarre than those met by Gulliver or Ulysses on their travels: a siren called Klara who is skilled in jiu-jitsu, a mysterious letter delivered at the witching hour of midnight, a monstrous opera singer called Brunelda who, Circe-like, is attended by the swinish Delamarche and Robinson, and the vast 'Theatre of Oklahoma' which recruits new actors on a racecourse where men and women dressed as devils and angels stand on pillars, blowing cacophonously on trumpets.[6]

In this new world Karl Roßmann finds his expectations repeatedly confounded by events. The reader faces similar difficulties if he or she attempts to make sense of the novel's irritating mixture of recognizable social reality and unfamilar detail by assigning Karl's travels in America to some established type of literary journey. There are, for example, echoes of the benign and malevolent characters in *David Copperfield*, which Kafka claimed his own novel had merely imitated (DW, 46), but one finds neither the crusading moral convictions nor the detailed descriptions of domestic and other milieux which map the route of Dickens's young hero onto Victorian England. Equally, when Karl is led through workplaces where people have to function with machine-like rapidity, Kafka's descriptions can seem at times to anticipate Chaplin's caricatures of industrial work in *Modern Times*, but other oddities in the novel, such as the muscular Klara or the obese Brunelda or Mack's half-built country house, do not suggest that Kafka's controlling purpose was to analyse the workings of modern capitalist society.[7]

The reader with a knowledge of the German tradition of the 'Bildungs-roman' ('novel of self-formation'), in which, typically, a talented young man sets out to improve both himself and the world, is likely to recognize certain parallels and contrasts with Goethe's *Wilhelm Meister's Apprentice-ship*.[8] Inasmuch as Karl is sent away from home rather than making a bid for creative freedom (as Wilhelm Meister does), and appears to undergo precious little inner growth during his travels, apart, perhaps, from eventually learning a little more caution in his dealings with people, a good case can indeed be made for reading *The Missing Person* as a parody of the classic Bildungsroman. Again, however, something else is needed if one is to understand why the world into which Karl Roßmann is sent to learn (or not to learn) his lessons about life should deviate so persistently, and at times so grotesquely, from social reality.

Karl's naive character neither causes him to be initiated into great mysteries, as happens to the 'stupid fool' turned quester hero, the Knight Parzival (although he is eventually admitted into the company of the mysterious Theatre of Oklahoma), nor quite conforms to the type of the 'ingénu', such as Voltaire's Candide, or of the 'holy fool', such as Dostoyevsky's Christ-like 'Idiot', figures who are sent out into contemporary society by their authors to reveal, simply by contrast with their innocent example, its malice, hypocrisy and corruption. Although a well-intentioned lad with a good heart, Karl, by contrast, has already been sufficiently instructed in the ways of the world by his upbringing to believe that there are times when a lie or a bribe are expedient. In short, *The Missing Person* contains elements reminiscent of various types of literary journey without conforming fully to any of them. If anything, the familiar elements in the novel have the effect of underscoring the puzzling quality of its overall organization.

In part the oddity of this fictional world derives from striking patterns of character, event or imagery which seem charged with significance but which do not yield up their meaning readily. It is strange, for example, how many of the characters Karl meets are of great physical size. The first such figure is the stoker on the ship, a 'gigantic' man whose bulk is further emphasized by the tiny dimensions of his cabin. At his uncle's house in New York Karl is introduced to 'two large, fat gentlemen' (V, 56), a certain Mr Pollunder and a Mr Green. When Green next reappears at Pollunder's country house his 'gigantic' frame immediately makes Karl lose heart; as things go from bad to worse in the course of the evening Green seems to Karl to have grown so large that he even wonders fleetingly whether he might not have 'eaten up' Pollunder. Karl also encounters a parallel sequence of oversized female figures, the first being the towering Statue (or 'Goddess') of Liberty in New York harbour to whom the new arrival looks up in awe, the second a kindly-seeming cook who takes him under her wing in the Hotel Occidental, and the third the gargantuan ex-opera singer Brunelda. Objects, too, form patterns of repetition. The Statue of

Liberty, for example, holds aloft not her familiar torch but an ominous sword, the sight of which may well contribute to Karl's decision to go back below decks instead of disembarking with the others. When Karl enters the chief purser's office one of the first things to catch his attention is the sword hanging at the captain's side. Although the man standing next to the captain is actually carrying a bamboo cane, Karl sees this, too, as sticking out like a sword. The motif is picked up again in a much later episode when Karl is prevented from escaping from his unwanted companions by a long black stick held out by a policeman.

The 'chance' appearance of this policeman on the scene at the very moment when Karl is getting out of a taxi is just one of a whole series of crucial coincidences on which the plot hinges and which carry the events of the novel beyond the limits of plausibility.[9] The first chapter alone is riddled with them: Karl happens to knock, at random, on the door of the stoker's cabin when he goes below deck in search of his umbrella, the loss of which he just happens to notice when it is time to disembark; this stoker just happens to be a man with a grievance who drags Karl along with him to the purser's cabin to complain; the captain just happens to be in the purser's cabin when they arrive, along with a stranger who eventually reveals himself to be Karl's uncle, although his surname is Jakob rather than Bendelmayer; the uncle in turn happens to be in the cabin at that very moment because a letter from the mother of Karl's child has just reached him, 'after many misdirections', on the evening before Karl's ship was due to dock. Many events of this kind are signalled by the phrase, 'just as...'; what happens next usually has damaging consequences for Karl although this may not immediately be apparent.

Such frequent and, for the purposes of the plot, highly convenient coincidences were once the hallmark of 'novelistic' writing, a residue of the novel's origins in the fanciful genre of romance. Whereas Goethe was still happy to lay a trail of coincidences through *Wilhelm Meister's Apprenticeship*, they came to be shunned as an inartistic device once novelists had decided that the world ought to be described 'realistically'. Yet Kafka, a passionate admirer of the supreme realist Flaubert, scattered coincidences throughout *The Missing Person* as freely as any novelist of the seventeenth or eighteenth century. Why? If Karl's uncle is to be believed, the coincidences are evidence that 'signs and wonders' (V, 34) are still alive in America. The phrase originates in a faith in a benevolent Providence who works in mysterious ways.[10] Inasmuch as the coincidences in *The Missing Person* apparently conspire to reward vice and punish virtue, one might read the novel as parodying the belief in a universal moral order which was propagated by the authors of the Enlightenment and which was still producing endings-with-justice in the novels of Dickens. Even allowing for some such parodistic intention, however, the question remains as to who or what has replaced benevolent Providence as the source of the many *malevolent* coincidences in the novel. What gives rise to its implausible patterns of repetition? What 'fate' governs the twists and turns of Karl's journey through this peculiar America? Why is the action structured as it is?

A possible or partial answer to such questions is to be found in Karl Roßmann's early experiences at the hands of his family. These reveal a structure of power which is reproduced at every stage of his journey across America and down through the ranks of its society.[11] Far from deserving the name of a 'New World' of hope and opportunity, the country in which Karl has landed proves to be as merciless as the old world of Europe from which he has been expelled. The (unsuccessful) 'éducation sentimentale' to which Karl is subjected here reflects Kafka's lasting distrust and resentment of all educators, particularly parental ones. The roots from which this strangely shaped world springs, in other words, are psychological and moral.

REJECTION AND BANISHMENT

What the opening sentence of the novel describes in an almost offhand way, in a subordinate clause, as the reason for Karl's journey to America is nothing less than a moral scandal.[12] Karl has been expelled from his home and banished from the country because the family maid seduced him and got a child by him. His new-found uncle compares his treatment to the ejection of an annoying cat from a room and speculates that Karl's parents were motivated by the desire to avoid any scandal or the obligation to pay alimony. Whatever their reasons, the parents' decision appears fundamentally unjust, in that Karl is punished for a sexual act in which he was the victim rather than the perpetrator. As the seventeen-year-old Karl remembers it, what he experienced at the hands of the thirty-five-year-old Johanna Brummer resembled a rape more than a seduction. Having locked him in her room, she had put her arms round his neck as if throttling him, asked him to undress her but in fact undressed him, laid him on her bed and, finally:

pressed her naked belly against his body, searched with her hand between his legs so disgustingly that Karl shook his head and neck clear of the pillows, then she pushed her belly against him a number of times, it seemed as if she were a part of him and perhaps this is why he had been seized by a terrible need for help. Finally, after she had said many times that she wished to see him again, he reached his own bed in tears. (V, 36)

The account resembles that of a child, or at least of someone quite innocent of sexual matters, who has been sexually abused.

Ironically, Karl's submissiveness towards the older Johanna, for which he is then punished by his parents, is a behavioural trait inculcated by his parents themselves. Even after being sent away from home, his attitude to his parents remains deeply submissive. Admittedly, his first reaction to his mother's announcement that he was to be sent away had been to vow angrily and 'irrevocably' (V, 106) that he would never write home to them. As the ship pulls into New York harbour, however, he thinks of them as his 'poor parents', a phrase intended by Kafka to convey 'uncomprehending sympathy' although without any particular emotional emphasis.[13] That this pity is bound up with feelings of guilt on Karl's part is suggested by his complicated response to a photograph of his parents which is perhaps the dearest of his few possessions. The figures are posed in conventional studio manner, with the father standing next to the seated mother, one hand on the back of her armchair. Seen through Karl's eyes, however, their gestures and expressions convey a quite personal message. Although small in stature, the father stands very erect, his clenched fist highlighted by contrast with the 'flimsy decorative table' (V, 106) on which it rests. As his bearing suggests, he is an ex-soldier, and one who inspires fear in his son. Revealingly, however, Karl now carries all his possessions in his father's old army trunk. As he scrutinizes the photograph, it seems to Karl that his father is refusing to communicate with him. He tries to catch his father's gaze from various angles, but his father refuses 'to come more to life' (V, 106) no matter how often Karl changes the picture by holding the candle in different positions. The complex image he 'sees' in the photograph is that of a powerful, angry, dismissive – and yet emotionally *lifeless* – father. Is this because of the shame Karl has supposedly brought upon the family? Karl deals with this patently disturbing reflection of his own admiration, resentment and guilt by telling himself, flatly, that the portrait is 'quite unlike reality' (V, 106).

His mother's image, by contrast, strikes Karl as almost too lifelike to be believable:

It was a rather better picture of his mother, her mouth was twisted, as if some hurt had been done to her and as if she were forcing herself to smile. This must be so plain to anyone looking at the picture, it seemed to Karl, that the impression struck him a moment later as being too clear and even absurd. How could a picture convey so convincingly, so indubitably, the hidden feelings of the person depicted? And he looked away from the picture for a while. When he looked back at it, his gaze fell on his mother's hand which hung down right at the front of the arm-rest, close enough to kiss. (V, 106)

This image of his mother may strike Karl as so implausibly lifelike precisely because he sees in it what he would dearly like to see, namely a much more acceptable response to the 'hurt' he has done her, a willingness to make the best of things (the brave smile) and even an offer of reconciliation in the hand held out 'close enough to kiss'. Presumably it is a kiss of submission and supplication that is being demanded, for which it would be necessary to bow or kneel down.

Indirectly, of course, kissing the hand of his mother would also express submission to his father, so much does their picture convey an image of conventional parental unity. For Karl, however, this would not be too high a price to pay for re-admission to the family from which he has been excluded, both in reality and on the photograph. He would prefer to have had another picture to look at, one he had not been allowed to take with him, in which he was at least shown in the company of his parents, albeit as the object of a severe gaze from both of them. As Karl lies down to sleep, pressing the cool glass (a beautifully ambiguous detail) of the photograph against his burning cheek, his feelings are still that of a child who is desperate to recover the love of his hurt, distant and angry parents, and who is therefore quite prepared to accept any 'guilt', whether real or merely invented, for being the cause of all this misery, if doing so will only gain him re-admission to the family. Although Karl is the one to whom wrong has *been done*, the need for love makes him willing to believe, even now, that he is being justly punished by his present unhappiness:

He was in the company of two down-and-outs in the garret of an inn outside New York and, what is more, he had to admit that this was where he really belonged. And with a smile he examined the faces of his parents as if it were possible to tell from them whether they still wished to receive news of their son. (V, 107)

This deeply rooted, submissive reaction of the child who has had love withdrawn from him is at the heart of all that happens to Karl in the novel.[14]

Kafka's bold and original method in *The Missing Person* is, then, to view the world from the static childhood perspective of submission to the absolute and unjust power of adults on whom the child is materially and emotionally dependent. The boldness lies in making the child-protagonist seventeen years old while the adults he has to deal with still exercise the kind of capriciousness and dominance normally reserved for the treatment of infants.[15] The central theme of the novel is the profoundly disabling, in this case ineradicable, emotional effect of childhood subjection to adult power. In its cyclical structure the underlying trauma of subjugation and rejection in childhood issues in an obsessive, self-perpetuating downward spiral into ever greater abuse. While Kafka may have taken over from Dickens the 'method' of estranging the practices of powerful adults by seeing them with the sensibility and imagination of a child, he applied the method with a new radicalism, with 'sharper lights' (DW, 47) taken from his times, so that arbitrary power is shown stripped of all the rational justifications in which it normally pleases to parade.

ADOPTION

The centrality of Karl Roßmann's experiences *as a son* to any understanding of his 'fate' is evident throughout the first chapter of *The Missing Person*, the only part Kafka considered worthy of publication. It appeared in 1913 under the title 'The Stoker' in Kurt Wolff's avant-garde series *Der jüngste Tag* (*Judgement Day*). So important was the theme to him that Kafka wanted to re-issue 'The Stoker' along with 'The Metamorphosis' and 'The Judgement' in a volume entitled *The Sons*. The stories clearly were closely linked in his imagination, for the manuscript of the novel occasionally refers to Karl as Georg,[16] the name of the hero of 'The Judgement', while Georg's second name, Bendemann, resembles Bendelmayer, the maiden name of Karl's mother; 'Bende' also has the same number of letters as both Samsa and Kafka. Kafka may have hoped that the joint publication of all three stories under a common title would produce a volume with more inner unity than he felt he had achieved in the remainder of the novel.

At any rate, the formative effect of Karl's experiences in the family pervades 'The Stoker' from the very first sentence. While his ship is slowing down in New York harbour Karl is shown gazing up at the

'Goddess of Liberty', her sword held aloft while 'free airs' swirl around her, with a new intensity, 'as if in sunlight which had suddenly become stronger' (V, 9). Karl's vision of the figure, presented by means of Kafka's favourite technique of free indirect speech, is charged with ambivalence. There is a sense of exhilaration in the energy of the wind[17] and in the upward thrust of her arm. The mixture of awe and excitement is even clearer in two sentences Kafka deleted in the manuscript: 'He looked up to her and discarded all he had learned about her. "She really is magnificent." '[18] Although he is gradually pushed towards the railings by the bustling porters, Karl nevertheless appears so reluctant to disembark that a fellow passenger is prompted to ask if he doesn't feel like getting off yet (V, 9). Karl responds with a laugh and a show of high spirits, but then suddenly remembers the umbrella he has left below, asks an acquaintance to keep an eye on his case and hurries off in search of the umbrella. One does not need to be a devotee of Freud to suspect that Karl's 'forgetting' the umbrella may express his unconscious need for an excuse *not* to set foot in America. After all, the 'goddess' he sees on its threshold brandishes not the torch of liberty but rather the sword of war or of justice (or perhaps even the flaming sword of the angel guarding the gates of paradise),[19] confronting him with a reminder of his punitive parents and his expulsion from his childhood home. Karl's impulsive abandonment of his suitcase, containing not just his clothes but his only reminders of home, may similarly express an unconscious wish to rid himself of his ties to his family. Equally disinclined to carry the burden of his past any longer or to accept Liberty's challenge to disembark, Karl flees back down into the innards of the liner.

The escape attempt, if such it is, is in vain. Employing another of his most widely and subtly used techniques, Kafka confronts Karl with a mirror image of himself in the person of the ship's stoker who then leads him into the first of numerous repetitions of the 'family scenes' of childhood. The outcome is to enclose Karl once again in a new version of the family, headed now by a very rich uncle rather than a relatively poor father.

The lower decks to which Karl returns have acquired in the meantime a nightmarish, labyrinthine quality by the closing of a familiar gangway during the preparations for disembarkation, so that he has to wander through countless small rooms, along corridors which constantly turn off in new directions, and up one short flight of stairs after another, until he is completely disoriented.[20] Eventually Karl hammers 'without thinking' on a little door chosen at random. Behind the door he finds another dream-like scene – a tiny cabin with a bed, a cupboard, a chair and a man, all close up against one another as if put into store (V, 10). The massive man opens and shuts the lock on a little case repeatedly, then pulls the hesitant Karl into the room, quickly closing the door behind him. The man's repeated gestures of closure and locking foreshadow what awaits Karl.

Karl's response to being locked in a room with a large stranger illustrates his ingrained habit of adopting a submissive posture to anyone who seems more powerful than he is. He asks himself (quite without evidence one way or the other) where he might find a better friend, but betrays his nervousness by wishing he still had his case containing the Veronese salami so that he could buy the stranger's goodwill. Karl had been taught this method of dealing with minor power-holders by his father: 'For such people can easily be won over by slipping them some little gift, Karl remembered that from his father who won over all the minor employees he had business dealings with by handing out cigars' (V, 15). In fact, however, the learned habits of submissiveness prove more damaging than helpful to Karl in the long run.

Karl begins to view the stoker rather differently when, prompted by Karl's xenophobic suspicions, the latter pours out his resentment at being treated unfairly by the Roumanian chief engineer. Lying on the stoker's bunk, Karl immediately identifies with him as another victim of unjust power: ' "You mustn't stand for that", said Karl excitedly. He had almost lost all sense of being on the unsteady deck of a ship off the coast of an unknown continent, so at home did he feel here on the stoker's bed' (V, 14). Karl then urges the stoker, very revealingly, to seek redress from the captain. Although his own unjust banishment makes him share the stoker's anger at injustice, the deeper need of the child within him to trust figures of authority prompts him to appeal to a yet higher authority for help. This ingrained need to believe that power can coexist with justice, mercy or love makes it extremely difficult for Karl to draw appropriate conclusions from his experiences. Instead of learning to distrust those with power, he constantly seeks to reinstate parental figures to a position of respect and to regain by his own righteous conduct the love his real parents have withdrawn from him.

Although initially sceptical of Karl's proposal, the older man is suddenly sparked into action by the return of the ship's band (which sounds to Karl's ears like the 'rattling as of weapons' – V, 16). Seizing Karl by the hand, he marches off with seeming boldness to confront his superiors – but not before tucking a picture of the Holy Mother into his breast pocket, a gesture which echoes Karl's attachment to an idealized vision of the

family. Inwardly no less cowed by power than Karl, the massive stoker
knocks 'respectfully' on the imposingly pillared door of the purser's cabin
and, like one nervous schoolboy to another, signals to *Karl* to enter 'without fear' (V, 18).

It is evident from Karl's conduct in the purser's office ('Hauptkassa')
that his ambition to win justice for the stoker is fatally flawed in three
closely related respects. Firstly, Karl shows himself to be strongly attracted
to and by power. From the moment he enters the room his heart beats
faster as he looks down on the scene of small and large ships criss-crossing
the harbour, at the steely gleam of the guns on passing warships and across
to the skyscrapers of New York which, he thinks, are spectators of a scene
in which he occupies centre stage: 'But behind it all stood New York,
watching Karl with the hundred thousand windows of its skyscrapers. Yes,
in this room you knew where you were' (V, 18). Secondly, Karl's conviction that the stoker has been unjustly treated rests on nothing more than
prejudice. Just as he readily shares the stoker's antipathy towards foreign-
ers, he simply accepts his complaints about the chief engineer at face
value, without asking for any evidence to support the charges or trying
to test them in any way. Plainly, Karl's failure to question the stoker's
version of events springs from his identification with another victim of ill-
treatment, while his demand for justice is motivated by his own contradictory desires to strike back at the powerful while at the same time
seeking to regain the approval of his parents:

> Karl felt stronger and more alert than he had perhaps ever been
> at home. If only his parents could see him now, fighting the good
> fight in a foreign land in front of people in positions of respect [...]
> Would they change their opinion of him? Sit him down between them
> and praise him? Look once, just once, into eyes that were so devoted to
> them? (V, 29)

Kafka's sardonic verdict on Karl's prejudice in favour of the stoker is to
have it answered by an equal and opposite prejudice on the part of those
in authority.

Finally, Karl's aim of achieving justice for the stoker is flawed because
he does not truly believe in the processes of justice. He recognizes from the
outset that the outcome of the stoker's case will be decided by the powers
of influence and rhetorical persuasion rather than by establishing the
truth. This is evident from Karl's own rather inflated way of addressing
the assembled figures of authority: ' "I permit myself to say [...] that in my

opinion an injustice has been done to this gentleman, the stoker [...] Thus it can only be some calumny which is obstructing his progress and denying him the recognition which would otherwise quite definitely be his"' (V, 20–1). Yet even as Karl is asserting that the justice of the stoker's case is beyond all doubt, he betrays his fundamental lack of trust in justice by 'cunningly' suppressing the fact that he has only just met the stoker. When the stoker begins to present his own case, Karl is so impressed by his controlled manner of referring to 'Mr' Schubal that he toys with the letter-balance on the purser's desk, pressing it down repeatedly out of sheer delight that the stoker's powers of persuasion seem to be tipping the scales in his favour. When the stoker's speech becomes a little clumsy, however, Karl tries to add to its persuasive force by staring with all his might at the captain as if he were a colleague of his (V, 23). Ironically, an answering gesture comes not from the captain but from a servant who feels sympathy for the sufferings of the 'little man' placed amongst and beneath the great and who nods to Karl 'as if to explain something' (V, 23). Such sympathy merely confirms that the existing power relationships are unlikely to collapse because of an appeal to justice. This, at any rate, is the lesson spelled out by Karl's uncle, a Senator with every interest in maintaining the status quo: '"Do not misunderstand the situation [...] It is perhaps a matter of justice but at the same time it is a matter of discipline. Both and quite particularly the latter are subject here to the captain's jurisdiction"' (V, 40). A further remark, subsequently deleted by Kafka from the manuscript, states the matter even more plainly: '"But justice and discipline do not mix."'[21]

Karl is unaware not only of his own prejudices but also of the extent to which he is attached to hierarchical values. Although he notices that the sympathetic servant is the only person not to become bored and distracted during the stoker's speech, Karl's own attention drifts away to the harbour scene visible through the porthole. Put to the test, he is as inattentive to the stoker's increasingly inarticulate pleas as those in authority. In contrast to his earlier demand for action, he falls into resigned contemplation of the natural hierarchy evident in the power of the sea and the relative impotence of human beings: 'A movement without end, a restlessness transferred from the restless element to helpless human beings and their works' (V, 24). As the stoker's cause gradually sinks amid the turbulence of his own indignant denunciations, Karl observes his behaviour critically, adopting the point of view of the captain who, however good a man he might be, 'was not an instrument one could play to destruction' (V, 25). Karl tries to help the stoker by advising him to present his complaints in a more orderly manner, claiming, quite untruthfully, that this is how he has presented them to Karl, and excusing his lie to himself with the sophistry that if they can steal suitcases in America he can surely tell a lie. (In fact the supposed theft of his case is just another of the stoker's unsupported assertions.) All of this is further evidence that Karl is less interested in establishing truth and justice than in winning the struggle for power. There is thus an apt if ironic chiasmus formed by the rise of Karl's fortunes while those of the stoker sink ever further, for inwardly Karl has already adopted the perspective and tactics of the powerful before being drawn over to their side.

This turn of events comes about in two stages. Firstly, the stoker rounds on Karl, hurt and angry, so that Karl feels guilty at having robbed him of all hope by his criticisms. Then the nameless 'gentleman with the bamboo cane' asks for Karl's name. At first Karl ignores the question and tries desperately to rally his forces, only to realize that the stoker has lost all ability to fight: 'He stood there, legs apart, knees slightly bent, head raised, while the air passed through his open mouth as if there were no longer any lungs inside to absorb it' (V, 28–9). Just as Karl's father appears to him to be 'lifeless' in the photograph, so the life now seems to be draining away from his newly adopted friend as a result of a confrontation urged on him by Karl. By the time Karl agrees to accept the uncle's claim on him, he has come to the painful realization that to join the uncle means sacrificing his instinctive sympathy with the stoker and his inarticulate demands for justice: 'And now Karl wept as he kissed the stoker's hand and took the cracked, almost lifeless hand and pressed it to his cheeks like a treasure that had to be relinquished' (V, 41). The recurrent death imagery, the kiss on the hand and the pressing of it to his cheek all parallel the mixture of guilt and attachment Karl feels towards the photograph of his parents. As in his own case, it is again not Karl who is responsible for the stoker's unhappiness but those in authority.

When Karl kisses the hand of his uncle it is to acknowledge his submission to a new, more powerful but equally stern father-figure who, in return for his protection, demands that Karl should distance himself from the stoker, share the uncle's detestation of his own family, and accept that discipline must take precedence over justice. As the uncle puts it, Karl must learn to 'understand his position' (V, 41). The choice before Karl is either to commit himself wholeheartedly to the emotional values embodied in the stoker, whatever the consequences, or to submit to the existing hierarchy of power. He chooses the latter. Seated in the boat that will ferry them ashore, Karl has lost sight of the stoker entirely – 'It really was as if the stoker no longer existed' (V, 44) – but he still doubts whether the uncle will ever take the place of the stoker. The core of childlike good-heartedness in him will ensure that Karl never becomes entirely consumed by the power to which he has surrendered. At the same time his dream of reconciling power with humanity will ensure that he succumbs repeatedly to those who regard power as something entirely sufficient unto itself.

DESIRE AND DISCIPLINE

Thanks to his adoption by his uncle, an American Senator and owner of a vast warehousing and transport company, the next stage of Karl's journey initially takes him even higher in the world than the cabin of the chief purser, to a spacious flat high above the streets of New York. By the end of it, however, he is quite literally down and out, sent out onto the highways of America to make his way as best he can. Having been raised by the power of his uncle, Karl falls because he fails to appreciate the price exacted by power in return for its protection and privileges.

The uncle's career in America had equally humble beginnings. He owes his present wealth and position to the principles of hard work, caution and self-discipline which, so he claims, he dare not forsake without risking the loss of all he has achieved. His treatment of Karl seems designed to inculcate these same principles so that Karl, too, may have a 'brilliant career' ('glänzende Laufbahn' – V, 31). Part of Karl responds readily to the 'Glanz' ('gleam' or 'brilliance') of power. Although probably fearful of her, he had thought the Goddess of Liberty 'magnificent' when he caught sight of her 'in sunlight that had suddenly become stronger'. Throughout the novel, however, things that gleam or sparkle (the eyes of Klara or Brunelda, for example) usually prove dangerous to Karl. When he moves into his uncle's flat, Karl immediately takes great delight in looking down from the balcony to the ever-changing street which fascinates him with its images of light, might, energy and even violence:

All this was seized and pervaded by a mighty light which was constantly being scattered by the mass of objects, carried off by them and busily brought back together, and which seemed to the bewitched eye so material that it was as if every second a pane of glass covering every-thing in the street were constantly being smashed to pieces with full force. (V, 46)

The phrase 'to the bewitched eye' ('dem betörten Auge') is for Kafka an unusually direct authorial indication that Karl has succumbed to a dangerously exciting illusion.[22] The uncle has his own reasons for showing his disapproval of Karl's liking for the balcony. He warns him against becoming 'captivated' by what he sees, urges him to be cautious in his judgements and advises him to refrain from gaping inactively at the 'work-filled New York day' (V, 46–7) like someone travelling for pleasure.[23] Noting his uncle's repeated looks of disapproval, Karl decides to deny himself the pleasure of standing on the balcony 'as far as possible'. As this phrase indicates, Karl finds it difficult in practice to resolve the conflict between his own desires and the self-discipline demanded by his uncle.

Karl is made to feel this conflict in a number of ways. His room contains, for example, an elaborate modern writing desk of a type his father had always coveted but had never been able to afford, even at auction prices. The child in Karl treats the contraption like a complicated toy, cranking its handle slowly or quickly by turns to produce ever new constellations of shelves and panels, and thinking back to the similarly operated nativity scenes he used to love watching at the Christmas fair. But just as his mother would put her hand over his mouth to stifle his childish shouts of delight, so his uncle, who only wanted him to have a 'decent' ('ordentlichen') desk without any such mechanism, seeks to suppress his playfulness by warning him not to use the allegedly delicate and fragile mechanism 'as far as possible' (V, 48). Although the uncle could easily have had the mechanism immobilized, however, he does not do so. It seems that he wants to expose Karl to the conflict between desire and discipline and to require him to suppress his *own* wishes in deference to his benefactor. Power, so the uncle seems to understand, operates most successfully when those who are subject to it carry out the work of repression for themselves.

A further clash between Karl's desire and his uncle's discipline comes about when he requests a piano. Again he does not meet with outright refusal but with reluctant consent followed by the attempt to harness his artistic impulse to a disciplinary programme in which there is no room for the 'free instinct of play'.[24] The uncle first gives Karl useful, backbone-stiffening music to practise – American marches and the national anthem – and then tries to persuade him to make a more serious commitment to musical training by suggesting that he might also learn other instruments. Karl, by contrast, likes merely to play an old soldiers' song full of sentimental longings which he heard in childhood and to dream of changing American life through his playing.

These episodes all contain echoes of Goethe's *Wilhelm Meister's Apprenticeship*, a model of the optimistic belief in personal growth which infused the German classical movement and inspired its emulators in the nineteenth century.[25] The young Karl's excitement at the mechanical nativity scenes recalls Wilhelm Meister's boyhood passion for his puppet theatre, while Wilhelm's ambition to change the life of the nation by reforming the theatre is a precursor of Karl's brief dream of exerting influence on the entire life of America through his (utterly amateurish) piano playing. The allusions help to highlight the fundamentally different premisses of the two novels. Superficially, Karl's merchant uncle shares the same stern attitude to children as Wilhelm's merchant father who expresses the view that adults should deny children their wishes 'out of conviction' and that 'one should appear earnest when they were enjoying themselves and sometimes spoil their pleasure lest their contentment should lead them to excess and high spirits'.[26] Yet although both Wilhelm's father and Karl's uncle appear to endorse the same adage about sparing the rod and spoiling the child, they actually differ fundamentally in their feelings towards children. Goethe employs a mobile narrative point of view which allows the reader to see that, behind his stern mask, Wilhelm Meister's father is really very fond of his son, however much he may make it a principle to conceal the strength of his love for his children. Because that concealment, inevitably, is far from perfect, Wilhelm sets off on his journey through life in the secure knowledge that he is the beloved child of kindly parents. Admittedly, Karl Roßmann also speaks of his uncle's 'love' when he accuses himself of disobedience in going away with Pollunder, but his panic at this point only confirms the impression that their relationship is not actually founded on love and trust but on domination, dependency and fear. Karl fondly imagines making a new start with his uncle, going into his bedroom and taking breakfast with him, but this wishful thinking contrasts starkly with the fact that his uncle has never allowed Karl even to share his dining table except to introduce him to his business associates, Green and Pollunder. The uncle's purpose in arranging the meeting with Pollunder may even have been to expose Karl deliberately to the temptations embodied in Pollunder's daughter Klara, just as he had previously introduced Karl to the spoiled millionaire's son Mack whose carefree existence offers a taunting and tempting contrast to the self-discipline demanded of Karl.

Wilhelm's father and Karl's substitute father differ most signally in the way they respond to the errors of the young. During his first long journey alone Wilhelm commits numerous mistakes, abandoning the commercial and educational programme which is the proper purpose of his trip, joining a troupe of strolling players, misjudging his companions and so on. Yet all the while his meanderings are being observed from a discreet distance by the members of the 'Society of the Tower', a kind of private freemasonry of the spirit, a group of substitute parents whose aim is to fend off the worst consequences of Wilhelm's errors. Karl's uncle, by contrast, not only rejects him with the same harshness as his original parents for committing just one error in an ambiguous situation, but he even colludes with Green, Klara and Mack to humiliate Karl before banishing him irrevocably. Where Goethe could once imagine a group of benevolent spirits acting providentially, Kafka has created a conspiracy of malevolence.

The trap is sprung as soon as Karl arrives with Pollunder at a villa (which is actually owned by Mack) on the outskirts of New York. They are welcomed by Klara Pollunder with the news that Green has arrived just before them. Pollunder, presumably sensing that something is afoot, wants to drive Karl straight back to his uncle's house, but Klara urges them to stay and Green comes out to hurry them into the house. It later emerges that Green is the bearer of a letter from the uncle expelling Karl from his household forever. The letter is to be opened at midnight. Karl might never have received the fateful news if he had carried out his sudden, remorseful decision to return to his uncle's house immediately to beg his forgiveness, but he is dissuaded from doing so by Green and Pollunder, who has presumably been drawn into the conspiracy during a hushed conversation with Green. In order to ensure that Karl does not receive the letter until after the witching hour, Green even insists he must say goodnight to Klara, thus using the object of his desire as an instrument of his humiliation.

None of this is the behaviour of a loving or, as he signs himself, a 'true' uncle genuinely concerned to educate his protégé, for a loving education will make allowances for the mistakes and even the hurt a child may do to parent or mentor. Edward Jakob's actions are those of a petty tyrant who will not tolerate even a single denial of his power and jealous possessiveness. In his letter of banishment, it is true, he addresses Karl as his 'beloved nephew', claiming that Karl would be the first person for whose sake he would be prepared – if this were at all possible – to abandon the 'principles' on which his entire existence has been built. But what are these principles and what laws dictate them? If the uncle's highest principles are discipline and self-interest, it is sheer hypocrisy to speak of his love for Karl. If there is no room in this beleaguered life for feeling, it can have been nothing more than possessiveness that prompted his boastful question to the ship's captain, ' "Don't I have a splendid nephew then?" ' (V, 37). If another millionaire like Mack is free to live a life of undisciplined self-indulgence, why should one believe the claim that a man of the Senator's immense wealth and influence would inevitably be destroyed if he allowed himself even the small indulgence of putting love and forgiveness for his nephew above the dictates of discipline?

Kafka was undoubtedly interested in the institutional forms and effects of power, whether in the shape of capitalist enterprises or systems of law, but his analysis of power in this novel is not so much sociological as moral and psychological. Karl's uncle does not simply live *by* power but also *for* power, power as an end in itself. His vast business and the capitalist system of which it is part are certainly shown to be inhuman undertakings, but material imperatives are not shown to determine his behaviour. At the hub of the business there sits a man who simply wants to possess and dominate others, who may even have adopted Karl to give himself the illusion of humanity in an inhumane world. If Kafka had wanted to depict the alienating effects of the capitalist *system*, he would have had to focus attention on the impersonal compulsions of money and markets. Instead he has depicted relationships between individuals where personal forms of power, such as possessiveness, jealousy and capriciousness, dominate. Thus, when Klara wrestles Karl to the ground, her motive for humiliating him is anger at his unwillingness to do her bidding or respond to her sexual invitation. Similarly, Mack has nothing to gain by mocking Karl from the luxury of Klara's bed except the sheer pleasure of malice. Whatever he may claim in his letter of banishment, there is no evidence that Karl's uncle is anything but a scheming and hypocritical bully.

Karl, for his part, provides the perspective of injury from which power is seen as in an enlarging and distorting mirror. At the same time Karl's victimization by the powerful is, in part, made possible by the fact that he is made of the same fragile and corruptible human stuff as his persecutors. If Edward Jakob is being selfish when he adopts Karl, Karl is also being selfish when he insists on going to Pollunder's house to meet Klara despite the evidence of his uncle's displeasure. Karl's readiness to desert his uncle temporarily is then answered by his uncle's willingness to sever their ties permanently. Something resembling the symmetry of 'an eye for an eye' appears to be at work, even if it is distorted by the unequal distribution of power between uncle and nephew. Having enjoyed, in Senator Jakob's house, the privileges power can bestow on the favoured few, Karl becomes one of its victims. While driving out to the villa in Pollunder's car he enjoys being cradled like a child in Pollunder's arm and savours the prospect of soon being a welcome guest in a well-lit country house surrounded by walls and guarded by dogs (V, 60–1), well away from the disturbed and choked streets of New York where masses of workers are striking against the power of those whose privileges Karl presently shares. Within the space of a few hours that secluded country house will have turned into a dark, labyrinthine trap from which Karl can only escape through grounds patrolled by the very same dogs whose protection he had sought.[27] The laws of this fictional world are harsh indeed. It is ruled by power alone. Although the powerful may speak of love, the price they demand for their protection is unquestioning submission. To accept or seek the privileges of the powerful is to run the risk of becoming their next victim.

'THE BEWITCHED EYE'

From time to time Karl becomes aware of how little he understands the world. As a child he had been fascinated to observe how the turning of a handle translated itself into the movements of the various mechanical figures in the nativity scenes. His childish enthusiasm and curiosity remain evident in his excitement at meeting the ship's stoker: ' "I have always been interested in technical things [. . .] and I would surely have become an engineer later if I had not been forced to travel to America" ' (V, 12). Later he is frustrated to discover that his post as a lift boy in the Hotel Occidental does not allow him to have anything to do with the machinery of the lift. All this is part of a wider desire in Karl to understand and influence the world, evident in his resigned contemplation of the ceaseless traffic in the street below, a 'small part of a mighty circulation which one could not simply bring to a halt without knowing all the forces which drove it around' (V, 50). Here Kafka's phrasing carries a faint echo of Faust's exorbitant desire to know 'what holds the world together at its inmost heart, and see the seed and driving force of all'.[28] Whether or not the parallel and contrast are intended, the novel reveals an ironic disparity between Karl's desire to know and act, and his repeated failures to perceive how things are in reality.

Thus, for example, when Green hands Karl a cap to replace his hat, Karl neither registers the social implications of the exchange (namely that he is about to descend the social ladder again) nor its proverbial implication (if the cap fits he should wear it).[29] In fact he does not even recognize the cap as his own until it falls from his head into the familiar surroundings of his suitcase. Kafka reinforces the point with another example of mis-perception during Karl's march to Ramses in the company of two ruffians, Delamarche and Robinson. During a pause they look back on New York (and Boston!) from a rise. Whereas Karl can barely see any difference between the large and the small houses and has the impression that everything in these great cities is 'empty and put there for no purpose' (V, 113), his companions excitedly point out well-known squares, gardens and other places of entertainment. Each, in other words, sees things through the lens of his particular experience and disposition. Karl's flat, empty gaze is one of melancholy exclusion from a world which had seemed so vibrant when seen from his uncle's balcony. The subjective element in his perception is perhaps most evident in the 'trembling' of the bridge over the river or the windows lining the road, for this is just how these things would appear to eyes filling up with tears.

Karl's subjective perceptions do him the greatest harm in the area of personal relationships. Not only does he still crave the affection of parents who rejected him quite unfairly, but he extends the same unjustified loyalty to his uncle and Mack. He deliberately ignores the evidence of widespread class conflict in America, preferring to side with his uncle rather than listen to Delamarche's criticism of the fraudulent methods used by Edward Jakob's firm to recruit new employees. Similarly he dismisses the complaints of striking building-workers about their employer, Mack's father, as merely the 'talk of ill informed and ill willed people' (V, 115). What makes Karl's behaviour so extraordinary is the fact that his own experiences at the hands of the treacherous Mack and his scheming uncle have given him no reason to think them admirable or trustworthy. The self-injuring submission to those who have injured him, a response to power learned early in life, is shown to be a powerful psychological compulsion governing Karl's behaviour in one situation after another. The chief irony in Karl's fascination with matters technical and mechanical thus lies in his persistent failure to understand the damaging psychological mechanisms at work *within* him.

The entire episode with Delamarche and Robinson illustrates the operation of these mechanisms in Karl. He is pitched into their company at a cheap lodging house where he seeks shelter after being expelled from the villa. Observing that they sleep in their clothes and that one even still has his boots on, Karl draws the (petty bourgeois) conclusion that they are an untrustworthy pair. In fact this eventually proves to be entirely correct, but Karl is so uneasy at the thought of sharing the room with a pair of suspicious strangers that he promptly re-interprets the evidence to conclude that they are really harmless hotel servants who sleep in their clothes because they must rise early to attend to the guests. This is much as he had behaved when, finding himself locked in the tiny cabin with the huge stoker, he asked himself where he could possibly find a better friend. Such childish wishful thinking is usually the prelude to a turn for the worse in his affairs.

The damage begins on the following morning, when Karl lets himself be persuaded by his new-found companions to sell his best suit for next to nothing. Karl knows he has been cheated but prefers to raise no protest. Delamarche and Robinson then proceed to rook him systematically, eating the Veronese salami he has kept in his case throughout his journey, and paying for the midday meal (plus an extravagant tip to the waitress) with his money. Karl is angry but he expresses his feelings in the inverted manner of a coward, refusing to eat and drink with them, just as he had done in the face of Green's aggressive, demonstrative pleasure in eating (including the carving of a dove!) at the villa. Nor is this the kind of tactical cowardice that simply waits for a suitable opportunity to escape or take revenge. When the three stop their march for the night Karl offers to fetch – and pay for – food at a nearby hotel and even feels guilty, although it is again not his fault, about the delay in coming back with their order. So ingrained is his habit of loyal submission to those he fears that he initially declines the hotel cook's offer of a bed in the hotel, ignoring her criticism of his stubbornness. Only when he discovers that Delamarche and Robinson have rifled his suitcase in his absence, and caused the loss of his parents' photograph, does Karl decide to take up the cook's offer. The arrival of a waiter sent out by the cook to look for him gives Karl the upper hand over Delamarche and Robinson but he plainly has never learned how to use power to his own advantage, for, rather than take revenge on them, he even offers money to his persecutors if only they will return the missing photograph of his parents. His distress at the disappearance of the picture serves to emphasize how much Karl remains in thrall to the values on which his internal image of loving or benign power rests.

WORK

While watching the ships in New York harbour, Karl is struck by the unending, restless motion of the sea and its power to spread its unrest to helpless human beings 'and their works' (V, 24). In Kafka's America the institutional equivalent of that restless energy and compelling power is the workplace.

Karl is given just a brief glimpse of the American way of working in the telephone exchange of his uncle's business, but he has his first direct experience of it as a lift boy in the Hotel Occidental, a name which indicates its representative significance. As in the telephone exchange, all work is carried out here with inhuman speed: waiters run, a typist's fingers race faster than the ticking of the clock, enquiries are answered so quickly at the information desk that each piece of information merges with the next. The demands of work conflict systematically with the needs of the workers, who suffer from a chronic lack of sleep, working till late into the night and beginning again very early next morning. The cook's assistant, Therese, tells of a little kitchen girl who had become so exhausted that she was admitted to hospital; Karl is employed to replace a young lift boy called Giacomo whom the head cook (Karl's new patron) finds asleep on his feet beside his lift. According to the cook, Giacomo will ultimately be made big and strong by working in America, but when Karl meets up with him again in the Theatre of Oklahoma Giacomo's condition shows no sign of the promised improvement. In this society, one person's gain means another person's loss. The conflict between work and nature is further expressed through the symbolism of clothing: the lift boys must stamp their feet hard to force them into boots that are too narrow; Karl is handed a fine uniform which is not only stiff and cold from the sweat of his predecessors but is so tight across the chest that he can hardly breathe. The wider background of exploitation is indicated by the masses of strikers glimpsed by Karl from the comfort of Pollunder's car and by Delamarche's criticism of the employment practices of Karl's uncle. That the consequences of unemployment in this society are even more terrible than the exactions of work is made plain by Therese's moving (and very convincing) account of her mother's death in a fall from some scaffolding; having made her living as a builder's labourer, her place of work becomes her place of death (V, 157).

Plainly, all this is a satirically pointed critique of modern working conditions. Yet if Kafka's intention was to denounce the pursuit of profit regardless of human cost, he set about it in a rather peculiar way, for nothing is said or shown of the business interests of the entrepreneurs or financial institutions which are served by this exploitative system. Nor can one imagine a hotel surviving long in which clients are treated as badly as they are here. At the enquiry desk, for example, any customer who formulates a question wrongly is simply met by blank silence until he reformulates it in a manner acceptable to the information-giver.

Hotels make their profits by flattering and pampering customers, not by humiliating them like this. The target of Kafka's criticism thus seems less the material acquisitiveness of capitalism than the senseless, frenetic energy which drives around the great 'circulation' in which all who live under this system, workers and customers alike, are trapped.

The most pervasive features of life in the hotel are conflict and the exercise of power. The constant fist-fights in the lift boys' dormitory are perhaps the least harmful expression of these principles. Yet Karl is initially persuaded to stay at the hotel by the apparently kindly, even motherly figure of the head cook, a stout single woman in her fifties who has already adopted one substitute child in the person of her assistant Therese. Various things make it easy for Karl to accept the proffered role of the cook's 'little one'. He recognizes in her advice to settle down and work his way up in the world by industry and attentiveness the same values as were preached by his uncle and his previous educators at home and at school. She has the added attraction of being more sentimental than his uncle, speaking fondly of Karl's home town of Prague and the Golden Goose inn where she used to work. She even keeps old photographs on her sideboard, just as Karl had once hoped to display the picture of his parents. Her combination of power, bourgeois ideals and affection seems to match exactly the ideal parental image with which Karl has replaced his real parents. Yet Karl's dream will prove to be just as illusory as the cook's nostalgia for an inn with a fairy-tale name which was pulled down two years previously. As her prompt dismissal of Giacomo from his post as lift boy indicates, her humanity is selective and self-interested. By taking advantage of the privileges her power can give, Karl exposes himself yet again to betrayal.

Karl tries to make the best of his third chance to prove himself a worthy son. He eschews the pleasures of the other lift boys, studying business correspondence in his leisure hours in order to better himself. He keeps the brass fittings on his lift brightly polished and learns how to accelerate it by pulling on the rope so as to serve more clients than the other lift boys. Yet all his efforts are defeated by a single incident when a figure from his past, Robinson, arrives drunk at the hotel one night. Robinson was able to track Karl down thanks to information from Renell, a pleasure-seeking lift boy for whom Karl has often done extra duties while he went out on the town. That Karl should be punished rather than rewarded for practising the virtues of industry and friendship may seem perverse, but Kafka makes it clear that he practises them out of self-interest, in the hope of either outdoing the other lift boys or gaining future favours from his older colleague, Renell. Equally, Karl deserts his post at the lift in order to conceal Robinson in the dormitory not out of altruism but because the intruder is an embarrassment and a threat to his new-found security. While Renell and Robinson are more blatantly selfish than Karl, the difference between them is a matter of degree rather than of kind. Karl is innocent at least in the sense that he accepts the values of bourgeois self-improvement at face value. The rogues, bullies and exploiters of whom he falls foul, however, reveal that the reality underlying the ideology Karl has accepted so naively is one of exploitation.

Karl's brief absence from his post is noticed immediately and reported to the head waiter who then summons Karl to his office to announce his dismissal. The head waiter will permit no appeal or defence because he is certain that he will only hear lies, and because any leniency, so he complains, would cause the entire discipline amongst the lift boys to collapse. The refusal to hear mitigating evidence is characteristic of other figures of authority in Kafka's fiction (such as the officer in 'In the Penal Colony') and suggests nervousness about the foundations on which the edifice of power rests. In any case, Karl quickly abandons all thought of making any plea when he realizes that every piece of evidence is being twisted against him out of sheer prejudice, so that he eventually stands accused, and hence effectively convicted, not only of deserting his post but even (quite wrongly) of theft. Both here and in Europe decisions are made 'in whatever way the judgement springs from the lips in the first heat of rage' (V, 178). The capricious conduct of the angry parent seems to serve as the model for the exercise of power wherever Karl finds himself in the world.

Gradually it emerges that the patent injustice, by normal standards, of the head waiter's conduct of the hearing is motivated not simply by fear of general indiscipline, but also by petty personal jealousy and self-interest of a kind characteristic of family relationships. The head waiter, who sees his own relationship with the head cook threatened by the fact that she has come to regard Karl as her 'little angel', has decided to deal with the threat by having Karl dismissed in disgrace from the hotel. When summoned to the hearing, the head cook appears at first to merit the trust Karl has placed in her (as a substitute mother) by questioning him in a much more reassuring manner than the aggressive style adopted by her male colleague. So habitual is it for Karl to feel guilty when being accused, however, that her support begins to unsettle him, making him feel that he has never deserved her kindness.[30] Unfortunately for Karl, her bias in his favour is balanced by an equal and opposite (but quite unfounded) conviction that the head waiter, her suitor, is a just man. The balance changes radically, however, the

moment she hears the (false) suggestion that Karl had an assignation with a
female opera singer. She turns pale, stands up, holds the hand of the
head waiter, supports herself against the chair, addresses Karl by his surname instead of his Christian name and finally rejects him with a trite
phrase: ' "Just things have a particular appearance" ' (V, 192). Although
Karl gives no sign of recognizing the fact, the grouping of head cook and
head waiter (with the addition of Therese in the role of faithful daughter)
reproduces, in slightly varied formation, the family hierarchy displayed in
Karl's lost photograph. Yet again Karl finds himself deserted by a substitute
parent as the cook/mother sides with the waiter/father in condemning and
banishing the 'wicked' child. As with his uncle, the motive for Karl's betrayal
is once more the adult's jealousy and wounded pride in possession. If the
uncle's implacable attitude resembles that of Karl's father, the cook's leave-
taking recalls his mother's slightly kindlier behaviour in that she does at least
give him the address of another place of refuge. Yet such 'kindly' condemna-
tion only makes it more difficult for Karl to recognize the betrayal for what it
is and to respond accordingly. Having been wrongly accused and humiliated
in the hotel, it is he who will feel guilty and unable ever to return there.

Before Karl can go anywhere, however, he must first escape the clutches
of the head porter. In this case the ill-treatment of Karl is motivated not by
jealousy or frustrated possessiveness but by sheer sadism. He tortures Karl
physically and adds mockery to his bullying: ' "Now that you're here I
want to enjoy you" ' (V, 203). His Slav name (Feodor) and his function
anticipate the frightening doorkeeper with the 'Tartar beard' in the parable 'Before the Law' (in *The Trial*); like the whipper in *The Trial* or the
officer in 'In the Penal Colony', moreover, he claims merely to be doing
his duty: ' "Orders, little Missy, orders" ' (V, 184). A figure of such sadistic
capriciousness strengthens the impression that the exploitative system of
the Hotel Occidental is not fundamentally the product of financial motives
or imperatives, but rather the reverse, that the force driving the 'circulation' of the system is the exercise of power as an end in itself. This
impression is confirmed by the following episode where Karl falls once
more into the hands of Delamarche and Robinson.

INNER AND OUTER IMPRISONMENT

Since childhood Karl Roßmann has had a great liking for security. He
recalls evenings spent doing his homework at the family table: 'How quiet
it had been there! How seldom had strangers come into that room! Even

as a little child Karl had always liked to watch his mother lock the door of their flat with the key as evening approached' (V, 264). The sentimental reminiscence contrasts starkly with Karl's present situation: 'She [his mother] had no idea that things had now come to such a pass with Karl that he was attempting to force open strangers' doors with knives' (V, 264).[31] The door in question belongs to a flat shared by the former opera singer Brunelda, Delamarche and Robinson, who has brought Karl here to act as their servant or slave. The irony in Karl's melancholy reverie lies precisely in the fact that he can see only the contrast between the past and the present. He is blind not only to the continuities between the two situations but also to the fact that his present condition, in part at any rate, is a consequence of his childhood experiences. His very nostalgia is evidence of emotional bonds within him of which his outer imprisonment is both reflection and result.

If childhood was a time of security for Karl, it was also a time of submission to the paternal power which protected him. When doing his homework at the table where his father was reading the newspaper, Karl would spread out his books on chairs in order to avoid being a nuisance to his father. In Brunelda's matriarchal ménage exactly the same rules apply: on no account must the lower orders disturb the head of the household. Karl's status as substitute child (he is Brunelda's 'little one') is underlined by an incident when he is awakened during the night by a cry from her, evidently in response to Delamarche's sexual attentions, and is sent out to the balcony with Robinson (his hateful older brother in this household) in order to spare her any further embarrassment.[32]

Karl finds himself in this situation of subjection to others because he has accepted, yet again, the protection of someone older and more powerful. While being chased down a street by a policeman, Karl is suddenly pulled into a doorway. On finding that his rescuer is Delamarche, he responds not with fear but with gratitude: 'Karl almost lay in his arm and pressed his face, half-fainting, to his breast' (V, 221). Karl is clearly unaware of the ominous parallel between Delamarche's embrace and those of both his uncle and Pollunder. Surprisingly, Delamarche appears at first to respond in a fatherly way, setting Karl carefully on the ground, kneeling down beside him and stroking his brow. Only when they have reached Brunelda's flat is the offer of protection revealed yet again to be merely the acceptable face of the exploitation practised by all the parental figures in Karl's life.

Karl's ingrained submissiveness towards figures of power or authority also plays a decisive part in the events leading up to Delamarche's Artful-

Dodger-like recapture of him.[33] Having escaped the head porter and reached the street in front of the Hotel Occidental, Karl's petty bourgeois upbringing makes him feel so ashamed of having to appear in public without a jacket, and so sure that everyone will see in this evidence of his criminal nature, that he chooses to join Robinson in his cab rather than be exposed to the public gaze. Not only do the unfounded accusations of the head waiter suffice to make the guilt-prone Karl see himself as 'suspicious', but when he has to deal with the next figure of authority, a patrolling policeman, he thinks of the head waiter and the head cook not as his unjust accusers but as having shown him kindness and understanding: 'And if he had not got justice from the kindness of the head cook or from the understanding of the head waiter, it was certainly not to be expected from the company here on the street' (V, 215). Although he is the object of the policeman's unwelcome, and unjustified, attentions, Karl again sympathizes readily with this representative of public order: 'Karl looked at the policeman who was obliged to maintain order in the midst of strangers, all concerned only with themselves, and something of his general worries was transferred to Karl' (V, 219). He even sees the coarsely muscular but clean-shaven face of his enemy Delamarche as proud and eliciting respect (V, 213). In these various situations Karl's inner shackles are mirrored in repeated scenes of encirclement (by children, by workers taking a lunch break) or enclosure (the inside of the cab, the door through which Delamarche pulls him, the locked door of Brunelda's flat, even Brunelda's massive bosom which pins him against the railings of the balcony).

During his imprisonment in Brunelda's flat Karl finally begins to loosen the inner bonds which have kept him subservient until now. On the one hand, this depraved ménage is just the kind of fate Karl's feelings of guilt might conjure up for him after he has proved himself 'unworthy' to live according to the ascetic, disciplinary principles of his uncle. In the morality of the nursery there is just one step separating obedience and cleanliness from anarchy and filth.[34] On the other hand, here at last Karl begins to see that power is underpinned not by morality but by self-interest. He is helped in this process by the negative example of Robinson whose puerile sexual fantasies about Brunelda are undiminished by her demand that Delamarche whip him across the face. This repels Karl, prompting him to declare that he will not allow himself to be similarly humiliated and abused: ' "What applies to you does not have to apply to me. Indeed such rules only apply to someone who puts up with them" ' (V, 233). The process of emancipation may also be advanced by the sight of even the brutal Delamarche pandering to the whims of such a grotesque figure as Brunelda who not only lacks all physical attraction (for Karl) but who virtually personifies the classic vices of gluttony, sloth, vanity, sensuality, anger, envy and avarice. In this pair power appears to be stripped of even the last vestiges of moral authority, dignity or humanity.

After his first bid for freedom is thwarted by Delamarche's physical strength and brutality, Karl is determined not to give up trying. However, his new-found resolve dwindles again after a late-night conversation with a student on the next balcony who works in a department store all day and studies all night, postponing sleep until he has completed his studies. When the student tells him how hard it is to find employment and that any work, even as the slave of Brunelda and Delamarche, is better than none, Karl decides to stay on in the flat 'provisionally', at least until a better opportunity presents itself in one of the offices nearby. Once more Karl's need for security proves itself to be much stronger than his desire for freedom or dignity. His dreams of a better life extend no further than hoping for a future as an office worker: 'that he might some day be a clerk seated at a desk and gaze for a while out of the open window like the official he had seen today while crossing the yard' (V, 272). Simply to gaze out of the open window, Karl believes, would be freedom enough for him. He would even abandon all thought of advancement through study and devote himself entirely to his duties and to the next father-figure: 'His good intentions crowded into his head as if his future boss were standing in front of the couch and reading them from the expression on his face' (V, 272–3). As with Gregor Samsa, Georg Bendemann and Josef K., who all seek a 'provisional' accommodation with life, the inner bonds of Karl's bourgeois upbringing prove even stronger than the locked door of the flat.

The evidence of the next, fragmentary chapter, entitled 'Brunelda's Departure', is even more contradictory. Here Karl is shown pushing Brunelda's vast bulk, covered with a cloth so that she resembles a load of potatoes, on a creaking hand-cart, when, as the reader has almost come to expect, a policeman suddenly appears from a dark doorway and begins to question him. By now, however, Karl has acquired enough experience in dealing with the police to remain unperturbed: 'Karl merely shrugged his shoulders, this was just the usual interference of the police [. . .] Contempt from the police was better than their attentions' (V, 292). When he finally reaches the mysterious 'Undertaking Number 25' (possibly a brothel), Karl is scolded by the man in charge for arriving late. Again, however, Karl simply shrugs off the reprimand: 'Karl hardly listened to speeches like this any more, everyone exploited his power and cursed anyone in a lowly position. Once you had become accustomed to it, it sounded no different from the regular striking of the clock' (V, 294). On the other hand, Karl remains enough of a petty bourgeois to be appalled by the moral degradation of the place despite its superficial concessions to order:

> Yet everything was greasy and repulsive, as if everything had been put to bad use and as if no amount of cleanliness could ever put things to rights again. Whenever he arrived somewhere new Karl liked to think about what could be improved here and what a joy it would be to take action immediately, regardless of the perhaps endless work it would cause. Here, however, he did not know what could be done. (V, 294)

Although no longer quite so much in awe of figures in authority, Karl seems to retain to the last a naive belief that the world can be made a better place.

'EVERYONE IS WELCOME'

The external evidence concerning the ending Kafka might have given Karl's story is both scanty and contradictory. The only evidence which comes directly from Kafka is a note concerning the respective fates of Josef K. (hero of *The Trial*) and Karl Roßmann: 'Roßmann and K., the guiltless and the guilty, both finally killed by way of punishment, with no distinction being made between them, the guiltless one with a lighter hand, more pushed to one side than struck down' (DW, 46). Max Brod, on the other hand, reports a conversation in which Kafka talked of a happy ending to the novel, with Karl regaining all that he had lost, including family and friends, 'as if by the magic of paradise' (DW, 45). Neither piece of evidence can be considered conclusive, however, since Kafka might have changed his mind and Brod may have misunderstood or misinterpreted what was said to him. The only evidence we have is some fragments of a chapter or chapters which show the author taking the same ambivalent attitude to the hero as he does in the rest of the novel. These fragments, which depict Karl's admission to the vast Theatre of Oklahoma (or Oklahama, as Kafka found it misspelt in his main source),[35] suggest that he considered giving the novel a parodistic Utopian ending and thereby completing the sequence of allusions to the classic German Bildungsroman evident in the early chapters.

At the end of *Wilhelm Meister's Apprenticeship* the hero is admitted to membership of the select Society of the Tower which, as we have seen, is dedicated to helping gifted individuals like Wilhelm and thus improving society at large. A Utopian project of this kind was necessary to complete the design of Goethe's Bildungsroman, for the formation of the hero's personality and the development of his creativity demanded a corresponding potential for improvement in the society in which he was to work. After breaking out of the conventional role initially offered him by bourgeois society, Wilhelm needs to be convinced that there is a more fulfilling and creative function to perform there before he can re-join society with a new-found faith in its values. Having set out on his travels with an excessive faith in the theatre, Wilhelm ultimately chooses the profession of medicine. In *The Missing Person*, by contrast, the preconditions for any such positive vision of personal and social development are entirely absent. It, too, is a novel concerned with education, but education as a process of social de-formation of the personality rather than of its formation by the development of personal creativity. Whereas Wilhelm's loving, if superficially stern upbringing has given him the self-confidence at least to attempt to realize his 'theatrical mission', Karl has only to think of intervening in American life for the dream to seem unattainable. Whereas Wilhelm dares to leave the route prescribed for him by his father, the downward spiral of Karl's journey through society results from no initiative of his own but from a combination of 'fateful' coincidences and malevolent conspiracies, threats and seductions on the part of others. In sum, Kafka's allusions to the classic Bildungsroman suggest that he thought it impossible to adapt its ethos to his own times: his hero lacks the creative energy to challenge social norms, while society in its turn seems incapable of humane improvement. Possibly because he was reluctant to follow the example of society by simply throwing his good-hearted, if naive young hero to the dogs, Kafka takes leave of him in a questionable Utopia.

The Theatre of Oklahoma has both a welcoming and a threatening aspect. What most attracts Karl to it is the promise of unquestioning acceptance on the posters inviting people to join the theatre:

> 'Everyone was welcome', it said. Everyone, that meant Karl too. Everything he had done until now was forgotten, nobody wanted to make a reproach out of it. He could apply for a job which was not shameful, something to which one could be invited in public. And equally public was the promise that he too would be accepted. He could ask for

nothing better, he wanted at long last to begin a decent career and this
was perhaps such a beginning. (V, 295–6)

Nothing could be more welcome to Karl than such unqualified acceptance, for he has constantly been the subject of the most unfair questioning
and suspicion throughout his stay in America. Usually he had answered
his interrogators truthfully, only to be met with disbelief or hostile distortion of his statements. So used has he become to such hostility that he now
begins to tell lies about his name and his background in order to secure
admission to the theatre. When it is discovered that he is not in fact a
trained engineer, he is simply sent to the appropriate booth, the least
impressive and most distant of all, the one for 'pupils of European middle
schools' (V, 305). It appears that the theatre has a booth for each and
every category of person. Here Karl tells another lie, claiming that his
name is 'Negro'.[36] The supervising official's demand for his papers of
legitimation is simply brushed aside by a junior clerk, however, who
declares that Karl has been accepted, and his new identity ('Negro,
technical worker') is run up on the board normally used to announce
the winning horses on the racecourse where the recruitment is taking
place.

Thus far, everything in the Theatre of Oklahoma seems to represent a
Utopian inversion of the hostile practices Karl has encountered elsewhere
in America (or back at home in Prague): hostile, suspicious interrogation
has been replaced by belief, rejection by acceptance, expulsion by admittance, while a new hierarchy of authority appears to place the lowly clerk
above the official whom he nominally serves. There are even overtones of
Paradise in the fact that Karl is reunited here with lost friends, Giacomo
and Fanny, and in the hint that this is a place where the race is not to the
swift. The suggestion that here is Paradise Regained corresponds structu-
rally to the Paradise Lost of the opening chapter where Karl's expulsion
from his childhood home had been occasioned by Johanna Brummer's
seduction of him, a model of fate which was then repeated and varied in
his expulsion by his jealous uncle (thanks to the machinations of Klara
Pollunder) and by the head porter (thanks to his jealousy of Karl and the
head cook's jealousy of Brunelda).[37] In each case Karl's 'Fall' into unhappiness involves a woman or what Kafka once referred to as 'the general
old miracle of the rib'.[38]

Yet there are suggestions, too, that the Theatre of Oklahoma is a
counterfeit Paradise which shares too many features with the world outside to seem entirely trustworthy. The invitation to join the theatre, for

example, contains threats as well as promises: ' "At twelve all will be closed and not opened again. Cursed be whoever does not believe us" ' (V, 295). Twelve o'clock, it will be recalled, was the hour at which Karl was banished by his uncle. The trumpet-blowing 'angels' who stand at the entrance are ordinary women perched on unstable pedestals whose lack of musical skill produces a hellish din rather than heavenly harmony; what is more, they are replaced from time to time by equally unmusical men dressed as devils. Although Karl joins here a community of the dispossessed who are sharing a meal, he also meets an individual whose suspicious remarks spoil his pleasure at being admitted to the company (V, 312–13). While those in charge of the operation appear not to want to accept the grateful applause of those they have admitted, a picture is passed around the table showing the President of the United States' private box at the theatre where they are destined to work. The box is vast, more like a stage than a box, with a golden balustrade and lavish decorations. If there is something calculated to inspire awe in all this grandeur, an even more disturbing effect is produced by the contrast between the mild white light at the front of the box and the 'dark emptiness shimmering with a reddish glow' (V, 314) which can be seen in its depths. Karl finds it hard to imagine the box being occupied by people, 'so lordly and sufficient unto itself did the whole thing appear'. Ominously, the motif of speed associated with inhuman methods of working in Edward Jakob's warehouse and the Hotel Occidental is suddenly reintroduced when the meal is interrupted by the announcement that the train will depart in just five minutes, so that the new recruits must stop eating immediately and run to join it. The racecourse, it seems, may have been an appropriate recruiting venue after all. Once Karl and Giacomo have boarded the train, their pleasure in the vast landscape is somewhat spoiled by some 'friendly' travelling companions who pinch them hard in the leg whenever they reach down to recover a fallen playing card. The very last image in the novel is of the boys' faces 'shivering' (V, 318) in the air rising from the cold mountain rivers tumbling beneath the train. None of this bodes well for the future.

The ambiguities of this dubious Utopia correspond to the mixture of sympathy and irony in the author's account of Karl's experiences throughout *The Missing Person*. Although Karl is a well-intentioned lad who deserves better treatment than he usually receives, the plot implicitly criticizes his habitual acceptance of the protection and privileges of the powerful in preference to the difficulties of self-assertion and freedom. When it was pointed out to Karl at one stage that he was free, for example, he did not welcome the fact: 'Nothing seemed more worthless to him' (V, 133).[39] Kafka's criticism of this attitude is implied by the harsh consequences such subservience has for Karl. At the same time he shows how difficult it is for Karl to escape this punishing spiral, given the crippling emotional effect of early discipline and his need to regain the love which has been denied him.

The structure of the novel is, then, a subjective one. Its pattern of theme and variations is rooted in the psychological trauma which has trapped Karl in a cycle of obsessive, self-damaging repetition of his experiences in the family. The world Karl moves through is constituted, that is to say, by the author's imaginative identification with Karl's traumatized condition: the world of adult power is seen in the perspective of a damaged and dependent child. The plot is also a form of symbolic action, whereby the author tries and condemns the patriarchal world which has condemned without trial the defenceless Karl Roßmann.[40] Here, in his fiction, Kafka could launch a counter-attack on those structures of power which had invaded and damaged not just his own personality but, he believed, the lives of his contemporaries.[41] In *The Missing Person* Kafka's imagination displaces the 'rational' structures within which power is normally practised and justified (as a means to 'progress'), and replaces them with the static emotional structure of the child's enthralment to its parents. Such stasis is the very antithesis of the optimistic belief in individual and social development on which the Bildungsroman was founded.

The ambivalent, half comical, half ominous Utopia of the Theatre of Oklahoma repeats once more the unresolved conflict which pervades the entire novel and which arises from a tension between implicit criticism of Karl's ingrained trust in authority on the one hand and the sympathetic author's wish to grant him release from the deformed and deforming world of power on the other. The Theatre of Oklahoma expresses for the last time the conflict between a child's dream of a world in which authority is not to be feared, in which faults are forgiven or overlooked, in which friends can stay together forever – and the melancholy knowledge that none of this can be.

4

The Trial

Towards the end of *The Missing Person* Karl Roßmann dreams of spending his days as a clerk seated peacefully and dutifully behind an office window. For Josef K., hero of *The Trial*, that dream, once realized, turns into a nightmare. Even having a large office with a large window in his capacity as chief clerk of a large bank offers no protection against the intrusion into his life of an unknown court which robs him of all peace of mind and eventually has him killed one night in a quarry on the edge of town.

Cross-references of this kind between Kafka's fictions may have been intentional or an unintended consequence of their overlapping or interwoven periods of composition, the writing of *The Trial* having been interrupted by resumption of work on *The Missing Person*, in the same way as the latter had been interrupted for the writing of 'The Metamorphosis'. In addition to thematic and compositional links there were biographical connections between the works of this period: 'The Judgement' was written just two days after Kafka's first letter to Felice Bauer, while work on *The Trial* was begun in August 1914 shortly after the dissolution of his (first) engagement to her in July. Having lent Felice's initials to Frieda Brandenfeld in 'The Judgement', Kafka also gave them to Fräulein Bürstner in *The Trial*, and shared out parts of his own name in various forms or disguises amongst Georg Bendemann (see DW, 23), Josef K., Franz (one of the guards who inform him of his arrest) and three officials from Josef K.'s bank who are present on the morning of his arrest, called *K*ullich, *K*aminer and *Rabe*nsteiner ('Rabe' or 'raven' being an ornithological relative of 'kavka'). The arrested, the arrestor and the witnesses, in other words, are all 'K's,. The raven's colour is then picked up as a motif in the black coat donned by Josef K. for his first meeting with an official from the court, in the black suits, coats or hats worn by the men who arrest and execute him and by those present at his first hearing before the court, in the black eyes of the advocate's nurse Leni and the 'darting black eyes' of the audience in the courtroom, and in the black 'Tartar' beard of the doorkeeper who is said to stand before the entrance to the Law.

As these few details indicate, the artistic structure which binds together the materials of *The Trial* is based on the same method of motif repetition and variation as Kafka had used in *The Missing Person*. The difference between the two novels lies in the intricacy and complexity of the patterns thus produced. Before attempting to answer the larger questions of Josef K.'s 'guilt' or the 'meaning' of his trial, it is necessary to examine in detail the links between the elements of the fiction created by means of this technique of interweaving.

STRUCTURE AND PERSPECTIVE

In one respect *The Trial* ought to be easier to understand than *The Missing Person*, since it does at least have a concluding chapter called simply 'End'. Malcolm Pasley has established from manuscript evidence that Kafka departed in this case from his usual practice of linear composition (through the 'dark tunnel' of his imagination) by writing the last chapter immediately after the first, presumably with the aim of preventing the work from 'running off in different directions' (DW, 39) and ultimately losing its impetus, as had happened with *The Missing Person* and other earlier and even more fragmentary attempts at extended works of fiction. If the overall shape of the novel could be established from the outset it might be possible to reproduce that coherence and feeling of inner connectedness that Kafka had been so elated to achieve in 'The Judgement'.

That the ending of *The Trial* was indeed intended to be a genuine bringing-to-a-conclusion of what had preceded it, rather than an arbitrary stop, is suggested by the particularly strong structure of correspondences linking the first chapter to the last. Thus the action which begins on the morning of Josef K.'s thirtieth birthday ends, neatly, on the eve of his thirty-first. The novel begins and ends with K. in a semi-prone position: he is sitting up in bed when he first sees a guard from the court, and is made to sit down by his executioners who then lean him against a stone on which they 'bed' his head. One of the executioners lays his hand on K.'s 'Gurgel' (windpipe), which is exactly where K. had kissed Fräulein Bürstner on the night following his arrest. There are two executioners in the last chapter just as there are two guards in the first, and just as one of the guards pats him on the shoulder at the beginning, so one of the executioners pats him on the back at the end. Just as Josef K. paces up and down the room during his first interview with the supervisor, so he is led back and forth in the quarry until a suitable spot is found for his execution. Having donned his best black coat to meet the supervisor in Chapter 1, K. awaits his executioners dressed in the same formal manner. Whereas the guards had instructed him to get dressed for his first interview, he is undressed by the executioners in the last chapter. If the 'tightly stretched' gloves Josef K. wears on the night of his death echo the 'tight fitting' garment worn by the first guard, which he thought resembled a 'travel suit', so this in turn foreshadows K.'s last journey through the town in the company of his executioners. As he walks between them he catches sight of a female figure who strikes him as being very similar to Fräulein Bürstner, the woman in whose bedroom the supervisor had formally announced the fact of his arrest. Puzzled by his strange arrest, K. had reflected that he lived in a state under the rule of law ('Rechtsstaat' – P, 12); on the way to his place of execution he sees several policemen whose duty it would be to enforce those laws if he were to appeal for their help.[1] On the morning of his arrest Josef K. is annoyed to see first an old woman and then an old couple watching him from a room across the street; on the night of his execution, similarly, he notices a pair of little children in a lighted window across the street. One of the last things K. sees before he dies is a single figure at a window in the distance. Like the many other parallels and echoes, the chiasmus (one, two; two, one) formed by these figures is unlikely to have been produced by anything other than highly conscious artistry. So closely do the two chapters correspond to one another, indeed, that they resemble pillars designed to carry the span of a bridge.

Certain aspects of Josef K.'s behaviour in the last chapter reinforce the impression of an action reaching its appointed and proper end. This is suggested, for example, by the fact that he awaits the executioners in formal dress although he has not been informed of their visit in advance. The impression that the action has a known and accepted goal to which it should move is confirmed when the sight of the patrolling policemen prompts K. to pull his executioners off at great speed in the opposite direction. Once they have reached the quarry, K. co-operates with the executioners' efforts to position him satisfactorily, and he 'knows precisely' (P, 241) that his duty would now be to take the butcher's knife from their hands and kill himself with it.

Conversely, certain other details of K.'s behaviour indicate that, as far as he is concerned. the ending does *not* bring matters to a satisfactory conclusion. Although he had anticipated a visit without it having been announced, the two executioners do not quite conform to his expectations. Although he eventually takes the lead, he at first resists being frog-marched through the streets by them. Although he takes up his position for the execution voluntarily, his attitude remains 'forced and unconvincing' (P, 240). His very last gesture is to raise his hands, with fingers stretched wide, in response to the distant figure he sees leaning out of a window and apparently stretching out its arms towards him. This indicates that, only moments before he dies, Josef K. is still ready to accept help and sympathy, still convinced that there remain objections which he had forgotten to make, still protesting that he has never seen the judge or reached the high court. In short, although the last chapter brings the action to an end, it appears to be riddled with unresolved contradictions.

This lack of resolution also contributes to the pattern of correspondences linking the end of the novel with the beginning, since the first chapter, too, had revealed peculiar contradictions in K.'s behaviour. Confronted with representatives of an unknown court who lack any form of legitimation, it occurs to K., quite understandably, that he should telephone an influential friend, the state prosecutor Hasterer. The supervisor agrees to the request, but adds that he can see no sense in it. K. finds this comment astonishing, yet his own decision *not* to call Hasterer after all is just as astonishing and self-contradictory: ' "You ask for sense and yet you are carrying out the most senseless thing there is. [...] What sense, you ask, is there in telephoning a state prosecutor when I am supposedly arrested? Very well, I will not telephone" ' (P, 21). One might speculate that K. changes his mind out of fear of reprisals, although the supervisor actually urges him to carry out the decision, pointing to the next room where the telephone is kept. Alternatively, the decision not to call Hasterer may reflect some sub- or semi-conscious acknowledgement on K.'s part that the appearance of the court in his life does indeed have little or nothing to do with the state prosecutor. K.'s response to the imminent departure of the guards and the supervisor is similarly ambivalent. As they make to leave, K. suddenly feels his independence of 'these people' increasing and imagines that he can now 'play' with them by running after them and 'offering them his arrest' (P, 23). However sarcastically intended, and however much at odds with his earlier objections to the announcement of his arrest, K.'s imaginary gesture may in fact mean just what it says, namely that K. is now asking to be arrested by this unofficial court.

Given that the last chapter of the novel still shows K. behaving towards the court with the same perplexing mix of co-operation and resistance as he had shown in the first, *The Trial* is clearly a very peculiar kind of crime story. In this genre final chapters generally solve the mystery, making it clear, at long last, who did what to whom, and why. In *The Trial*, by contrast, the usual question, 'Which criminal fits this crime?' is inverted, so that the reader is left asking, even at the very end, what crime, if any, the arrested and executed Josef K. has committed. Indeed, so thoroughly does Kafka re-orient or subvert the genre that things normally taken for granted in crime fiction, in particular the justice and practices of the arresting authority, seem to require at least as much investigation and justification as the actions of the accused. The moral scandal of Karl Roßmann's banishment for a sexual offence in which he was the injured party seems to be repeated and magnified here in the treatment Josef K. receives at the hands of a court which offends against all principles of natural justice. Because K. is not informed of the charges against him, he is unable to offer a defence; because he does not know his accusers, he cannot cross-examine them; because the judge is anonymous, there is no way of knowing whether he or she is disinterested; because the crime is not stated, at least not to the reader as representative of the public, it is not possible to assess the 'proportionality' or fitness of the extreme penalty in relation to the offence. Justice, by any normal definition, is simply not seen to be done.

Kafka's choice of narrative perspective adds to the reader's difficulties.[2] Anyone reading the novel in English translation faces additional problems, however, since they are likely to be misled by its very first sentence: 'Someone must have been telling lies about Josef K., for without having done anything wrong he was arrested one fine morning.'[3] The problems begin with the 'must have', a phrase which suggests that the narrator is offering this as a possible explanation for the arrest. This impression is then reinforced by the statement, 'without having done anything wrong', which looks like an assertion of K.'s innocence by an authoritative narrator. Provided they pay very close attention to Kafka's phrasing, German readers ought not to be misled in the same way (although many of them have been). The 'mußte' in the statement, 'Jemand mußte Josef K. verleumdet haben', for example, is more likely to indicate a speculation by the *character* rather than the narrator; if the latter were offering the opinion as his own, the verb form ought, strictly speaking, to be 'muß', since the point at which the narrator would make the conjecture would be the narrative present. The subjunctive 'hätte' (rather than the indicative 'hatte') in the clause, 'ohne daß er etwas Böses getan hätte', makes it even clearer that the narrator is reporting Josef K.'s version of events; the 'mußte' is then confirmed as being the character's reaction to his supposedly unjustified arrest. The recognition that Kafka is narrating here from the point of view of K. removes at least one source of confusion from the novel: we are not reading the story of a man who is arrested despite the *fact* that he is innocent, but rather the story of a man who *maintains* that he has been wrongfully arrested. This is not the end of the problem, however.

If Kafka's chosen technique of free indirect speech means that the reader is obliged to explore the new world which has suddenly opened up before Josef K. along with the hero, and to interpret its features as they are apprehended by his eyes, ears and mind, how can the reader hope to understand events which puzzle K.? If the protagonist dies with a set of unresolved questions on his lips, is the reader not bound to be left in the same state of confusion? This, at any rate, was the conclusion drawn by Friedrich Beißner whose conviction that Kafka's method of narration was always strictly mono-perspectival led him to argue that *The Trial* presents the psychologically disturbed visions of a man trapped in a persecution complex from which there is as little escape for the reader as there is for Josef K.[4] As many critics have pointed out, the chief weakness in this argument is that the narrative perspective is not in fact identical to that of the protagonist at every point in the novel. Two of the clearest examples of shifts in perspective occur at the beginning of Chapters 7 and 10. Chapter 7 opens with a description of K. seated at his office desk one winter's afternoon. Instead of working, he turns around in his chair and slowly rearranges some objects on his desk, but then, 'without knowing it' (P, 118), he leaves his arm stretched out over the table top and just sits there motionless, with his head hanging. Here K. is seen from the point of view of someone else present in the room, in fact from that of the conventional 'omnipresent' narrator who can convey information independently of any of the characters in the story. For years German paperback editions of the novel have carried on the cover a drawing by Kafka of a figure seen from just this point of view and in roughly this position (with his head resting on his hands rather than just hanging). Similarly, Chapter 10 begins by describing the arrival of two gentlemen wearing seemingly unmovable top hats who are to kill Josef K. After a little formality at the door of the flat about who should enter first, the same formality is repeated, rather more elaborately, outside K.'s door (P, 236). None of this is being observed by Josef K., who is seated inside his room, pulling on his new, close-fitting gloves, while these formalities are taking place outside.

Although such distinct changes of perspective are relatively rare, it is not unusual for the narrator to draw attention, as in the phrase 'without knowing it', to the fact that some of K.'s behaviour is unconscious, involuntary or unintended. Some of these comments could be taken to represent K.'s observations of his own behaviour, as when he goes through a door 'more slowly than he wanted' (P, 10). At other times, however, one can hear quite clearly the amusement of the narrator as he records some contradiction between K.'s view of his own conduct and the evidence of his involuntary behaviour.[5] Just after his arrest, for example, K. pours himself a glass of schnapps and then another for courage, 'as a precaution against the unlikely possibility that he might need it' (P, 17). While drinking the schnapps, however, he is so startled by a shout from the next room 'that his teeth knocked against the glass'. There is irony, indeed comedy, in the way the narrator shifts back and forth between K.'s attempt to assert that he is in control of the situation, and the uncontrolled reflexes of his body. It is reported that Kafka laughed so much at certain points that he could hardly carry on reading this chapter to his friends.[6] The numerous laughing or smiling figures encountered by Josef K. incorporate this response to his behaviour into the body of the novel. Kafka was clearly not laughing *with* K., who is disturbed and frightened during most of the chapter, but *at* him, looking at him from the distinct and, at times, even distant point of view of an ironic narrator whose descriptions filter and colour Josef K.'s sense impressions and thought processes.

The ironic mode of narration and the structure of corresponding motifs are two forms taken by the same organizing intelligence in the novel which makes it possible for the reader at least to consider events from a point of view distinct from that of the protagonist. As the narrator is otherwise very reticent, rarely commenting explicitly on K.'s situation or behaviour,[7] the only way the reader can discover what, if anything, his account communicates is by studying closely the images and the patterns they form.

LIKENESS AND DIFFERENCE

Seen from the point of view of Josef K., the court is a strange organization. He is struck above all by the differences between the practices of the court and those of the world with which he is familiar. The guards who arrest him, for example, present no written authority when asked to do so. He is shocked to learn that bribery determines what happens to any clothes taken into the court's depot. The court sits not in the palace of justice but in a tenement house, where its offices lack all the dignity he expects of a court, housed as they are in the attic of the building amidst rows of washing hung up to dry. Whereas K. has a large, well-lit office at the bank, he hears that the advocates attached to the court have to be careful not to put their feet through a hole in the floor of their room. Where K. is so punctilious about order that he insists on pointing out to his neighbour, Fräulein Bürstner, the slight rearrangement of her photographs during his first interview with the supervisor, the books he finds in the courtroom are tattered and dusty. Even less salubrious are the burst sewer pipe and the rats he encounters as he enters the building in which Titorelli, painter to the court, lives and works.

For all that it strikes K. as very alien, the court, seen from the rather different perspective of the reader, has many characteristics which mirror K.'s life and world to a remarkable degree. To begin with perhaps the most obvious similarity, both the world of the court and K.'s world are hierarchical and bureaucratic. His initial contact is with two guards, but they soon usher him into the presence of a 'supervisor' who receives him from behind a makeshift desk. When introduced to the offices of the court, K. passes rows of people sitting in the corridor, all waiting to be attended to, just as his clients at the bank have to wait outside his office until he is ready to deal with them. Titorelli's account of the different categories of 'exoneration', 'apparent exoneration' and 'delay' (P, 160) is couched in the language of the bureaucrat, full of convoluted explanations and multiple qualifications. The equally complicated processes of supplication and influence outlined by K.'s advocate go beyond even Dickens's descriptions in *Little Dorrit* or *Bleak House* of the patience-sapping efforts involved in petitioning any public authority.

The hierarchical character of K.'s everyday world is attested by numerous details. When asked at his first hearing if he is a housepainter, for example, he retorts indignantly that he is the chief clerk of a large bank. Since his rank is just below that of the deputy director, he rejects equally firmly the supervisor's description of three juniors from the bank as 'colleagues' (P, 24). K.'s sense of hierarchy extends beyond the bank to his relations with others, as when he tells himself that his designs on Fräulein Bürstner are bound to succeed since she is only 'a little typist' (P, 252) who will not be able to resist him for long. The officials of the court belong to a similar hierarchy, and their conduct is equally governed by mutual suspicion and ambitions for advancement. A young student of the law, for example, is someone to be feared because it is expected that he will become a judge some day. As if being whipped for a misdemeanour were not punishment enough, one of the guards complains to K. that they have now lost all prospect of being promoted in their turn to the office of whipper: 'Our career is over, we shall have to do much more menial work than guard duty' (P, 88–9). The current whipper then adds insult to injury, claiming that all this talk of career prospects is ridiculous. Within this oppressive hierarchy loyalty, even between colleagues at the same level, cannot be expected; thus the guard, Franz, makes a whispered plea to K. to intervene at least on his behalf since his older colleague, Wilhelm, is less sensitive to pain and has already lost his honour. K. naturally applies his own experience of hierarchies to the court, reassuring himself that the difficulties he is experiencing with the guards will be cleared up as soon as he is able to speak to someone of equal rank to himself (P, 15), but then resenting just as much the 'pedantic' tone of the supervisor who turns out to be younger than he is. Whether there truly is a person of high – or highest – authority in the world of the court, K. is never allowed to discover.

The court also shares certain bourgeois insignia with K. It is expected of him, for example, that he put on a black suit (i.e. formal dress, according to German convention) to meet the supervisor. As the latter prepares to leave, he in turn picks up his 'hard round hat' (the typical headwear of the lower middle class) from Fräulein Bürstner's bed. The other accused men who line the corridor of the court offices, and who mostly seem to belong to the same class as K., keep their hats, the most obvious symbol of their social status, under their seats while they wait. After K. has been helped out of the court offices by two officials, he finds his hat on the pavement beside him; and K.'s last action before leaving his flat with the executioners is to pick up his hat.[8]

Josef K. is surprised by the entry into his life of officials belonging to an authority which is unknown to him. Yet unofficial forms of accusation, judgement and punishment are in fact part and parcel of his everyday world. Even before he knows that he has been arrested, K. decides that his landlady must 'answer to him' (P, 10) for the intrusion. K. for his part expects that he will have to give an account of himself for arriving late at the bank and therefore considers calling on Frau Grubach as a 'witness' (P, 16) of the events which detained him. When Frau Grubach later passes judgement on the character of Fräulein Bürstner, whom she 'suspects' (P, 31) of sexual impropriety, K. considers 'punishing' his landlady by handing in his notice, but then immediately 'suspects' that his own motive for wanting to move out of the flat is the fact that he had been arrested there that very morning. At the end of his interview with K. the supervisor explains that his task had been to inform K. of his arrest and to see how he 'takes the news' (P, 23). K. in his turn assumes the role of the observer when, during the days that follow his arrest, he has the three junior clerks who had been present come to his office repeatedly, 'for no other purpose than to observe them' (P, 26–7). At the moment of his death, it is again K. who is the object of just such an investigative gaze as his executioners put their faces close to his, 'in order to observe the decision' (P, 241).

The court which arrests Josef K. mirrors, it would seem, a number of important features of his life 'outside' the court. As he has organized his life, so the court which will take his life appears to be organized. Yet the court also *inverts* the normal order of K.'s life. Whereas he has been used to judging and punishing others, for example, it is now he who is subject to judgement and punishment. Having occupied a high position in the hierarchy of the bank and in Frau Grubach's lodging house, he is now willing to seek the help of even such lowly creatures as the court servant and his wife. Just how little status an accused man has in the world of the court is made plain by the sight of the merchant Block crawling around in front of his advocate, little better than a dog (P, 205), as K. observes. On the point of death K. will apply the same verdict to himself.

The inverted image presented by the court is expressed partly in social terms. Although the supervisor and the executioners wear bourgeois clothes, almost to the point of parody in the case of the latter, the court generally seems to be a poor organization and to be associated with poverty. One of a row of uniform, tall, gray tenements occupied by poor people, there is nothing to distinguish it from the neighbouring buildings in a distant suburb which the well-situated K. has never visited before. What is more, the court's offices are located in the poorest part of the building, high up in an airless attic. Admittedly, the court employees do what they can to conceal its poverty by scraping together enough money to ensure that at least the information-giver's elegant uniform creates a first impression of dignity (an effect spoiled, however, by the man's habit of laughing constantly). The elaborate throne shown in a judge's portrait, so K. is told by Leni, is in reality an ordinary kitchen chair.

Josef K., by contrast, attaches importance to the fact that he is fairly well off. He enjoys having an elegant suit with a waist so fashionably tight that it has attracted the attention and comments of others (P, 18). The fact that he has been able to lend Frau Grubach money when she needed it gives him power over her, and presumably contributes to his status as her 'best and dearest lodger' (P, 27). So attached is K. to the outward signs of wealth and status that he fancies his social position must give him an advantage over the court officials who are housed in mere attics, whereas he himself has a large room in the bank with an antechamber and can look down on the town's lively square through an enormous window pane

(P, 71). According to the guards, who finger his fine shirts with evident envy, K. can now expect to wear much poorer shirts. In the event K. is not subjected to impoverishment by the court, but he is partially stripped of his bourgeois clothes for his execution, so that the loss of reassuring status symbols is combined with the shame of public nakedness.[9]

The parallels and inversions in the relationship between K. and the court reinforce one another. Where his position in the bureaucratic hierarchy of the bank once enabled him to enjoy a life free of poverty, a bureaucratic, hierarchical organization now confronts and threatens him with poverty and humiliation. The court thus embodies the fears which haunt a bourgeois life, holding up a mocking mirror to it (the laughing information-giver) and subjecting K.'s previously secure existence to experiences from which he has been at pains to distance himself both physically and socially.

WOMEN

Another important source of fear exploited by the court is K.'s sexuality. In this area, too, the court both mirrors and inverts features of K.'s behaviour. Until his arrest the women in his life have been restricted to the stereotype antithesis of mother or 'pure woman' and whore. After the shock of his arrest he feels at first that the only person he can speak to is an old woman, one whose sexuality offers no threat. Seated at the table with Frau Grubach and sliding his hand into socks from the pile she is mending, K. regresses to the condition of a little boy seeking comfort from his mother. Frau Grubach has the added advantage of being a *substitute* mother, chosen by K. himself, rather than the real mother he has failed to visit, even on her birthdays. Whereas real parent–child relationships are often difficult and even painful, with Frau Grubach he is free to switch out of the role of the comfort-seeking 'son' and back into that of the powerful creditor and lodger whenever she does or says things he does not like.

Control is also central to K.'s relations with Elsa, a barmaid who only receives visitors from her bed during the day-time; one such is K., who visits her weekly as part of his well-ordered routine. (That Elsa shares a name with the passionate heroine of Wagner's *Flying Dutchman* may be sheer coincidence, but it adds to the bathos of the relationship.) Otherwise K. leads an almost solitary existence, preferring to spend the few leisure hours which work permits alone or in the company of other officials or drinking beer with a group of older men. This kind of arrangement with a prostitute was not at all unusual in European society at that time, not only amongst bachelors like K. but even amongst married men.[10] Polite society condemned publicly but (possibly more readily than now) condoned tacitly such arrangements as providing a necessary, if regrettable outlet for the 'animal' desires of men. Prostitution had the merit of keeping sex at a safe distance, conveniently out of sight in those parts of town where it could give no offence to respectable ladies and gentlemen.

In the ambit of the court, by contrast, sexuality is not hidden away. As K. makes his way to the courtroom for the first time on a Sunday morning, he passes the windows of working-class houses where men in shirt sleeves can be seen holding children, where bedclothes are hung out to air and the still tousled hair of a woman can be glimpsed. As he climbs the stairs in search of the courtroom, K. passes many children playing on the stairs or running in and out of open doors, through which he sees half-grown girls apparently dressed only in smocks, women cooking, some with infants on their arms, and all the beds in the rooms still occupied by figures who are asleep or sick or pulling on their clothes. The domestic idyll *surrounding* the court, however, contrasts sharply with the aggressive and disruptive behaviour of the court officials towards women (including married women) within the narrower confines of the court. On his second visit to the courtroom K. finds it deserted except for the wife of a court servant, later joined by her husband, who together explain what it means to be dependent on the court. Because the court meets in their home, they have to clear out all their belongings whenever it is in session.[11] The disruption also affects their sexual life; even as the woman is speaking to K., a student of the law appears and carries her off (rapes her in the original sense of the word) to serve a higher official. During K.'s first visit to the court this same student had interrupted K.'s address to the court by engaging in demonstrative sexual activity with the same woman at the back of the courtroom, screaming at the top of his voice as he did so, while the public, far from intervening on the woman's behalf, had crowded round eagerly to watch.[12] Both the ordinary family life surrounding the court and the sexual exploitation practised by its officials present a challenge to Josef K.'s bachelor existence. If the outer circle shows life as he has chosen *not* to lead it, the behaviour of the officials is uncomfortably like his own habitual attitude to women.

As a result of the court's intrusion into his life, K.'s relations with women are disrupted in various ways. Even the supposedly unthreatening Frau Grubach does not give him the reassurance he seeks on the evening following his arrest, for her tearful advice not to take matters so seriously (P, 28) shows how little he can conceal the extent to which he has been disturbed by the day's events. Having put her in the role of substitute mother, and thereby invited a more confidential response than usual, K. now recoils from her motherly show of concern, telling himself that any agreement from 'this woman' (P, 30) is worthless. Frau Grubach unwittingly makes things worse by confiding her suspicions about Fräulein Bürstner's sexual freedom, which provokes K. to unconcealed rage. The vehemence with which he rejects Frau Grubach's allegations, and the lies he tells in doing so, indicate that her remarks have touched a raw spot. He does not in fact know Fräulein Bürstner 'very well' (having hardly exchanged greetings with her), but claims to do so in order to assert her innocence and thereby disavow his own growing sexual interest in her which has been apparent ever since his eye was caught by the white blouse hanging at her bedroom window on the morning of his arrest. When Frau Grubach now shows him Fräulein Bürstner's empty bedroom, his gaze immediately and revealingly goes straight to the window to check whether the blouse is still there. He next looks at the pillows piled 'strikingly high' (P, 30) on her bed. The sexual interest implied by these glances is confirmed by his disapproval of the late hours she keeps, a remark which indicates just how closely he has been observing her habits for some time past. When Frau Grubach addresses the question of her sexual propriety more directly, however, K. claims she has misunderstood his remarks, springs to Fräulein Bürstner's defence, but then retracts his defence immediately: ' "Besides, perhaps I've gone too far, I won't stop you, tell her what you like" ' (P, 31). These contradictions reveal a man out of control in an area where it is clearly very important to him to be in control.

The court's choice of Fräulein Bürstner's bedroom for K.'s first interview is nicely calculated to arouse anxiety in him by confronting him with a source of contradictory feelings. Sexual attraction causes his tidy and disciplined life to be invaded by fear and desire in equal degree, the fear feeding the desire, and the desire the fear. K.'s loss of control during the conversation with Frau Grubach culminates eventually in a loss of physical restraint when Fräulein Bürstner returns to the flat late that evening. As he lies waiting for her to appear, the mixture of desire, resentment and guilt he feels is displaced into blaming her ('sie war schuld' – P, 32) for the fact that he has missed not only his evening meal but also the (sexual) visit to Elsa he had planned for that evening. As he talks to Fräulein Bürstner in her room, his frustrated sexual desire again focuses his gaze on the way she crosses her legs, props her head on the cushions of the couch and strokes her hip with her free hand.[13] Whether she intends to do so one cannot tell, but seen through K.'s eyes Fräulein Bürstner appears to be continuing the work of 'seduction' initiated by the court's choice of her bedroom for his first interview; conversely, her resistance to K.'s advances recalls the discipline imposed by the guards. In the end, while Fräulein Bürstner is leading him to the door, he seizes her and kisses her 'on the mouth and then over her entire face, like a thirsty animal chasing with its tongue over spring water it had found at long last. Finally he kissed her on the throat, where the windpipe is, and let his lips lie there for a long time' (P, 39). The gesture suggests both a form of vampirism, as if he wished to suck the air from her (he will later struggle for air in the offices of the court and at the house of Titorelli), and a threat to avenge the disturbance produced by the desire she has aroused in him. Before actually carrying out the assault, K. calls out his own name very loudly, ostensibly to imitate his earlier summons to the supervisor, and thereby alerts the rest of the house to his presence in Fräulein Bürstner's room at this unusual and improper hour. The shouted name is both a boast and an act of self-denunciation, and as such typical of the way self-gratification and self-chastisement are inextricably intertwined in his psyche.

K.'s sexual attitudes are reflected back to him in two ways when he revisits the empty courtroom: in some books he finds there and in the court's mimicry of his treatment of women. In neither case does K. appear to recognize himself in these reflected images. One of the tattered and dusty books he finds lying on the table of the examining judge bears the title, 'The troubles Grete had to endure from her husband Hans', while the other contains an 'indecent' picture:

> A man and a woman were sitting naked on a couch, the crude intention of the draughtsman was clearly recognizable, but his awkwardness was so great that in the end the only thing one could see was just a man and a woman who protruded from the picture in an all too physical way, were seated in an excessively upright position and who, as a result of the wrong perspective, turned to one another with great difficulty. (P, 62–3)

K.'s evaluation of these images as 'indecent' and 'crude' reveals more about him than it does about the picture, which could equally well be described as 'sad' since it shows two people in an intimate situation but incapable of communication. That K. should condemn such an image of embarrassment and alienation as 'indecent' shows him caught in a vicious, self-defeating circle, unable to acknowledge the melancholy of sexuality without emotional closeness. It may be that K. recognizes in some corner of his mind that the 'false perspective' is his own rather than that of the artist, but he shows as little sign of admitting this as he does of seeing a connection between the couch ('Kanapee') in the picture and that in his own room (on which he lay waiting for Fräulein Bürstner) or the ottoman in Fräulein Bürstner's room.

The mimicry of K.'s sexual conduct within the court begins when the law student assaults the court servant's wife in the middle of the proceedings, and screams to attract attention just as K. had shouted loudly in Fräulein Bürstner's room. K.'s selfish and, at times, manipulative attitude to sex, whether with the prostitute Elsa or Fräulein Bürstner or the wife of the court servant, is matched by the patent self-interest of the court servant's wife in offering herself to K. in the hope of escaping life in the service of the court. K. calculates that it is worth yielding to the temptation she presents, because it offers an opportunity to strike back at the court, there being perhaps no better way of taking revenge on the examining judge and his hangers-on than by depriving them of this woman and taking 'possession' (P, 68) of her for his own pleasure. Appropriately enough, his plan is immediately frustrated by the arrival of the law student to carry the woman off to the judge, which forces K. to acknowledge his first 'undoubted' (P, 70) defeat at the hands of the court. K. tries to console himself with the thought that he had only sustained the defeat because he had sought the fight, but the symmetry of events adds more meaning to his words than he knows, in that his intention to use the woman as a means to an end has been frustrated – or punished – by the court's use of her in exactly the same way.

The same cycle of temptation and humiliation is to be found in all K.'s relationships with women throughout the period of his trial. At the house of the advocate Huld he is immediately attracted by the dark eyes of Leni, the young girl who tends the old and reputedly sick advocate. The advocate appears to be well connected with the court, for he is in conversation with the official in charge of the court chancery when K. is shown to his bedroom. K. throws away the opportunity presented by this chance meeting, however, when he simply walks out of the room to visit Leni, who has attracted his attention by crashing a tray to the floor. By this action K. rebels against his uncle's eagerness to have him pursue his case by the usual means and more generally against the procedures of the court which demand subordination and supplication from him. Yet he leaves the room slowly, 'as if giving the others a chance to hold him back' (P, 111), presumably in the hope of being saved from the foreseeable consequences of placing desire above discipline. Ironically and appropriately, Leni's motives appear to be as mixed as his, for she urges him to yield and confess to the court even as she presses her body against his, promising, quite illogically, that only if he confesses is there a chance of slipping out of the court's clutches. Whereas K. flatters himself that he has made yet another conquest, it is she who takes possession of him and who provides yet another mocking echo of his treatment of Fräulein Bürstner as she bites and kisses his neck. The predictable punishment comes in the form of his uncle's anger at the wasted opportunity and in the advocate's later humiliating revelation that Leni treats all accused men in the same way: ' "She throws herself at all of them, loves them, seems admittedly to be loved by all of them; to amuse me she then tells me about it sometimes, when I permit it" ' (P, 194). In other words, K. is no more and no less attractive to Leni than 'that miserable worm', the merchant Block. Whether he yields to impulse or relies on his habitual calculation of tactical advantage, both of which are elicited by the court, it seems that K. is facing too powerful an enemy.

Finally, K. meets a number of little girls who laugh as they crowd around him on the stairs leading to the room of the artist Titorelli. One in particular, a thirteen-year-old hunchback whose knowing looks and hitching up of her short skirt indicate to K. that she is already 'completely corrupt' (P, 148), confronts K.'s sexual desire with its object in its most taboo form. Like everything and everyone else he encounters, these girls 'belong to the court' (P, 158). K. is further humiliated by having to take off his coat while the girls peer excitedly through the cracks in the walls of Titorelli's overheated room. As Titorelli explains, they think he is about to undress in order to be painted. The motif of undressing links this scene with that of K.'s execution in the quarry where he is exposed, not to the stifling, airless heat he finds in all the rooms belonging to the court but to its complement, the cold, deadly air of the night. The shame Josef K. feels as he dies half naked brings into final, concentrated focus the conflict within him between desire and discipline which has been exposed and intensified by the eruption of the court into his seemingly orderly life. K.'s sexuality is not the only thing which reduces him to the condition of a 'dog' at the moment of death, but it is one of the most powerful contributors to that overwhelming sense of shame.

POWER AND VIOLENCE

Josef K.'s death at the hands of the court is the culmination of a series of violent experiences reaching back over the year of his trial. Just as the court's intervention in his life elicits unaccustomed sexual conduct from him, so it unleashes violent impulses in him more or less simultaneously.

As he waits to be summoned to the supervisor, the thought of suicide goes through K.'s mind: 'K. was surprised, or at least thinking about it from the point of view of the guards he was surprised, that they had driven him into the room and left him here alone, where he had the opportunity to kill himself ten times over' (P, 16). The response is that of a coward who prefers to turn his aggression on himself in imagination rather than on those who threaten him.[14] K.'s suppressed anger tends to be expressed in thought rather than action, or in his treatment of people weaker than himself. On discovering that Frau Grubach has tidied up the remains of his breakfast (which the guards have eaten), for example, K. imagines himself behaving quite differently. He would perhaps have smashed the dishes on the spot, he thinks, but he would certainly not have been able to carry them out of the room (P, 27). Later, when he disturbs some children playing on the stairs leading to the courtroom, it occurs to him that on his next visit he must either bring sweets to win them over or a stick to beat them (P, 45). In reality, however, K. allows two annoying little boys to cling to his trouser legs because, if he had tried to shake them off, he would have hurt them, and he feared their cries. It is not concern for the children which inhibits his violence but fear of the consequences it could have for himself. The response is typical of him, for whenever he is dealing with anyone who has even a little power his violent impulses are usually restrained by caution. The weakness of Frau Grubach or Fräulein Bürstner, by contrast, permits some physical expression of his feelings by slamming the door shut on the one and forcing his attentions on the other. Only occasionally do his impulses get the better of him, as when he jumps down from the podium in the courtroom 'recklessly', threatening to strike an old man who has come very close to him, but then he flees, avoiding the eyes of the examining judge and putting up the merest show of defiance by laughing at the door!

Again K.'s behaviour is mirrored in the world of the court. Thus the court servant returns from a spurious errand (during which his wife has been carried off to the judge) and pours out his desire for revenge to K.:

'If I were not so dependent I would have crushed the student against the wall here long ago. Here, next to the notice board. I always dream about it. Here, a little above the floor, he is crushed flat, his arms outstretched, his fingers spread apart, his crooked legs turned in a circle, and splashes of blood all around. So far it has only been a dream though.' (P, 72–3)

The servant speaks as the frustrated K. feels, but when he suggests that only someone like K. could give the student a thorough beating ('durch-prügeln'), K. responds first with caution (since he, too, has cause to fear the student's influence), then with a boast that he will indeed give not only the student but other officials of the court the treatment they deserve. When put to the test, however, he proves to be just as impotent as the court servant.

An opportunity for action occurs one evening when K. witnesses a beating which has been ordered by the court. While passing a lumber room in the bank he hears a sigh and opens the door (a familiar dream event) to find a man in the stereotypical leather outfit of an executioner preparing to whip the two guards for behaviour of which K. had complained before the court. Despite his earlier boast that he would never offer a bribe, K. now does precisely that in order to save the guards from the consequences of his complaints. The whipper refuses the bribe, demands that the guards strip naked and proceeds to beat Franz, causing him to produce an unbroken scream that fills the entire corridor of the bank. Fearful that the cry will attract the attention of other bank officials, K. pushes Franz to the floor where he writhes under the continuing lash of the cane. Having thus directed his aggression, characteristically, not at the whipper but at the victim he claims to pity, K. then shuts the door and tells some curious officials that the noise they heard came from 'a dog in the courtyard' (P, 91). The mention of the dog, the undressing of the victim and the fact that the moon is shining into the courtyard below are all details which recur in the scene of K.'s execution and confirm that the punishment of the guards foreshadows his fate at the hands of the court. K. justifies his action, or rather inaction, to himself, arguing that he could not be expected to sacrifice his own reputation for the sake of the guards: 'Really nobody could demand this self-sacrifice of K. If he had intended to do that, it would almost have been simpler for K. to have undressed and offered himself to the whipper as a substitute for the guards' (P, 92). Having consistently declined to take action against the agents of the court, K. in the end assumes fully the role of victim with which he had already identified himself implicitly.

Although K. refuses all responsibility for what happens to the guards, blaming their cruel treatment entirely on the high officials of the court, it was in fact his complaint which had led to this outcome. His desire to punish them was no less real than his avowed intention to punish the high officials (P, 93). In the whipping scene it is thus not only the guards who mirror K.'s impulses but also the whipper and the punitive authority in whose name he acts. As with his sexuality, K. flatly refuses to acknowledge the reality of his own violent impulses as they are reflected back to him by the court. Yet the beating of the guards flows so directly from his anger towards them that his relationship to the court goes beyond reflection to one of near identity. In the end K. will not take the knife from the hands of his executioners, just as he would not take the whip out of the hand of the whipper, but he has waited quietly for their unannounced visit, and as they walk to the quarry executioners and victim appear virtually inseparable and indistinguishable from one another: 'They now formed such a unity that, if one of them had been smashed, they would all have been smashed. It was a unity of the kind which can almost only be formed by lifeless things' (P, 237).

In *The Trial* violence, like sexuality, is repeatedly associated with dirt or disorder. A stickler for order, K. feels that Frau Grubach's home, and particularly Fräulein Bürstner's room, has been so sullied by the intrusion of the court that only his departure could restore its cleanliness: ' "If you want to keep your boarding house clean [or pure]" ', he shouts through the door to Frau Grubach, ' "you must first give me notice" ' (P, 31). In fact the physical disturbance of Fräulein Bürstner's room is so slight and so easily corrected that she would have overlooked it, had K. not insisted on drawing her attention to a few photographs which one of the junior clerks (Kaminer) had dared to touch ('in die Hand genommen' – P, 35) and rearrange. What makes K. feel so strongly implicated in the 'disordering' of the room caused by the intrusion of the court is clearly not the minor disturbance of the photographs but the implied, metonymic touching of Fräulein Bürstner and the feeling of moral or emotional pollution he associates with it. If anything, Josef K. seems even more powerfully disposed than Karl Roßmann to accept guilt in situations where he is the victim rather than the wrongdoer. Perhaps the corrosive effects of life in a hostile, judgemental society have simply had more time to eat into the substance of the older and, in terms of this society's standards, more successful man.

In contrast to the court's claim to want to 'bring order' (P, 261) into K.'s complicated case, the dusty, untidy lumber room where the guards are beaten is part of a rising curve of physical pollution reaching from the touching of Fräulein Bürstner's photographs through the dusty and all- egedly indecent books in the law court to the open sewer by the door of

Titorelli's house. The floor of the lumber room is covered with 'useless old printed samples and upturned, empty earthenware inkpots' (P, 87).[15] On discovering that the beating is still going on a day later, K. again slams the door shut, but on this occasion he orders some minor employees to clear out the room: 'We're sinking in dirt here' (P, 94). Scenes of washing complement and intensify the accusations implied by the motif of pollution.[16] Thus K. sees women washing in the tenement rooms on his way to the court; there is nothing but a large washtub in the room he must pass through to reach the court; washing is hanging up to dry in the attics housing the offices of the court. In order to dispel his worries about the court K. goes to the wash-stand in his office and washes in cold water. When K. orders the lumber room to be cleared he is bent on getting rid of any evidence linking him with what he feels to be the filth and violence of the court. By the end of his year on trial, by contrast, it is no longer dirt which upsets him, but the attempt to remove the signs of it from the faces of his executioners: 'He felt nauseated by the cleanliness of their faces. You could virtually still see the cleansing hand which had gone into the corners of their eyes, rubbed their upper lips, and scratched the dirt out of the lines on their chins' (P, 237).[17] The feeling of disgust is presumably prompted by this physical reminder of his own earlier attempts to cover up the moral and emotional pollution in which he felt implicated by the court's forced entry into his life.

The violence Josef K. feels, witnesses and is subject to during the year of his trial is simply the most palpable expression of the power which pervades all relationships, both within the court and outside it. Significantly, the court first enters his life in response to a gesture of power: when K. rings a bell to call for his breakfast the first guard comes into his room. It later emerges that the ringing of a bell marks the beginning of a trial; thus K.'s exercise of power as a lodger is followed by his exposure to the power of the court. This is characteristic of the way the court both mimics and inverts central features of K.'s life.

At the bank K. is engaged in a power struggle with his immediate superior, the deputy director, while the deputy director in turn is exploiting the illness of the director to secure his own position. K. knows, or at least he believes, that declining an invitation to a party on the deputy director's yacht implies a humiliation for the latter, since it looks as if K. is rejecting a gesture of reconciliation. Yet he feels he must refuse because he is due to make his first appearance before the court on the Sunday morning concerned. Having to deal with the power of the court thus weakens K.'s ability to exercise, gain or consolidate power outside it.

Progress in one of these areas is incompatible with progress in the other. Preparing a submission to the court, for example, will cost him time and energy just when he needs all the time and energy he can muster for his competition with the deputy director. As the weeks go past, K.'s constant fretting about the trial makes him grow ever more tired and unable to concentrate on business. One morning he is close to fainting and therefore quite incapable of following the arguments being put to him by a manufacturer who is an important client of the bank. Initially K. feels relieved when the deputy director appears in the doorway and takes over the negotiations, but his gratitude is soon undermined by the bitter thought that his moment of weakness has given the deputy director an advantage in their contest. K.'s bodily gestures during this incident illustrate with particular clarity the parallels and connections between the power structures in which K. has lived all his life and the power of the court to which he is now exposed. In a desperate attempt to concentrate on the documents presented to him by the manufacturer K. 'inclined his head as if in response to an order' (P, 136). He bows his head again when the deputy director looks at him for an answer to the accusation that he has shown little interest in the client's proposal. While the client and the deputy director stand conversing next to his desk, K. tries to follow events from his seat: 'It seemed to K. as if negotiations concerning himself were being conducted above his head by two men whose size he exaggerated in his imagination. Slowly he tried to discover what was happening up there by carefully turning his eyes upward' (P, 136–7). So intertwined are his thoughts of the court with his feeling of being on trial at work that he places one of the client's papers in the palm of his hand and stands up, proffering it to the client and the deputy director (or 'Herren' as he calls them). As he does so, he is thinking of nothing specific, but acts simply out of a feeling that this is how he will have to act some day when he has completed the great submission to the court which will unburden him of all charges.

The same constellation of a conversation or action being conducted above K.'s head occurs repeatedly in the course of K.'s trial. The two guards who arrest him are taller then he is and they stand very close to him while talking above his head: 'he looked up and saw a dry, bony face with a strong nose twisted to one side, which did not match this fat body at all, communicating with the other guard above his head' (P, 12). On his way to the court for the first time, K. hears men and women at the windows laughing 'directly above' him (P, 44); here Kafka exploits an ambiguity in German, for the phrase 'gerade über K.' could also mean

'particularly *about* K.'. When the stuffy air in the court offices brings him
close to fainting, K. is content simply to lie there and listen to a girl and
the information-giver talking above and about him. K. says nothing and
does not even look up, but simply tolerates them negotiating about him 'as
if he were a thing, indeed this suited him best' (P, 83). At the advocate's
house Leni climbs onto K.'s knees, from where she bends over him to kiss
and bite his neck. In the cathedral the prison chaplain first addresses him
from a high pulpit. As part of the novel's intricate structure of correspondences these incidents invert the relatively high position K. occupies in the
bank, from which he can look down, both literally and metaphorically, on
the doings of others. The final element in the pattern is again to be found
in the execution scene where K. lies on the ground while the two executioners, their cheeks touching, lower their faces close to his to observe how
he dies.

By being made to see things increasingly from below, both in the bank
and in the world of the court, K. joins the many other figures in the novel
who are forced to bend their heads or backs. The accused men waiting in
the corridor outside the officials' mean offices, for example, all adopt a
crouched posture, never standing completely upright, their backs bowed,
their knees bent, like 'street-beggars' (P, 75). The little merchant Block sits
with his back so bent that K. is forced to bend down low to hear his words.
The implication of this imagery of humiliation is that K. is made to
become the very thing he and his uncle fear most, namely the 'disgrace'
or 'shame' ('Schande' – P, 98) of the family whose pride and honour he had
embodied before his arrest. Thus K. dies thinking that 'the shame would
outlive him' (P, 241). Yet it is not only the accused who are forced to adopt
a posture of humility in this court. The gallery in the courtroom, for
example, is built so close to the ceiling that the public can only stand
bowed, with their heads and backs pressed against the ceiling, so that they
have to bring pillows with them to ease the discomfort. Both the whipper
and the two guards have to stoop in the low space of the lumber room.
One little girl on Titorelli's stairs is 'rather hunchbacked' while Titorelli
himself receives K. with a deep reverence and is 'bent down low' (P, 154)
as he works on a judge's portrait. Even the prison chaplain is not spared
the necessity of bowing his head. The pulpit from which he addresses K.
has an unusually low canopy so that even a man of medium height could
not stand up in it without constantly having to bend out over the parapet.
The whole thing seems to K. to be meant ('bestimmt' – P, 219) to torture
the preacher, and he cannot understand the need for this pulpit, given that
another large one with highly wrought ornamentation is available. To

judge by what K. sees of it, the court is an organization which is 'meant' to force all who are involved with it, its servants as well as the accused, into a posture of submission.[18]

'DO NOT DECEIVE YOURSELF!'

The word 'bestimmt' – 'meant', 'intended', 'designed' – which is applied to the 'torturous' pulpit in the cathedral recurs at another key moment in the same chapter. The prison chaplain tells K. a story or parable about a man from the country who seeks entry to 'the Law'. It ends with these words, addressed by the doorkeeper to the man: ' "No-one else could gain admittance here, for this entrance was meant [*bestimmt*] only for you. I am now going to close it" ' (P, 227). What makes this ending so cruel and unexpected is the fact that the doorkeeper had answered the man's initial request for admission with the statement that he could not admit him 'now'. This little story (the only part of the novel actually published by Kafka, as a separate story entitled 'Before the Law') has attracted a vast number of commentaries, even measured by the standards of Kafka criticism.[19] Read within the context of the novel, however, the phrasing and imagery of the story have specific resonances. The door which is 'bestimmt' for the man from the country echoes the description just a few pages earlier of the pulpit that seems to be 'bestimmt' to torture the preacher. By telling the man at the moment of death that the door is 'meant' only for him, the doorkeeper has made of the door an instrument of a last, sharp torture, just as his withholding of this information until this point has made it an instrument of slow torture during the man's long years of waiting before it. Since the story does not say that the doorkeeper was deficient in his duty or that he deceived the man, one may fairly conclude that the door was actually intended to be closed in this way. It was both 'bestimmt' for the man *and* 'bestimmt' to be shut before he could enter it. Such a timid man and such a fearsomely guarded door are 'meant' for one another in the sense that 'fate' is a mirror of character.[20]

Like K. and many other characters in the novel, the man from the country 'bückt sich' ('bends down') in order to see inside the door. By the end of the story the difference in size between the man and the doorkeeper has become so great that the latter must bow down deeply to hear the man's last question (just as K. has to bend down low to hear the words of the merchant Block). Taking the chaplain's story and the novel together, then, both the servant of the Law and the supplicant are forced to bow or bend their backs. Like Josef K. (who is in bed when the guards enter his room), the man from the country ends his life in the same low posture as he adopted for his first sight of what lay beyond the door. Whereas K. initially refuses to remain in this posture, however, by immediately leaping out of bed and walking about, so that he gradually has to be forced into submission by the court, the man from the country appears to be submissive from the start. He neither demands entrance to the Law nor attempts to enter by force. Instead he simply asks ('bittet') for entry. But if the arrogance and violent impulses of Josef K. contrast with the humility and gentleness of the man from the country, the one is actually just as much of a coward as the other. Although the doorkeeper expressly challenges the man to attempt to enter 'despite my prohibition', the doorkeeper's great nose, his long, black, Tartar beard, and his warning that there are many more doorkeepers within, each mightier than the last, combine to intimidate the man so much that he decides he would rather wait for permission to enter. His character is the opposite of Hans Christian Andersen's soldier with his tinder box who has no fear even of guard dogs with eyes as large as dinner plates. Consequently the man's story has the opposite outcome to that of the resolute soldier; whereas the latter makes his fortune, the man from the country sits down and dies without fulfilling his desire to enter the Law. Like K. during the whipping scene, the man tries bribery to no avail, he even asks the fleas in the fur collar of the doorkeeper's coat to help him, and he curses 'unfortunate chance' (P, 227) for his fate, just as K. repeatedly blames his experiences on others or on circumstance, but never, consciously, on himself.[21]

K.'s reaction to the man's story confirms this ingrained habit: ' "So the doorkeeper deceived the man" ' (P, 227). When the prison chaplain had introduced the story, however, it was to warn him of the dangers of *self*-deception: ' "Do not deceive yourself ", said the priest. "About what am I supposed to deceive myself, then?", asked K. "You deceive yourself about the court", said the priest, "In the introductory writings to the Law it says of this deception[...]" ' (P, 225–6). How the man from the country ought to have conducted himself (if indeed he had any possibility of behaving differently) one cannot tell, but he has plainly deceived himself, perhaps out of fear of the doorkeeper, if he believes that patient supplication is the best way to gain admission to the Law. Although the priest (as he himself warns K.) is not necessarily trustworthy, there are many indications throughout *The Trial* that Josef K. deceives himself in like manner about the nature of the court's power, and that this self-deception is intimately connected with the kind of person he is, or has become.

AUTHORITY AND ILLUSION

About one thing Josef K. is certainly not deceived, namely that the court
exercises power over his life and that of others. It does so in many, varied
ways. It exercises physical power, for example, by having the wife of the
court servant carried away bodily, by having the guards whipped and by
having K. executed. Like the doorkeeper before the Law, it also exercises
emotional power, with the result that K. does not telephone his friend, the
state prosecutor Hasterer, goes to his first hearing 'freely' (i.e. without
physical compulsion), returns to the courtroom for a second time although
he has not even been instructed to do so, and is unable to put thoughts of
the court out of his mind in order to go about his normal business, as the
supervisor assures him he might. The court also exercises the power of the
unknown, the inaccessible and the inscrutible. Because K. knows neither
the law, nor his alleged offence, nor his judges, and has only the rumours
of minor officials and satellites of the court to go on, it is impossible for
him to defend himself.

The fact that the court exercises emotional power over K. does not,
however, mean that it carries moral authority. The actions of its officials
are morally offensive, from the guards who steal K.'s breakfast and try to
extort money from him, to the student of the law who rapes the wife of the
court servant, and the examining judge who orders the woman to be taken
from her husband. Actions (purportedly) commanded by the court are
equally immoral. The ceaseless whipping of the guards for minor larceny,
and the cutting of K.'s throat for some unstated offence are not actions
informed by ethical principles or any sense of the appropriate balance
between offence and retribution, but appear rather to be merely the
disciplinary or even sadistic obverse of the officials' indulgence of their
own immoral inclinations.

Nor, equally, is the power of the court based on reason. On the
contrary, its procedures are thoroughly contradictory. When K. wonders
what he has been accused of, for example, the supervisor says that he does
not know whether charges have been made, only that he is arrested. When
K. tries to leave his room he is driven back into it by the guards, and when
he resists briefly the pull of his executioners they respond by tightening
their grip on his arm. Yet he is informed that his arrest does not mean any
disruption of his normal way of life, that the court will receive him if he
comes and let him go if that is his wish. K. is told that the court has made
no mistake (P, 14) in arresting him, yet at his first hearing he is asked, quite
erroneously, if he is a housepainter. He is assured by one of the guards that

the court does not seek out guilt in the population but rather is 'drawn to guilt' ('von der Schuld angezogen' – P, 14). This appears to be confirmed when, at his first visit, he finds the court behind a door which he chooses at random. When K. visits the court for a second time, however, he finds that the room has been turned back into a living room in which there is neither judge nor public but only the washerwoman who lives there. Does this mean that K.'s guilt has suddenly disappeared, or has it lost its ability to attract the court, or has the guard given a misleading account of the relation between the court and guilt? The supervisor, after all, speaks disparagingly of the 'chattering' (P, 20) of the guards. These contradictions may, in part, be explicable in terms of the contradictions within K. himself, but that would simply point yet again to the irrational source of the court's power.

The lack of reason in the court reaches its most disabling expression in the paradoxical words the prison chaplain cites to K.: ' "Correct understanding of something and misapprehension of the same thing do not exclude one another entirely" ' (P, 229). One can attempt to resolve the paradox by contextualizing it in particular ways, by pointing out, for example, that failure to perceive irony or sarcasm in a speaker's words could mean that their literal meaning was correctly understood while the speaker's intention was misapprehended. The contradictions between K.'s conscious intentions and his physical reflexes, such as entering a room more slowly than he would like, could also be taken to illustrate the coexistence in him of contrary modes of apprehension, one of which may be 'correct' while the other is 'false'. Yet the contradictoriness and obscurity of the court are such persistent features that one must not attempt simply to explain them away, since that would be both to block the source of its most disabling power and remove an important parallel to and inversion of K.'s misguided reliance on calculation.[22]

The verbal contradictions surrounding the court are matched by its visible signs. K. sees Titorelli, for example, painting a contradictory figure on the back of a judge's throne. With the painter's help K. identifies the figure as the goddess of justice, her eyes bound and with scales in her hand, but then he notices that the figure has wings on her heels and is running.[23] Titorelli explains that he was instructed to depict her thus, as the goddess of justice and victory in one. K. criticizes the combination of these two figures on the grounds that justice must rest, otherwise the scales will sway and a just verdict will not be possible (P, 153). Despite his criticisms he feels strongly, if reluctantly, compelled to watch Titorelli as he paints a mysterious reddish[24] halo around the judge's head and transforms the contradictory figure of the goddess still further until she resembles the goddess of the hunt (called Artemis by the Greeks and Diana by the Romans). The merging of the figures in the painting results in a paradoxical representation of Justice as a partisan figure eager for prey.[25] Nevertheless, the combination has the power to fascinate K.

While discussing the painting with Titorelli, K. learns something else about power in the court, something so important that it is astonishing how little effect it has on his conduct:

> 'You have painted the figure as it really is represented on the throne.' 'No', said the painter, 'I have seen neither the figure nor the throne, that is all invention, but I was given instructions about what I had to paint.' 'What?', asked K., deliberately acting as if he did not entirely understand the painter, 'surely it is a judge sitting on the throne?' 'Yes', said the painter, 'but it is not a high judge and he has never sat on a throne like this.' (P, 153)

The solemn pose and fine setting, in other words, are part of a fraud created by a set of rigid, anonymous conventions on the one hand and, on the other, by the vanity of this minor judge who has asked to have his portrait painted in quite unsuitable pastel shades because it is intended for a lady. (Given this fact, it is ironical that the figure of Justice on the back of his throne should be indistinguishable from the avenger of womankind, the huntress Diana: behind and above the male judge–pursuer is his mythical female counterpart by whom he in his turn may be judged, defeated or hunted down.) Yet Titorelli's information does nothing to diminish K.'s attraction to the 'high distinction' (P, 154) he discerns in the play of reddish shadows around the head of the judge. So great is the power of illusion, or so great is Josef K.'s susceptibility to it, that even as he watches the fraud being perpetrated by brush strokes on canvas he responds to the emotive and imaginative suggestiveness of the image. Kafka uses the same verb 'anziehen' ('to draw' or 'attract') to describe both K.'s reponse to the painting and the reputed response of the court to guilt ('it is drawn to guilt'). Given that this is a relation of mutual attraction, the question arises whether the guilt to which the court is drawn is as illusory as the images of dignity and authority which so fascinate K.

Once before, during his visit to the advocate, K. had been drawn to a very similar portrait of another judge. This, he subsequently learns, is a flattering and aggrandizing distortion of a person who in reality is tiny and

absurdly vain and seated on a kitchen chair (P, 113).[26] Whether intentional or not, the repetition makes it clear how important it was to Kafka
to stress both the personal insignificance of the men in whom the authority
of the court is invested, as compared with the image they wish to project,
and the strength of K.'s attraction to the *illusion* of power, regardless of its
substance. After Leni has told him that the subject of the portrait is merely
an examining judge, K. is disappointed but undeterred in his hope of
eventually seeing a high judge. Indeed, despite all the dis- illusioning
scenes he witnesses in the year of his trial, K.'s last thought before his
death is of the 'high court' to which he has never gained access. Yet he has
been given as little evidence that any such ultimate authority truly exists as
the man from the country, who only has the word of the doorkeeper that
other and more frightening doorkeepers lie behind the door, and whose
only evidence of the Law he seeks is a gleam in the darkness behind the
door. What is more, that 'inextinguishable' gleam, like the reddish halo
around the judge's head in Titorelli's painting, may rest on nothing more
than an optical illusion: ' "Finally his eyesight becomes weak and he does
not know whether it is really growing darker around him or whether it is
just his eyes deceiving him" ' (P, 227). Significantly, the man is described as
seeing the gleam 'wohl', an utterly ambiguous adverb which is equally
capable of conveying affirmation and reservation. No less dubious is every
other sign of authority K. sees in his dealings with the court.

K.'s reluctance to pay any heed to the fraudulent nature of the judges or
their portraits contrasts with his willingness to regard the lower agents of
the court as mere 'actors'. He thinks of his executioners, for example, as
'old, subordinate actors' (P, 236) whose double chins remind him of tenors.
The theatrical comparisons are part of K.'s strategy to maintain some
ironic distance from what is happening to him and to observe things to the
end with his 'calm, analytic reason' (P, 238). The metaphor does not have
the desired effect. On the morning of his arrest K. would like to believe
that the bizarre events are a practical joke arranged by colleagues in the
bank for his birthday: 'If it was a comedy he would play along' (P, 13). In
supposing that others could be deceiving him, K. is actually making a
desperate attempt to deceive himself. No sooner has he formulated this
thought than his mind switches to other, quite different and contradictory
ones, which show him caught up in the reality of his arrest: 'He was still
free [...] In his room he immediately tore open the drawers of his writing
desk, everything lay there in great order, but in his excitement he could
not immediately find the legitimation papers he was looking for' (P, 13).
His panicky actions are not those of someone playing his role in a friendly

prank. Finally, although K. is still trying to act the part of willing victim during his death scene, his attitude or pose as he lies on the execution stone is 'forced and unconvincing' (P, 240).

The irony in K.'s decision to 'join in the comedy' consists in the fact that he is generally unaware of his own play-acting.[27] Lying on his bed and eating an apple to replace the breakfast the guards have eaten, for example, K. re-interprets events in the theatre of his own imagination where he can take the part of a man in control of things:

> Now it was his only breakfast and in any case, so he assured himself at the first bite, much better than the breakfast from the dirty all-night café he could have got by the grace and favour of the guards. He felt well and confident; admittedly he was absent from duty at the bank this morning, but that was easily excused, given the relatively high position he occupied there. (P, 16)

That K. actually feels anything but well and confident is indicated by the thought that he will have to excuse his absence from the bank, which leads to his resolve to give the real reason, citing Frau Grubach as his 'witness', an implausible plan which is immediately overtaken by his realization that the guards have left him alone where he could so easily commit suicide. In his imaginary drama K. then invites the guards to watch him go to the cupboard, drink one glass of schnapps in place of his breakfast, followed by another for courage just in case, 'quite improbably' (P, 17), he should need it. The internal theatre collapses abruptly, however, when K. hears his name called out so loudly from the next room that he bites the glass in fright. Again he tries to recover control of the script, as it were, by telling himself that it was only the abrupt, military manner of the shout that had startled him, whereas, 'The command itself he welcomed very much. "At last!", he called back, shutting the cupboard and hurrying immediately into the next room' (P, 17). He even gives himself the credit for hurrying proceedings along, secretly believing that he has achieved an acceleration of the whole affair thanks to the fact that the guards have forgotten to force him to take a bath. K.'s self-deluding play-acting is complemented by the numerous spectators of K.'s behaviour scattered throughout the novel, many of whom disturb him by their smiles or laughter, such as the giggling little girls who peer through the cracks in the walls of Titorelli's room 'to see the play' (P, 164) for themselves. During K.'s address to the court, when he claims to be speaking not on his own behalf but for all those who are persecuted by it, his insincere words are greeted by applause from the audience and ironic-sounding shouts of ' "Bravo! Why not indeed? And again bravo!" ' (P, 52).

Like the flattering portraits the judges require Titorelli to paint, K.'s play-acting shows him to be a vain man. When re-enacting his interview with the supervisor, for example, ostensibly in order to explain to Fräulein Bürstner what had happened in her bedroom on the morning of the arrest, he begins with a description of how the participants had been positioned relative to one another: ' "Oh yes, I'm forgetting about myself. The most important person, which is to say me, stands here in front of the little table" ' (P, 37).[28] The re-enactment also shows something else, however: in taking the part of the supervisor, literally sitting in the same place and adopting the same attitude, K. presents his relationship to the court as being one of identity rather than simply one of parallelism or mirroring. Yet despite the fact that he plays the role of his own accuser here, K. refuses to acknowledge the relevance to his conduct of the mirror images presented by the court. Instead he remains incorrigibly insincere. Thus, when asked by his uncle to give an account of recent events, K. resolves on 'complete openness' (P, 103), yet his account makes just one, fleeting mention of Fräulein Bürstner. This he justifies to himself on the grounds that she is irrelevant to his case. K. is thus caught in another vicious circle. Being unwilling or unable to acknowledge his own insincerity, he pays little heed to the signs of insincerity in his persecutors, insisting to the last that there must exist some high court behind the appearance of immorality, violence, self- interest and deceit presented by the agents of the court. K. evidently *needs* to believe in such an authority in order to explain and justify to himself what has happened to him. Far from compelling the reader to take the same view, however, the imagery of the novel puts events in a rather different light. The authority and dignity of the court are shown to be as spurious as the various illusions K. nurtures about himself. Despite this quality of unreality attaching to the court's authority, however, the 'comedy' initiated by its agents has the power to compel K. to participate. One is thus compelled to ask where the source of this power can lie.

PROGRESS AND STASIS

Like that of Georg Bendemann in 'The Judgement' and Karl Roßmann in *The Missing Person*, Josef K.'s life has been built on the idea of progress. He takes pride in having worked his way rapidly to a relatively high position in the bank and he resents the fact that the court has intruded into his life at a time when he is still rising and needs all his energy for his contest with the deputy director. For some of the time he believes that he will be able to make the same kind of rapid progress in his dealings with the court. When contemplating the preparation of a submission to the court, for example, he resolves to work at it uninterruptedly in order to complete it as soon as possible: 'anything but stopping halfway [*auf halbem Wege stehenbleiben*], that was the most senseless thing one could do, not only in business but always and everywhere' (P, 133–4). However, when he sees this faith in progress mirrored in the behaviour of his bustling and eager little uncle from the country who insists on taking K. to consult an advocate, K. becomes reluctant, tries to delay things and eventually aborts the consultation by walking out of the advocate's bedroom to visit Leni. The same ambivalence is evident in the way he first resists the pull of his executioners and then tows them along behind him, or in his curious behaviour on his initial visit to the court, first hurrying along to be there by nine o'clock, the time he himself has fixed, then strolling slowly down the street once he has found it, so that he eventually arrives in the courtroom an hour and five minutes late for the hearing. From these and many other such instances where he decides one thing and promptly does another, it is clear that K. is neither the resolute man of the will he likes to consider himself, nor someone so consumed by feelings of guilt that he wishes only to be condemned and punished.

The court reflects back to K. his contradictory attitude towards making progress with his trial. Initially it claims to share his desire to bring things to a rapid conclusion, but when K. appears for a second hearing, admittedly having ended the first by shouting that he was not interested in any further hearings, the courtroom is empty. Everything he later learns about the court's procedures from Titorelli, the advocate and the merchant Block indicates that delays are the rule rather than the exception in this court. One of the first instructions he receives from the guards is to 'wait' (P, 11), while the patient Block and the row of men lining the corridor in the attic give the impression that waiting is an essential element in the experience of all who are accused by this court. Block, who was once just as eager for 'progress' (P, 187) in his case as the less experienced K. is now moderately proud of having 'trundled along' (P, 185) his case, Sisyphus-like, for a whole five years. In the two paintings of judges K., is again shown a mixture of stasis and dynamism which mirrors his own behaviour. The allusion to the huntress–goddess Diana in the second of these pictures, an image which corresponds to the urgent, ambitious and restless side of K., is picked up in Leni's sympathetic observation towards the end of the trial, ' "They are harrying [*hetzen*] you" ', to which K., the exhausted quarry, can only reply, ' "Yes, they are harrying me" ' (P, 215). Conversely, K.'s lack of progress in understanding the obscure court and his underlying reluctance to make any progress towards a resolution are reflected not only in the (literally) static images painted by Titorelli, but also in the whipping scene in the lumber room where time seems to stand still so that the guards' punishment is repeated endlessly.

In another of Titorelli's paintings (of which K. is persuaded to buy several identical copies) stasis is represented in 'natural' imagery which suggests that the theme has wider significance in K.'s life beyond his relation to the court. The picture shows two 'weak' trees set at a distance from each other on an otherwise empty heath and outlined against a garish, multi- coloured sunset (P, 171) reminiscent of a theatrical back-drop. This constellation recalls two other images seen by K. The first is the 'indecent' drawing of two naked figures seated on a couch, turned towards one another but unable to make contact. The second, glimpsed on the night of his execution, is the sight of two infants in a play-pen reaching out to one another with their hands but not yet able to move from their respective places (P, 236). In all three pictures stasis is associated with isolation. The first of them, with its setting sun, further links this pair of motifs to that of transience. This theme is also implicit in a *sequence* of three pairs of human figures to which the other two images (the drawing and the children) belong. The first pair in this sequence appears on the morning of K.'s arrest when K. notices, with some irritation, an old couple looking into his room from the building opposite, their arms clasped around one another (P, 15). Here transience – ageing – contrasts with the enduring affection of the couple for one another. As the plot moves forward, the pairs of figures become progressively younger, ending with the two infants vainly reaching out to one another. As K. moves towards death, so these images suggest, he remains isolated and trapped in the condition of a helpless infant. Beneath the surface of professional and social progress lies emotional stasis. While K. may insist that ' the most senseless thing of all is stopping halfway ', his underlying awareness – and fear – of the stasis in his life is reflected back to him repeatedly. It is suggested, for example, by the many beds he sees, with their multiple connotations of rest, sex, procreation, sickness and death. It is conveyed even more plainly by the wall he sees from his office window, the wall to which the sick advocate turns his face, the alcove in the wall where Block has his bed, the walls lining the narrow staircase K. climbs to reach Titorelli's room, the wall he has to feel his way along in the darkened cathedral and, finally, the quarry wall ('Bruchwand'), beneath which he dies at the age of thirty-one – 'stopping halfway', as he might once have put it.[29]

PROXIMITY AND DISTANCE

Thoughout the novel images of separation are complemented by images of closeness and even of fusion. This pattern begins on the morning of K.'s arrest when he makes a strange, sudden movement, as if tearing himself away from the two men who are actually standing far away from him (P, 10). The motif of proximity then switches back and forth from metaphor to bodily closeness or contact. While one of the guards repeatedly presses his belly against K., thus making it difficult for him to concentrate, the other criticizes K. for irritating them – ' "us, who are probably closer to you than anyone else" ' (P, 14). K. must then squeeze past Wilhelm on his way to the supervisor. When K. exclaims that the proceedings are 'sense-less' ('sinnlos'), the three 'gentlemen' ('Herren') turn round to look at him earnestly but 'entgegenkommend' (literally 'coming towards him', i.e., expressing agreement or cooperation) (P, 21). Although still protesting about the stupidity of the duty the officials have performed, K. in turn draws very close to the supervisor just before his departure, so that he and the officials are all gathered together in a narrow space by the door (P, 23). In the courtroom the press of the crowd pushes K. very close to the judge's table (P, 49). In the attic corridor some of the accused men come so close to K. that they have to be shooed away by the servant leading him. In the advocate's house Leni finds K. sitting bent over and very close to the accused merchant Block who has just been telling K. about the forlorn hopes he, too, had once entertained of 'palpable progress' in his dealings with the court. They are sitting so close to one another that they would be bound to bump their heads together if they turned even slightly (P, 189). K. then complains of the advocate's inaction at a time when the trial is ' "getting ever closer to me" ' (' "mir [. . .] immer näher an den Leib rückt" ') (P, 197).

Apart from those occasions when he is seducing or being seduced by a woman, K.'s physical proximity to others is at its greatest at two points: when he is being more or less carried out of the court's offices by two servants, and when he is walking to his death between the two execu-tioners. K. is so close to losing consciousness in the stuffy air of the court offices that he would collapse were he not being supported by the girl and the man: 'He was utterly dependent on them, if they let him go, he would be bound to fall like a board' (P, 84). A similar phrase is used to describe the group of K. and his executioners: 'It was a unity of the kind which can almost only be formed by lifeless things' (P, 237). The consistent implications of the imagery seem clear: K. is drawn physically close to others in situations involving sexual domination, arrest, accusation, punishment, senselessness and lifelessness – but never, significantly, affection.[30] An isolated life lacking any 'sense' other than the pursuit of power and pleasure is subjected to an equally 'senseless' trial. A man who habitually treats others as objects of his will to 'progress' is disposed of, whether he will or no, by two executioners as lifeless as himself.

Having felt 'harried' to the point of exhaustion during his trial, K. is struck by the 'naturalness and calm which is given to no other light' (P, 240) of the moonshine in the quarry. There is irony in his observation, not only because the place is about to become a scene of violence, but because the moon has appeared repeatedly in the novel and always in scenes of danger to K. It shines onto the pillows in Fräulein Bürstner's bedroom on the night of his assault on her, it shines into the courtyard on the night K. discovers the guards being whipped, it is shining into the advocate's study when Leni summons him there and, finally, it lights the path of K. and his executioners to the quarry. The goddess of the moon is Diana, the same figure as is portrayed in her role as huntress on the judge's throne. Diana is also the goddess of fertility and childbirth and, as protectress and avenger of women, a goddess of death. Unwittingly, K. passes through her territory in the tenement building where he sees many women cooking, tending children and washing clothes. Diana's last, vengeful appearance is signalled by the moonlight illuminating the death of a bachelor whose life of sterile isolation and exploitation of women for his own purposes has offended against all that is under the goddess's protection.

POETIC JUSTICE

The multiple correspondences and inversions in *The Trial* produce the symmetrical structure which is the chief characteristic of poetic justice. Just as feelings of guilt need to be distinguished from actual guilt,[31] the distinct term 'poetic justice' implies that the concept is not quite coextensive with that of justice, whether moral or legal. When matters are being judged legally or morally, we may take account of mitigating circumstances, of mercy, or of the relation of a particular action to a person's general conduct of life, while in determining a punishment our culture attaches great weight to the 'proportionality' of misdeed and retribution. Very often poetic justice disregards such matters in the name of the primitive symmetry of an eye for an eye. Where the imagination is guided by this principle it devises some witty connection between crime and punishment or action and consequence. Thus Lucifer, brightest of the angels, is cast into nether darkness, King Oedipus puts out his eyes to punish them for what they have seen but not seen, Tantalus is condemned to eternal hunger and thirst because he has presented his own son as food to the gods, King Edward II has a burning poker thrust into his bowels to punish him for his homosexuality. By the same principle of symmetry, the bureaucrat Josef K. is persecuted by a bureaucratic organization; as someone who habitually tells himself that his own questionable judgements are 'beyond doubt', he is arrested by a fallible court which claims to make no mistakes; having made others wait before his office, he is obliged to wait by the court and its adjuncts; his pride in his grand office is mocked by a court housed in the humblest conditions; having risen to a high position in the bank, he must now climb stairs time after time to enter the mean, dilapidated and airless rooms of the court; having once attracted attention for the daring cut of his clothes, he is now exposed to the humiliating gaze of neighbours and colleagues, and is stripped half naked for his execution; the outward progress he has sought in life contrasts with the stasis of his trial; having once scorned the dog-like behaviour of the merchant Block, K. himself dies 'like a dog'; having lived for himself, he dies alone.

The correspondences are precise and ingenious, but they are not 'just' in any sense of the word other than its poetic one. Perhaps Josef K. could have lived a life of greater emotional fulfilment and generosity, but it is equally arguable that he could not. Selfish he may be, but he is at least sufficiently decent for Frau Grubach to regard him as her favourite lodger. On the scale of human evil his failings are relatively modest, more sins of omission than of commission. If he merits death by the butcher's knife, what penalty does this court of justice have in store for those who are actively cruel to others? In any case, how is the 'good' life to be defined, even within the terms of the arguments with which Kafka wrestled? Is it a life committed fully to marriage and the raising of children, one which expresses faith in the 'indestructible'[32] core of human life by the simple fact of living it out patiently? Or is it a life of self-destructive asceticism, filled with a 'wish to die'[33] thanks to some sudden insight into the deluded and illusory nature of human existence? Or is the human consciousness which asks such questions of life unwittingly in the situation of the misguided creature in the following aphorism: 'The animal wrests the whip from the hand of its master and whips itself in order to become master – and does not know that this is only a fantasy created by a new knot in the master's whip' (GW 6, 232)? Does the individual have free will or does choice lie at such a deep and metaphysically prior level of being that, in practice, 'there is no room for a will, neither for one that is free, nor for one that is unfree' (GW 6, 247)? Kafka arrived at no clear or consistent answer to such questions in his notebooks. His way of dealing with their complexities and relativities in *The Trial* was to construct and simultaneously to undermine a system of poetic 'justice'.

Although he regards it as an alien intruder, the court which exacts poetic justice from Josef K. in these various ways not only mimics his life, but is intimately connected with it. It is his ringing of the bell to summon Anna, Frau Grubach's cook, which calls the first guard into his room. It is his pretence of looking for a carpenter called Lanz which leads to his being ushered into the room where the court is sitting. These and many other connections suggest that one source of the trial is to be found within K., in the lumber rooms and attics of his personality, as it were, where the unacknowledged or repressed anxieties of his ambitious and outwardly well-ordered bourgeois existence lie waiting to mock him. One critic has described the whipping scene aptly as a 'synecdoche' of the entire trial, with K. taking three roles simultaneously, namely those of the whipper, the whipped and the observer or judge.[34] How and why does this come about?

On the one hand, Kafka implies that there are social and psychological mechanisms at work in this process (the German 'Prozeß' – or 'Proceß', as it is spelled in the critical edition – can mean both 'process' and 'trial'). Like Karl Roßmann, K. has imbibed the values of the bourgeois family. He knows that he embodies the honour of the family and that he owes it to his family to 'give an account' of himself (P, 99). This feeling derives, in part, from the disciplinary and judgemental role of the family in bourgeois society, a role which both supports and is shaped by the disciplines of the workplace. K.'s success in rising to a position in the bank where he is 'acknowledged by all' (P, 132) means that he has satisfied outwardly the requirements of a society in which the individual is expected to discipline himself and to *give proof of* his or her worth. To put it the other way round, the educative principles of this society leave the individual who identifies with them as completely as K. does with the feeling that he or she has no worth *unless* it has been demonstrated by outward achievement. The motif of K.'s growing tiredness during the year of his trial, together with the fact that it begins while he is in bed, may indicate that, at the age of thirty, the demands of ambition and competition have already wearied him sufficiently for the fundamental self-doubt built into bourgeois education to precipitate a crisis. The power of the court is also fed by the inner weakness of a life that has been devoted to the pursuit of aims – power, progress – which, as K. knows but is reluctant to acknowledge, ultimately offer no refuge from the annihilating fear of ageing and death.

Some of the clearest evidence of the social and psychological foundations of K.'s behaviour is to be found in the unfinished chapters of the novel. One of these, entitled 'State Prosecutor Hasterer', is particularly illuminating in this regard. It describes the centre of K.'s social life, a 'Stammtisch' (a 'permanently reserved table' at an inn or pub) with a membership drawn mainly from legal circles. It is an exclusively male club with a strong sense of seniority and hierarchy. K., who has no legal training, is very conscious of the honour he has gained by achieving admission to this exclusive group and is especially proud of his close relationship with one of its leading members, the state prosecutor Hasterer, with whom he would walk home arm in arm after an evening at the Stammtisch. It has taken K. a long time to get used to walking like this alongside this gigantic man who could have hidden him in his cape without anyone noticing (P, 255). There is a strong suggestion here that the relationship had begun like that of a small son to his father, although this aspect has become less marked as the friendship has developed. When the director of K.'s bank sees them together, he is so astonished that he drops in for a rare talk with K. It is, above all, the director's way of addressing K., as if he were a child or a youngster about whose well-being his frail and overburdened superior is deeply concerned, which 'enchants' K. (P, 260). The 'weakness' in K. which makes him susceptible to the director's show of concern may, he himself suspects, derive from the fact that 'there was still really something childish in him in this respect, since he had never known the care of his own father, who had died very young, had left home very early and had always tended to reject rather than elicit the tenderness of his mother' (P, 260). K. is strongly oriented, this suggests, towards father-figures whose affection he needs to gain and whose power he seeks to emulate. The 'Fürsorge' ('concern' for his welfare) which K. craves from his superiors in the bank is readily accepted as a substitute for paternal affection, despite his awareness that it may be nothing more than a calculated ploy to gain the loyalty and hard work of officials for years to come in return for a brief show of kindness; as with the authority of the judges, K. is captivated by the illusion of paternal care, regardless of its substance. The unattainable affection of his dead father is sought now in the deferred, never perfectly achievable and never entirely reliable approval on which the bourgeois ethic of striving is based. In the patriarchal world of the court, however, where the courtroom appears to be filled almost entirely with bearded men, K.'s dependence on male approval, undermined as it is by his doubts about the manipulative intentions of power holders, reveals its obverse, the fear of failure and disapproval underlying the constant struggle for social recognition. The unseen 'high court' puts the possibility of self-justification at an unattainable distance, leaving the accused man with the feeling of irredeemable failure: 'it was as if the shame would outlive him' (P, 241). In the symmetry of Josef K.'s trial the 'justice' exacted from him is the sadistic complement – or masochistic obverse – of a life educated in and dedicated to power and 'progress'.

The crude system of bribery and chastisement on which early socialization so often rests flashes up momentarily in K.'s own mental reaction to the children who obstruct and pester him on his way to meet the court for the first time. If deferred or conditional approval or affection is one of the mainstays of bourgeois education, punishment, or the threat of it, is the other.[35] In the mirror-world of the court, the power which pervades human relations in a hierarchical society is translated out of the sublimated or 'merely' verbal forms it assumes in habitual social intercourse and back into physical violence, the form in which the infant all too often first experiences power. This topic was clearly of such urgent concern to Kafka that he broke off work on *The Trial* to expose physical cruelty as the primitive source of 'discipline' even more graphically in 'In the Penal Colony', where a broken law is literally engraved into a man's flesh by a machine.[36] As in Karl Roßmann's story, the violence of the poetic justice exacted by the court emerges from the damaged child deep within K. – and is understood by the child in Kafka's readers – who remembers the discipline exacted by the recognition to which it is obliged to aspire, but who knows no alternative to fraternizing with the 'gigantic' Hasterers of this world.

FANTASY AND TRAUMA

Kafka's sharp and painful insights into social and psychological processes in *The Trial* are embedded, admittedly, in a fictional world which lies at an oblique angle to 'normal' reality. This is no conventional novel of personal and social development. Nor does Josef K., any more than Gregor Samsa, simply dream the scenes of humiliation, frustration and violence to which he is exposed. Rather, he and the world around him are 'metamorphosed', to borrow his uncle's expression (P, 101), by the appearance of the court in his life. How is one to understand the novel's systematic erasure of the boundary which normally keeps 'reality' and fantasy safely apart?

The mysterious nature of the court, together with the fact that a cathedral is the setting for K.'s conversation with the prison chaplain, have disposed a number of critics to regard the court as the expression of some higher, metaphysical or religious reality which erupts into and disrupts the social world.[37] In support of such a view one can also draw on evidence from outside the text, such as Kafka's (later) aphorisms where he was much exercised by the relationship between our everyday world and another level of reality hidden from us by man's fall from innocence and expulsion from paradise.[38] Some of Kafka's positive comments about writing as an inspired state in which he drew strength from touching the 'Boden' or 'ground' of his being can also be adduced in support of this kind of transcendental reading. Yet, as we have seen, these statements must be balanced against others where Kafka denounces writing as a 'devilish' activity, a form of self-indulgence and narcissistic vanity, in which the writer flutters like a moth around his own mirror image. In another such letter Kafka cited, as an entirely apt description of his own writing, Mörike's verdict on Heine: 'He is a poet through and through, but not a quarter of an hour could I live with him because his whole being is a lie' (DW, 163). The poet as inspired visionary, or plaything of demons, or liar – Kafka himself swayed between these different views. Given the corrupt, self-interested and harsh actions of the court's agents, one might fairly conclude that *if* some metaphysical impulse is at work in the cruel imagination which devised the poetic justice of Josef K.'s demise, then it is buried so deeply under the sediment of a traumatized personality that it is barely discernible, except, perhaps, as silent horror at its own violent imaginings. Whether or not some other, deeper voice speaks through the voice of the narrator, the mysterious power which transforms reality in order to punish K. for the empty success of his life, appears, in the first instance, to be the demiurge of Kafka's own hurt and retributive imagination. As Kafka tried to explain to his father in the letter he never sent, Josef K.'s fear that the shame of his death would outlive him drew on Kafka's own memory of the 'limitless' feeling of guilt instilled in him during childhood by his own, all too earthly father (GW 7, 41).

The barbarous, unreasoning, disproportionate character of the poetic justice enacted on Josef K. may also have been inspired by another element in Kafka's own experience, the recent dissolution of his engagement to Felice Bauer which left him with feelings of guilt, emptiness and self-loathing.[39] At the same time Kafka hoped that the 'dialogue with himself' initiated by his work on Josef K.'s story would give his 'orderly, empty, crazy' bachelor existence some 'purpose' ('Sinn') and 'justification' ('Rechtfertigung') (DW, 78). Such 'justification' he defined elsewhere as the depth of the 'wound' (GW 11, 161) laid bare by all his successful episodes of writing. In this sense *The Trial* 'justified' vicariously the dissolution of Kafka's engagement to Felice Bauer by showing Josef K.'s character to be incorrigibly that of a bachelor, self-centred, obsessed with his own 'progress', manipulative, unable to see women as anything other than objects of exploitation or, conversely, as sources of temptation and threat. What is more, by spending the months following the broken engagement utterly absorbed in writing *The Trial*, Kafka was living out the writer's version of precisely that obsession with 'progress' (in his case, that of the novel) which the novel chastises.[40] Yet this 'justification' of the separation from Felice and his choice of isolation, on the grounds of the guilt inherent in the writer's calling, was threadbare, a half-truth at best, not free of the 'tricks of the advocate', perhaps even no more than a devilish excuse for indulging in the pleasures of writing,[41] while at the same time putting the responsibility somewhere else – on the society that moulds or deforms the Josef K.s of this world, or on the unique 'organism' of the fated writer from which there spring involuntary visions of a world transformed by the workings of some anonymous and inaccessible power. The imagery of theatre, pretence and delusion spreads Kafka's ironic self-doubt throughout the novel. Knowing that he was judge, jury and executioner in the imaginary trial of his proxy, the bachelor Josef K., the trained lawyer Kafka must also have known that he was contravening one of the most fundamental principles of justice which debars anyone from judging a case in which he is an interested party.[42] Indeed Kafka's awareness of this impropriety is reflected in his choice of the partisan and vengeful Diana as the emblem of the 'justice' pursued in this court: the two wrongs of K. and the court do not make a right. As Karl Roßmann's uncle observes, ' "Justice and discipline do not mix." '[43]

In *The Trial* Kafka arraigned not just the sterile, empty show of Josef K.'s existence, the society which had instilled the pursuit of power in the protagonist, and the vengeful female goddess who demanded excessive retribution for a life thus led, but also his own literary undertaking, the very process of reaching a verdict on a proxy self in the court of the imagination. The ironic, self-undermining, theatrical 'poetic justice' of *The Trial* was the best he could achieve. His last, ambiguous verdict on the enterprise was to abandon it unfinished and to ask his friend Max Brod, whom he knew to be the greatest admirer of his work, to burn it.

5

The Castle

> It was late evening when K. arrived. The village lay deep in snow. There was nothing to be seen of the castle mount, mist and darkness surrounded it, not even the faintest glimmer of light suggested the great castle. K. stood long on the wooden bridge which leads from the highway to the village and looked up into the seeming emptiness. (S, 9)[1]

With this characteristic leap *in medias res* Kafka plunges the reader into K.'s story, much as he would plunge himself into the 'stream' of images in his mind with the hope of capturing them in writing.[2] The abrupt beginning forces readers to ask a series of questions in an attempt to find their bearings in an ill-defined and unfamiliar world: What village? Which great castle? Who is K.? At the same time the method places the reader both inside and outside the mind of the protagonist. We are shut out by the fact that he knows things we do not (where he has come from, who he is), but we are drawn into his point of view by his frustrated expectation as he peers up into the darkness, looking for an invisible hill and castle he is convinced *should* be there. His long hesitation on the bridge before entering the village suggests that it is, above all, 'the' castle (one he already 'knows' about) which he has come in search of. But why this castle, and what does he want from it?

Although the novel leaves questions about the exact location of village and castle unanswered, this has not deterred commentators from speculating about the originals on which they might be based.[3] Yet nobody (normally) asks which forest the grandmother of Little Red Riding Hood lives in. It is The Forest, a place of danger and imagination, the kind of place appropriate to the story we are about to hear. Thus it is with Kafka's unspecified castle: it is The Castle, the place where K.'s quite particular adventures can best take place.

Perhaps it is because mysterious castles and adventures are most commonly found together in the genre of chivalric romance that some critics have likened K. to one of the last, deluded devotees of the chivalric ideal, Don Quixote.[4] Admittedly, the place to which K. has come has features no less strange than those found in and around the enchanted castles of romance. Time and space, for example, have peculiar characteristics here. As Peter Beicken puts it, 'The world of the castle shifts all the co-ordinates.'[5] On the morning after his arrival K. sets out in bright sunshine immediately after breakfast to walk from the Bridge Inn up to the castle, but has to abandon the attempt just two hours later as darkness suddenly closes in around him. Not even the most zealous positivist commentators have concluded from this strange fact that the original of the castle must lie somewhere close to the Arctic Circle! In the village beneath the castle mount K. meets several people who appear to age with extraordinary rapidity. The father of the supposed messenger Barnabas, for instance, who now moves with the infinite slowness of the very old and frail, was reputedly a hale and hearty leading member of the fire brigade until just three years ago. The process is even more rapid in the case of Jeremias, one of K.'s childlike assistants, who ages overnight after having been separated forcibly from his companion Artur. On the other hand, the features of the official Bürgel are a curious mixture of the aged and the infantile.[6] The most obvious *spatial* oddity is the fact that the road K. follows to the castle never actually reaches it, but gets close and then veers off, apparently deliberately, whereas it seems to permit other characters (such as the assistants) to move between village and castle without difficulty. Do they take another, possibly secret route, or does the road only behave like this when K. traverses it? Another such oddity is the unusual number of confined, narrow spaces or rooms K. comes across, such as the cramped sleeping quarters of the gigantic landlady of the inn, or the cubicle-like rooms in which the castle's officials work. Spaces here, in other words, often have the dream-like quality familiar from Kafka's other novels.[7]

Bureaucratic and social practices here are no less peculiar. The village superintendent's filing system, for example, consists simply of stuffing papers to bursting point into a bedroom cupboard, after which, if they have not already been lost, they are assigned to the barn. When a new pump is donated to the village fire brigade by the castle, it is inaugurated in a ceremony which has overtones of an archaic fertility rite. Although admittedly less surreal than Gregor Samsa's transformation into a creature resembling a bloated cockroach or Josef K.'s execution by top-hatted men in a quarry, the conditions described in *The Castle* are sufficiently different from those prevailing in the world with which we are familiar to compel us, in the first instance, to look to the internal organization of this fictional world for clues to its understanding.

If the geographical and historical location of K.'s story is vague, the information supplied about the protagonist's background is only marginally more generous. Kafka has pared it down to the bare minimum, in line with his reduction of the hero's name (Karl Roßmann, Josef K., K.) in each successive novel. Of K.'s life up to his appearance on the bridge leading to the village we learn only that he has made a long journey to reach this place; that he has left behind a wife and child in order to make this journey (although his passing thought that he might have done better to pay one of his rare visits to his old home [S, 17] suggests that the family at home may be as much of an invention as his claim to be a land surveyor proves to be); that the church spire in his home town is more regular and pointed than the tower of the castle; that, as a boy, he once succeeded in scaling the sheer wall around the churchyard, and that he has happy memories of his time spent as a soldier. Sparse though these details are, they suggest the outlines of a character which the unfolding plot will both confirm and make more complex.

Thus K.'s long upward gaze from the bridge to the invisible castle becomes a detail of characterization when one relates it to the fact that he was already drawn to high, scarcely accessible places in childhood. As the graveyard beyond could be inspected simply by entering at the gate, there was no practical purpose to be achieved by climbing the churchyard wall. The desire to do so was evidently prompted by a fascination with difficult challenges as ends in themselves rather than as means to some further end. Equally significant is the fact that K.'s childhood obsession with climbing the wall was no individual quirk, for many other boys before him had made the attempt. Thus the impulse to reach the top was also a competitive, which is to say a social one, and K.'s reward for defeating the wall was to know that no-one was greater than he was (S, 40) at that moment and in that place.[8] The influence of shared values on K.'s behaviour is also apparent in his admiration for the church spire at home which, as he recalls, symbolized an aspiration to higher things by its definite and unhesitating upward movement.

These traits mark K. out as belonging to the type of the quester hero who appears in many guises throughout Kafka's work. Sometimes this travelling or climbing figure is contrasted with another who is static or prone; at others the climber or traveller is himself (it is usually a 'he') forced to be static or prone. The hunter Gracchus, for example, who dreams repeatedly of ascending to a light at the top of some stairs only to find himself still lying in his ship, marooned in earthly waters, belongs to the latter category.[9] An early example of the contrast between the climbing man and the static man is to be found in some fragments of a story in Kafka's diary of 1911.[10] Rather as Coleridge's unfortunate wedding guest is accosted and detained by the Ancient Mariner, the 'climber'–narrator in this fragment is stopped on his way up to a party by a strange bachelor ('the little occupant of the ruins') whom he finds lying in the gutter. Having initially promised himself that joining the party or society upstairs ('Gesellschaft' can mean both) will fulfil all his wishes, the climber gradually comes to recognize in the fragmented being of the bachelor in the gutter 'the truth which cannot be shown in such purity anywhere else' (GW 9, 90), a truth which the bachelor has come to embody at a crucial turning point in his life when some insight prompted him to lie down, 'just as children sometimes lie down in the snow in winter in order to freeze to death' (GW 9, 91). Kafka returned to the 'truth' of the prone figure in a later fragment, in which a first-person narrator describes his affinity with certain 'savages' who, when 'death desires them', simply lie down in the sand on the shore, never to stand up again. In contemporary society, he goes on, it is difficult to yield to this impulse thanks to the throng of others all around who prevent anyone from simply sinking to the ground for no reason and just lying there, because the others fear 'the stink of truth that would rise from him' (GW 7, 85). The crowd will not permit the individual to collapse, in other words, because they do not wish to be reminded of the enemy they carry within themselves. On his way through the village K. will meet several such static or prone figures.

CHALLENGE AND RESPONSE

If, as his gaze up to the castle suggests, K. belongs to the type of the quester hero, what does he seek in this place? His own statements about his goals are inconsistent and hence unreliable. Hardly has K. arrived in the village than he is told he must leave again immediately because he does not have the necessary permission from Count Westwest, the owner of both castle and village, to spend the night in the village. Whoever sleeps in the village, he is informed, sleeps, in a certain sense, in the castle (S, 9). K. retorts that he is the land surveyor sent for by the Count himself. At first his claim is rejected on the telephone by an official of the castle, only to be confirmed by a second telephone call a few moments later. K.'s surprised reaction to this second call shows that his initial claim to have come here in answer to a prior summons was, in all likelihood, a lie: 'So the castle had appointed him as land surveyor, then' (S, 13). If K. had come here in the belief that he had *already* been appointed land surveyor, he would not now be *concluding* that this was the case. He is responding rather to something new, namely the castle's surprising endorsement of his claim to be the surveyor, which he takes to be evidence that the occupants of the castle have accepted his challenge to combat, and that they are confident about their ability to defeat him. The subsequent appearance of two unknown young men from the direction of the castle who claim to be his 'old' assistants (although they carry no instruments and admit to knowing nothing about surveying) confirms, in his view, that someone up there has decided to repay his opening gambit in the same coin by supplying the spurious surveyor with spurious assistants. Although K. will re-state from time to time his claim to have come here to work, most of the evidence suggests that his main aim in coming to this place is to pick a fight with the authorities in the castle.

K. likes to make a show of his pugnacity. No sooner has his appointment as a land surveyor been confirmed than he shifts his ground slightly, insisting that he expects to be paid well, and pointing out that he is not timid by nature but can speak his mind, even to a count if necessary (S, 14). In the house of Barnabas the family only needs to begin debating whether K. will be permitted to enter the other (and better) inn in the village – the 'Masters' Inn' ('Herrenhof') – for K. to resolve on going there straight away. Having reached the inn, he insists on sleeping there despite the landlord's warning that he may go no further than the tap-room. On hearing that one of the 'masters' from the castle, his own superior Klamm, will be spending the night at the inn, however, K.'s readiness to defy authority suddenly and surprisingly appears to have reached its limit. Although prepared to challenge an anonymous opponent, he tells himself, he is reluctant to hurt an individual to whom he owes a debt of gratitude (S, 46–7). Nevertheless, he resents his own inability to overcome such feelings, and attributes his attitude to his subordinate position. Whether K. is actually motivated by embarrassment or by fear (although he denies this) is not entirely clear, but the upshot is his decision to spend the night in the humble home of Barnabas's family. K.'s conduct in this situation confirms something that he had confided to the landlord of the Bridge Inn earlier, namely that he, too, feels 'respect' for the powerful, even if he is less honest than the landlord about the fact (S, 16). Whether deferring to authority or challenging it, it is clear that K. is always fascinated by power.

K.'s combative disposition is also evident from his habit of categorizing those he meets either as potential allies or as enemies. What first attracts him to the serving girl Frieda, for example, is the superior look he detects in her eyes. This tells him that she has already dealt with things which concern K., although they are as yet unknown to him (S, 48). With the intention of enlisting her help in his own struggle, he offers to help Frieda in hers, arguing that the resistance of the world increases in proportion to the magnitude of one's goals, and that the help even of a 'little man' who is prepared to fight can be valuable (S, 51). Exactly what Frieda's or K.'s ultimate goal might be is not discussed. He simply assumes that they each have one and that he has found a kindred spirit in someone who has already shown 'exceptional strength' (S, 51) by fighting her way up from stable maid to serving girl.

In K.'s case the goal seems to be open to constant re-definition in the light of his current circumstances. Thus he claims at one point that he simply wants to obtain his 'rights' as an employee of the castle (S, 93), at another to work quietly and as far out of sight of the castle as possible (S, 35), at another to speak to the official Klamm in his private capacity (S, 107), and on yet another to walk past Klamm and on into the castle (S, 138). However K. may define his aims, one thing remains fairly constant: his desire to assert his will in defiance of the hierarchy linking village and castle.

If K. has come here looking for a fight with a hierarchically organized society, has he come to the right kind of place? Practically everyone he meets is certainly well aware of hierarchical relationships, and most seem to be respectful of them. Schwarzer, the young man in whom K. first encounters the castle bureaucracy, is the son of one of the lowest ranking under-castellans. Nonetheless, this rank is enough to make him a powerful man in this society (S, 15). When Schwarzer telephones the castle to discuss K.'s apparently unauthorized presence at the inn, various gradations of authority become apparent. He first asks a certain Herr Fritz to enquire about the matter in the central registry. The second call he receives in reply to his enquiry countermands the first, the head of the office having intervened personally to confirm that K. has been appointed after all. At this, Schwarzer immediately addresses K. as 'Herr' land surveyor. Although it involves at least three levels of command, this little episode is an instance of unusually direct (if not particularly reliable) communication with the authorities. In the days which follow K. is required to receive his instructions from the village superintendent, who is in turn subordinate to Momus, Klamm's 'village secretary', beyond whom there are further 'linking secretaries' such as Bürgel. Later K. hears Olga, Barnabas's sister, describe a room in the castle where Barnabas waits for messages to deliver. Although filled with officials, clerks and servants, all of them apparently very busy, this 'office', says Olga, is probably not an office at all, but merely an antechamber, or perhaps not even that – perhaps it is just a room designed to detain those who are not allowed to enter the offices proper.

Although he casts himself in the role of challenger, K.'s attitude to this complicated hierarchy is not one of simple opposition or rejection. He is neither the Messiah nor a revolutionary. Thus, when he announces that he is the new land surveyor, he observes with some satisfaction that the peasants huddle together anxiously, the arrival of a land surveyor being 'no small matter' (S, 11). Once the appointment has been confirmed, he dismisses the now submissive Schwarzer haughtily and is pleased to see that all withdraw hurriedly from the room, fearful, so he believes, of being recognized by him on the following morning. (That they might be turning their faces away to hide laughter does not occur to him.) On a later occasion, having just criticized Olga, Barnabas and others for their excessive reverence ('Ehrfurcht') towards the authorities, K. goes on to contradict himself flatly: ' "If an authority is good, why should one not feel reverence for it?" ' (S, 223–4). K., the self-styled challenger of established power, is apparently quite capable of venerating authority and relishing the subservience of his supposed inferiors.

It would appear, then, that K. is correct in expecting to find a hierarchical society in this place, but is he also correct in assuming that power is used oppressively here, and that he must therefore fight to procure his interests? In the Bridge Inn he sees clear evidence of oppression in the peasants' 'tortured' faces: '[. . .] the skull looked as if it had been smashed flat on top and the features as if they had been formed during the pain of being struck' (S, 32). Admittedly, this could be a distorted impression produced by K.'s own prejudices (many of his impressions do indeed prove to be false), but there is considerable evidence to support his view that the hierarchy does operate in an oppressive and aggressive way, or at least that individuals within it do so. As far as it affects K. personally, the hurtful use of power ranges from the mild sarcasm of the village superintendent, who remarks that K.'s land-surveying skills should come in useful for keeping the flower-beds straight and tidy in his new capacity as school janitor (S, 115), to more serious humiliation and even physical violence. Thus the accommodation assigned to K. and Frieda is a school-room which they are required to clear of all signs of habitation before lessons begin each morning. Not having been told of this arrangement in advance, they are not ready for the arrival of the class on the first morning and have to pull on their clothes while hiding from the eyes of the children behind makeshift screens. The teacher then knocks their breakfast off her desk deliberately, breaking their only coffee pot and spilling sardine oil on the floor for K. and Frieda to clean up in front of the whole class. Humiliation seems to be built into their conditions of employment in various ways: because the couple are allowed no cooking facilities in the school, they have to depend on whatever food the villagers offer them; although the village lies deep in snow, they are permitted no access to the wood-store to heat the building outside school hours. As if these various humiliations were not enough, the teacher Gisa draws her cat's claws across the back of K.'s hand in punishment for an alleged (but unproven) injury to the animal.

K.'s humiliating treatment in the school could be regarded as part of a pattern of tit-for-tat retribution. After all, he had arrogantly considered declining the offer of work as a janitor in order to demonstrate that he regarded this 'concession' from the authorities as inadequate (S, 114–15). Before being injured by Gisa, K. himself had inflicted violence on others, throwing a snowball at the head of the old man Gerstäcker who had saved him from being stranded in the snow (S, 26), and striking one of the assistants for creeping into Frieda's place in their improvised bed (S, 157). This pattern of correspondence does not deserve to be called moral, however, except in the sense of the primitive kind of nursery morality practised by a particularly mean-minded Mistress Bedonebyasyoudid. Although on a smaller scale, the same lack of proportionality between 'crime' and punishment is evident in the treatment of K. as it was in the cases of Karl Roßmann and Josef K. While one might argue the moral or educative case for giving the lowly position of janitor to a man who had laid claim fraudulently to a higher one, this surely does not need to entail public humiliation and material harm. If the teacher's sadistic actions are in turn sanctioned by the castle's officials, the moral authority of the hierarchy is further diminished thereby.

The more closely one examines the punitive practices of individuals in the world of village and castle, the less they appear to be morally justified. If K.'s appointment as janitor is meant to punish him for his arrogance, why should Frieda also be subjected to the same deprivation and humili-ation? It could be argued that this is just an example of the rough justice routinely inflicted on wives, mistresses and other dependants. Perhaps it is even because she has rejected Klamm in favour of K. The treatment meted out to Amalia's family cannot be shrugged off so easily, however. Amalia's crime (although not declared to be such by the authorities) was to reject the unwanted sexual attentions of an official, Sortini, whose desires had been apparently conveyed 'in the foulest expressions' (S, 240).[11] Since then, the entire family had been ostracized by the villagers, a consequence for which the officials admittedly disclaim all responsibility. Either, as Amalia's sister Olga believes, all this is the work of the castle, in which case the authority itself is actively unjust, or the family's punishment is the work of the villagers, in which case the castle is morally negligent in condoning the villagers' actions.

POWER, ITS AGENTS AND ITS OBJECTS

Whether any events in the world of castle and village are actually attributable to 'the' castle, as K. assumes and Olga maintains, is debatable, however, since the official or unofficial status of actions performed by individuals is seldom clear. Yet even if K. is wrong to assume that the castle is an institution with a unified will, his attack on the hierarchy is not entirely misplaced, for the social organization linking village and castle is deeply implicated in the actions of individuals. Whether of high rank or low, the agents of the castle treat the villagers badly, and do so with impunity, thanks to the social norms prevailing here.

The official Klamm, for example, has earned the epithet of 'commander over the women' (S, 240) by his habit of making a woman his mistress for a while and then discarding her summarily. Having once been treated like this, the landlady of the inn spends the rest of her life pining and grieving for her few days of glory. When officials like Klamm come down from the castle to spend the night in the village they are accompanied by a number of servants. These servants, who are said to behave quietly and with dignity when subject to the laws within the confines of the castle, throw off all restraint in the village, where they are particularly troublesome to the serving girls at the inn. As the master ('commander over the women'), so the men; the difference is one of style, not substance. If the servants' licence in the village serves to compensate them for their discipline in the castle, the effect on their personalities of the alternation of licence and discipline is to bring them close to the level of animals. As they dance ever more wildly around Olga, their cries, 'hungry, hoarse' (S, 52), rise and merge almost into a single cry, until Frieda, in anger and disgust, takes up a whip, making them flee across the yard and into the stable where they will be kept quiet during the night by Olga, who prostitutes herself to serve their 'insatiable appetites' (S, 269). As far as physical gratification is concerned, these servants are 'the true masters in the castle' (S, 268). The moral cost of compensating repressive discipline with licence in this way, however, is the degradation of the men themselves and of the women prostituted to satisfy them.

The social order linking castle and village is implicated quite particularly in Olga's willingness to play the role of prostitute to the officials' servants, in that she hopes thereby to end the punishment imposed on her family by the villagers and condoned by the officials. The episode which had given rise to the family's disgrace was in its turn intimately tied up with the repressive conditions of the higher officials' service, for Sortini's passion for Amalia had been a sudden, violent departure from his normally very reserved manner and selfless devotion to work. His crude manner of address to Amalia, Olga suggests, may have been prompted by the conscientious, overworked official's anger at having the peace and concentration of his ascetic routine disturbed and invaded by the impression she made on him (S, 235).[12] Thus, in different ways, the lives of both Sortini and Amalia (and, by a form of collective liability, her family) are damaged by the hierarchical arrangements in village and castle. Admittedly, the patriarchal system sees to it that she and her family are hurt much more grievously than he.

By rejecting Sortini's summons to the Masters' Inn Amalia appears to have offended against one of the fundamental principles governing the social order of village and castle. As Olga puts it, the relation of women to the officials is both very hard and very simple to judge:

'There is never a lack of love. There is no such thing as unhappy love for officials [. . .] We know that women are unable to do other than love officials if the latter once show interest in them; indeed they love the officials even before this happens, however much they may try to deny it.' (S, 240–1)

Olga's acceptance of the blessings bestowed by a male-dominated hierarchy seems to be shared by most of the other women. The chambermaid Pepi, for example, considers that she took a great leap upwards on becoming Frieda's temporary replacement in the tap-room of the inn, since this gave her the opportunity to attract male attention with the frills and flounces of her dress and thereby prove that her charms were much superior to Frieda's. No less vain is the ageing landlady, massive, of door-filling proportions, ailing, still obsessed twenty years on with her erstwhile rank as Klamm's mistress, and still bent on attracting admiration for her dress. Despite her rejection by him, she seems still to venerate Klamm, comparing him to an eagle, in contrast to K. whom she declares to be no better than a 'Blindschleiche' (the English equivalent, 'slow-worm', conveys neither the implications of blindness nor of crawling connoted by the German). So great is the difference of rank between the two men, she insists, that K. should abandon all thoughts of ever being permitted to deal directly with Klamm. In this society, it appears, even those who suffer from the hierarchical arrangements generally remain astonishingly loyal to them.[13]

The initial contrast between K.'s determination to challenge authority and the villagers' attitude of submission and even reverence towards the officials becomes progressively less clear-cut. K.'s underlying attraction to the very power he seems bent on challenging is confirmed, for example, by his adoption of the landlady's awe-struck comparison of Klamm to an eagle:

> He thought of his distance, of his unassailable dwelling, of his muteness, interrupted perhaps only by cries, the like of which K. had never heard, of his piercing downward gaze which could never be proved nor disproved, of the circles, indestructible from K.'s depths and visible only for moments, which he traced high above in accordance with incomprehensible laws; all this the eagle and Klamm had in common. (S, 144)

The parallel between K.'s attitude to Klamm and that of the adoring landlady is further strengthened by the fact that both are eager to peer through a peephole to see him (the landlady even kneels down to do so). Kafka uses irony to remind us of the parallel in a later chapter when K., seemingly unaware of his own limitations, accuses Pepi and the other chambermaids of having a restricted, keyhole vision of the world (S, 369).

Conversely, the submissiveness of the women is not quite so wholehearted as they claim it to be. At one point even Olga questions the unity which supposedly embraces village and castle:

> 'They say of course that we all belong to the castle and there is no distance between us and no gap to be bridged [. . .] but unfortunately we have had occasion to see that this is not true at all, particularly when it matters.' (S, 239)

Similar resentments are expressed with varying degrees of openness by Pepi, Frieda and even the landlady. According to Pepi, K. had fallen into a trap when he became involved with Frieda, who desperately needed something to revive her flagging fortunes as an attractor of men, and who had therefore seized the opportunity of having a scandalous affair with an insignificant and unsuspecting newcomer to the village. According to this account of things, Frieda is no innocent victim of K.'s manipulation (as the landlady maintains), but a secretive and 'deceitful' (S, 349) person, a 'spider' (S, 348), who ensnares K. and uses him to defend her own threatened status in the social–sexual hierarchy. Olga's (admittedly reciprocated) distrust of Frieda suggests that Pepi's resentful analysis may contain at least a grain of truth. As in the song of 'Pirate Jenny' from Brecht's *Threepenny Opera*,[14] the hurt and disappointed child in Pepi longs to see the complete destruction of the Masters' Inn:

> Pepi is the victim and everything is stupid and all is lost and the man who would be Pepi's chosen one today would be any man who had the strength to set fire to the whole Masters' Inn and burn it, utterly and completely, so that not a trace was left, burn it like paper in a furnace. (S, 350)

The landlady's determination to drive K. into marriage with Frieda, now that he has allegedly ruined the girl by taking her away from Klamm, also looks suspiciously like an act of revenge for the unhappy marriage to which the landlady had consented, with the greatest reluctance, after her own rejection by Klamm many years previously. Whether her attitude to K. is truly inspired by motherly love for Frieda or by concealed resentment of a system she so stubbornly defends, the landlady's attempts to dictate his future and that of Frieda are further evidence that K. must be prepared to fight if he wants to assert his own will in a society where all human relationships are affected by the influence of hierarchically organized power. That he should now find himself in this situation, admittedly, has much to do with the kind of wilful person he is, or has become, thanks to the values prevailing in the society in which he grew up.

'AN EARTHLY BUILDING – WHAT ELSE CAN WE BUILD?'

As he walks out on the morning after his arrival, K. sees the castle for the first time, plainly outlined in the clear air. Seen from this distance, he tells himself, the castle largely conforms to his expectations, being neither an ancient keep nor a grand modern palace but an extensive collection of buildings which one might have taken for a small town if one did not 'know' it was a castle. Yet K. (like Josef K.) habitually asserts that things or people match his expectations when in fact they do not. On being told that he needs official permission to lodge in the village, for example, his immediate impulse is to obtain the necessary permission; as soon as Schwarzer says that this is impossible, however, K. claims to have known as much all along (S, 11). His dislike of ever having to admit to others or to himself that he is not in mental or emotional control of a situation is again evident when Schwarzer reaches for a telephone above K.'s head to call the castle. K. had previously overlooked the telephone in his drowsiness, and is now surprised to find that the village inn is equipped with one. Nevertheless he tells himself that only the details surprise him, and that on the whole things are as he had expected. One of the clearest examples of his self-deceit occurs when the castle confirms his appointment and thus (so he believes) declares its readiness to fight him: 'And if they thought they could keep him permanently in a state of terror by acknowledging his status as a land surveyor with such a show of intellectual superiority, they were deceiving themselves; he was shivering slightly, that was all' (S, 13). His very denial of his fear betrays the true reason for his shivering.

K. *may* have expected, as he claims, to find a castle composed of just a few two-storey buildings and many low ones built close up to one another, but his observation that the castle has 'just one tower' (S, 16) indicates that he was expecting more.[15] As he draws closer to the castle, K. is forced to acknowledge his disappointment:

> It turned out to be just a rather miserable little town, assembled from village houses, its only distinction being that the whole thing was perhaps built of stone; but the paint had gone long ago and the stone appeared to be crumbling. (S, 17)

Even K.'s small home town was scarely less impressive than this 'supposed' (S, 17) castle; indeed the church spire at home was actually more impressive than the tower on the castle. With its definite, unhesitating upward sweep the church spire was 'an earthly building – what else can we build? – but with a higher goal than the low mass of houses and with a clearer expression than the gloomy work-day has' (S, 17). The tower of the castle, by contrast, strikes K. as 'uncertain, irregular, broken, as if it had been drawn by the timid or careless hand of a child' (S, 17), while its windows suggest madness as they flash in the sun. The impression created by the whole is of some melancholy occupant of a house, who ought by rights to be locked away in its most inaccessible room, but who has broken through the roof to show himself to the world. Whereas the spire at home evidently pleases K. because it expresses aspirations like his own, the tower of the castle presents an image of immaturity, uncertainty and derangement with which he plainly does not want to identify. The more we see of K., however, the more he seems to resemble the irregular tower of the castle rather than the idealized church spire in his memory.

As he stands contemplating the castle, K. meets the schoolteacher and tries to strike up a friendship with him, explaining that he feels as if he belongs neither to the peasants nor to the castle. The teacher tries to correct this impression, denying any difference between the peasants and the castle (S, 19). The remark chimes in with the message conveyed by the architecture of a castle apparently 'assembled from village houses', but K. simply brushes the observation aside, claiming that it does not affect his position. Perhaps K. is simply incapable of taking in a message so much at variance with his preconceptions about authority. At any rate, something similar can be observed in his attitude to Klamm. His one and only sight of him, gained (significantly) through a peephole, reveals a man of middling stature whose sagging cheeks show the first signs of ageing as he sits dozing over his beer. Nevertheless, as we have seen, K. later transforms this unremarkable figure in his imagination into an eagle soaring above its impregnable eyrie, just as he restores to the castle its mysterious aura after his disillusionment on that first morning (S, 123). In creating his own subjective vision of Klamm, K. behaves no differently from the rest of the villagers whose 'rumours and various falsifying ulterior motives' (S, 215) have created reports of Klamm so variable that the only common factor is his dress, a black frock-coat with long tails.[16] The differences in the reports, Olga maintains, are the result, not of any magic but of the subjective condition of each particular observer, the infinite gradations of hope or despair felt by those who glimpse Klamm (if it is indeed him) for an instant.

None of this deters K. from believing in the mysterious grandeur of the castle and its officials. Whereas Barnabas, whose visits to the castle give him direct experience of the difficulties of communicating with or through the tangle of servants, clerks and officials, is prey to disabling doubts, K. insists to Olga that there is a single will embodied in the castle and that there is a purpose in everything which happens there. Whether or not the man whom Barnabas talks to in the castle is a proper official, K. maintains, 'someone has put him there and has done so with some purpose. What I mean by all this is that there is something there, something is being offered to Barnabas, something at least, and it is the fault of Barnabas alone if all he can achieve with it is doubt, fear and hopelessness.' (S, 225)

Yet K.'s belief in the castle's unity of purpose is as little borne out by the evidence of the actual workings of the bureaucracy as his idealizing images of Klamm and the castle match what he sees on closer inspection. His preference for his own preconceptions over the evidence of his eyes is apparent in the assurance with which he looks forward to a forthcoming interview with the village superintendent. He feels confident because, he is sure, some definite principle has been promulgated which is outwardly very favourable to the treatment of his affairs, but also 'because of the admirable unity of the apparatus serving the castle, which one sensed to be particularly perfect precisely where such unity appeared to be missing' (S, 73). For K., in other words, black can be white, if he so chooses.

The fact that K. is so resolutely convinced that the officials are defending 'distant, invisible things' in the name of 'distant, invisible masters' and on behalf of 'some public order unknown to him' (S, 73) makes him the object of irony bordering on farce when he finally enters the house-cum-office of the village superintendent. Not only does the latter conduct business from bed, but when he asks his wife to look for a file, she pulls pile upon pile of rolled-up papers (which look suspiciously like fire-lighters) from a cupboard until the floor is half covered with them. Needless to say, no trace can be found of the original edict relating to the appointment of a land surveyor. Many papers have gone missing, the superintendent admits without the least sign of concern, but there are still plenty more out in the barn. He then gives a long, involved account of the series of mistakes, confusions and accidents which may have resulted in the unnecessary issuing of a summons for a land surveyor, but insists nevertheless that nothing happens here without due deliberation; even the summons to K. was supposedly ' "well considered, but attendant circumstances intervened to cause confusion" ' (S, 79). Despite such confusions, the village superintendent shows not the slightest doubt about the official ideology, insisting that it is a principle of the bureaucracy's work that the possibility of errors is ruled out entirely, a principle justified by the 'excellent organisation of the whole' (S, 82), and one which ensures that matters are dealt with expeditiously. The superintendent goes on to undermine the significance not only of the letter from Klamm but also of the telephone calls from the castle relating to K.'s appointment, by revealing that there is no central switchboard in the castle to direct enquiries to the appropriate position, and that any answers to such enquiries should be regarded as private jokes on the part of some bored official on night duty. Having heard all this and having witnessed directly the 'ludicrous tangle' (S, 80) of the administration, K. might be expected to change his view of the castle. His later conversation with Olga about Barnabas's unavailing efforts to receive or deliver messages shows, however, that the revelations have had no lasting impact on him other than to make him feel that the grandeur of the castle is simply 'unentwirrbar' ('incapable of being disentangled') (S, 226).

K.'s conviction that the castle houses a single organizing intelligence and source of high authority is as impregnable as he, in his more awe-struck moments, perceives the castle to be. Admittedly, this view of the all-controlling power of the castle is shared by some of the villagers he meets. Olga, for example, is convinced that the punishment of her family is the work of the castle, however much the officials might claim it had nothing to do with them: ' "Everything originates in the castle" ' (S, 245). Frieda similarly sees Klamm's hand in all that happens to her and K.: ' "Klamm wants nothing more to do with me. But not, of course, because you came, darling, nothing like that could ever have upset him deeply. But I strongly believe it is his doing that we found one another down behind the counter; blessed be the hour, not cursed" ' (S, 66). The villagers waiting outside in the snow at night for an interview with the official Erlanger are equally sure that responsibility for their inconsiderate treatment lies not with the official but with the landlady: 'Of course it was not Erlanger's fault; on the contrary, he was very obliging, hardly knew about it and would certainly have been very annoyed if it had been reported to him' (S, 291).

All these characters have one thing in common with K.: they are convinced about something for which there is either no evidence or, worse still, evidence which indicates the very opposite of what they believe. In the case of K., this attachment to a preconceived notion of the castle's authority makes him deaf to warnings that things may be rather different in reality. When Momus mockingly contrasts K.'s eagerness to meet Erlanger with his earlier refusal to submit to a hearing, K. replies: ' "You people think only about yourselves. It is simply out of regard for the office that I refuse to answer – today as on the last occasion" ' (S, 294). So eager is K. to meet Erlanger that he does not give even a moment's consideration to Momus's ominous retort: ' "Who else should we think about? Who else is here apart from us?" ' (S, 294). Momus's question implies that K.'s belief in a source of power and authority lying behind, beyond or above the officials is simply misguided: there are *only* officials here, no-one else. Although Momus is not necessarily to be trusted, his words reinforce the teacher's earlier comment that there is no difference between the castle and the peasants. His words accord, too, with a 'supposed' castle which looks as if it has been 'assembled from village houses' set on a hill. As these details accumulate, a phrase from the very beginning of the novel begins to take on a new dimension. K., it will be recalled, stood long on the bridge and looked up into the 'scheinbare Leere' (S, 9). For someone arriving with K.'s preconceptions there was of course only 'seeming emptiness' above the village, because the castle and its mount were temporarily hidden from view by mist and darkness. Yet the phrase 'scheinbare Leere' could also mean that K. was looking up into 'emptiness without light', a nuance suggested by a phrase in the preceding sentence: 'auch nicht der schwächste Lichtschein deutete das große Schloß an' ('not even the faintest glimmer of light suggested the great castle'). Such emptiness is perhaps what is implied in Momus's mocking question: '"Who else is here apart from us?"' If, as the author suggests, earthly buildings are all we can build (S, 17), what else could the castle contain?

THE FOUNDATIONS OF POWER

In the absence of any sound reason to believe in the perfection of the castle's governance, one is bound to ask what keeps this structure of power in place. After all, as we have seen, not everyone who is subject to the rule of the castle or its officials accepts it unquestioningly. Even the generally acquiescent Olga questions the supposed lack of distance between castle and village on one occasion, while Frieda shows disrespect for authority even more boldly than K. Not only does she tell the landlord that the inn is empty when in fact K. is concealed at, or rather under, her feet behind the counter, but she refuses to go to Klamm when summoned and even bangs with her fist on Klamm's door, shouting that she is with K. (S, 56). Some of the peasants, led by Brunswick, had apparently demanded the appointment of a land surveyor long before K.'s arrival because they were not satisfied with the existing distribution of land (S, 84–5). There must be a spark of Brunswick's rebellious spirit in his son Hans, too, for although the boy is much more attached to his mother than his father, he offers to help K. after seeing him wounded and humiliated in the school. K. is thus not alone in feeling the need to challenge the authority of the castle. Yet the structure remains in place. Why?

If Amalia's rejection of Sortini is the clearest case, apart from K.'s, of a challenge to the social order of village and castle, Olga's account of the family's resultant ostracization throws most light on the workings of power here. As soon as news of the incident between Amalia and Sortini spread, the rest of the village had broken off all business and social contacts with the family, although not, initially, in a hostile manner. Despite the fact that the officials had taken no action in response to Amalia's behaviour, and indeed denied that they had any involvement or power in the matter, the villagers had felt it their duty to withdraw from the family until the matter was settled, partly out of fear and partly to spare themselves the embarrassment of having to talk to the family about the issue. According to Olga, what caused the villagers to move on to the next stage of openly despising the family and withdrawing all forms of material or emotional support was the family's own inability to come to terms with the incident (S, 257). Their inner debility and bondage is clearest in the case of the father, whose shame at being expelled from the fire brigade in order to preserve its 'purity' (S, 249) was so great that he fell silent, aged prematurely and spent all his days and all the family's money in vain attempts to plead for help or forgiveness from the officials. The rest of the family felt paralyzed, unable to act without a lead from the resolutely silent Amalia, until, that is, they 'betrayed' her by undertaking their own initiatives. Had the family been able simply to dismiss or forget the matter and to act as if normal relations could be resumed, says Olga, the villagers would have been only too happy to respond in like manner. What the villagers could not tolerate, she says, was the family's patent inner weakness:

> 'They noticed that we did not have the strength to work our way free of the business with the letter and they resented that very much [. . .] If we had overcome it their respect for us would have been correspondingly great, but because we failed to do so, they did conclusively what they had done only provisionally up to that point: they shut us out of every circle.' (S, 257)

The response of the villagers to the family's impotence is a variant of the attitude taken by the milling throng who will not allow the weary individual to drop to the ground because of the 'stink of truth' that would rise from his prostrate figure. As the Barnabas family has already 'fallen', its fate challenges the precarious social consensus which maintains that all is (generally) for the best in the best possible world of village and castle. The family must therefore be driven away, lest the sight of its misfortune should disturb the lives of others, for the suffering of the family proclaims the supposed unity of rulers and ruled to be based on unadmitted coercion. What is worse, the fate of the family shows this coercion to be self-imposed or at least self-maintained. In this sense Olga is right to assert that everything 'originated in the castle', even if the officials took no visible action, for the villagers' submission to the internalized power of 'the castle' means that there is no need for the officials to act. The sanctions imposed by the other villagers are implicitly endorsed by the family's own self-abasing conviction that, whatever the rights or wrongs of Amalia's behaviour towards Sortini (and Olga, at least, regards it as 'heroic'), the authorities must be appeased and their forgiveness or mercy sought. Amalia's uncompromising silence shows that there is an alternative to submission to the hierarchical power structure, but also that it demands the strength to live entirely outside the community. Otherwise the family must remain a thorn in the villagers' flesh, despised and detested because Olga's prostitution and the father's supplications only serve to publicize the humiliating *inner* dependence on the hierarchy which is the foundation of the villagers' own protested faith in the lofty and infallible authority of the castle.

Kafka's exposure of the psychological foundations on which the structure of power rests throws some light on the rambling and decaying appearance of the castle which so disappoints K. The collection of village houses placed on the hill above the village proper makes visible the nature of power in this society. Not only is the 'supposed' castle, like the church in K.'s home town, an earthly building ('what else can we build?'), but it embodies, in effect, the villagers' submission to their own conception and construction of a higher power. Just as the stones of the castle have apparently been gathered together from village houses, so the power exercised over the villagers from that higher place is a power built from the stuff of their own lives and maintained by their subordination to it.

THE TEMPTATIONS OF POWER

But what of K.? Why does he, an outsider, cling to his belief in the higher authority of the castle despite all the evidence of its disorganization, fallibility and dubious moral character? His responses to Amalia and Olga respectively are instructive. On learning about the episode with

Sortini, his first reaction is to support Amalia and condemn such abuse of official power outright. Increasingly, however, K. comes to dislike the cold, detached look in Amalia's eyes and her scorn for Olga's tales of the castle which so fascinate him. If he had to choose between them, he reflects, he would favour Olga's character over Amalia's (S, 282). His explicit reasons for the preference are Olga's moral qualities: her courage, her prudence, her sacrifice (by which he means her readiness to play prostitute to the servants of the officials) for the sake of the family. Yet Amalia also sacrifices herself for the family, working tirelessly and showing infinite patience in caring for her aged parents, particularly her helpless, childish father. She, too, has moral qualities, equal to or even greater than Olga's, for she is principled, resolute and incapable of the hypocrisy, deceit and self-deceit which are all part of Olga's strategy. However much K. may supply moral reasons for his preference, it rather looks as if he is repelled by Amalia and drawn to her sister because he recognizes in Olga a kindred (subordinate) spirit for whom contact with the castle is of paramount importance, whatever the costs. By thus placing K. between the contrasting pair of sisters, Kafka underscores the obsession with power underlying his super-ficially rebellious attitude. To 'rebel' as he does is, in reality, simply another way of paying tribute to the structure of power, whereas Amalia's silence shows that she neither fears nor seeks the favour of the authorities. Had there been more Amalia and less Olga in him, so to speak, K. would have had no need to seek out the castle in the first place. As he is, so is the world he encounters.

Although K. casts himself in the role of an 'attacker' who will force his presence on Klamm and even walk past him into the castle itself, his attitude to the castle is clearly much too ambiguous and contradictory to be contained within such a simple definition. That K. does not merely have secret respect for the powerful (as he confesses to the landlord of the Bridge Inn) but actually longs for their approval is suggested by his behaviour on discovering one night that Klamm's horse-drawn sledge is waiting for him in the yard of the Masters' Inn. After standing around for a long time in the cold in the hope of intercepting Klamm, K. eagerly accepts the driver's offer of some brandy which is kept inside the sledge. Hardly has K. opened the door when he feels an irresistible compulsion to slip inside. Once seated, or rather lying, in Klamm's place on piles of furs, pillows and rugs, he feels immensely comfortable, convinced that however much he were to toss or turn he would always sink back into warmth and softness. It is perhaps odd that K. should have such feelings of womb-like comfort and security inside the sledge of a father-figure like Klamm, but this is presumably intended to convey the intensity of his paradoxical desire for oneness with a figure whom he seems to want to challenge at every opportunity. It suggests that all K.'s combative posturing is actually a form of attention-seeking.[17] K. effectively says as much when he learns of Klamm's supposed approval of some land-surveying work which he has not in fact performed: ' "And of course I cannot interrupt work I'm not doing, I cannot even arouse bitterness in the gentleman [*Herr*], so how am I supposed to earn his recognition? And I can never be comforted" ' (S, 148).

When K. opens the brandy bottle inside Klamm's sledge (and later spills it in fright) his situation resembles that of a youngster illicitly sampling the pleasures of the adult world. The smell of the brandy brings an involuntary smile to his face, for it makes him think of being treated kindly by some (unidentified) male figure of whom he is very fond:

> The smell was so sweet, so flattering, it was like hearing praise and kind words from someone you love very much, and you have no real idea what you are being praised for and you have no desire to know, but you're simply happy to know that it is he who is speaking. (S, 129)

Not surprisingly, the rough, hot taste of the brandy does not live up to the seductive promise of its aroma, but K. carries on drinking long and deep nevertheless. Even if the reality of the brandy proves rougher than in his imagination, he still finds comfort in it. By analogy, the same is true of his relationship to figures of authority.

K.'s drinking is interrupted by the approach of another of the 'Herren' who asks him to leave the courtyard with him. K. refuses and is left quite alone in the yard. His stubbornness allows him to lay sole claim to the place, but it proves to be 'a victory that brought no joy' (S, 132). Once almost all the lights in the inn have been extinguished, K. feels both free and utterly abandoned:

> It then seemed to K. as if they had broken off all contact with him and as if he were now freer than ever before and could wait for as long as he wanted in this place which was normally forbidden to him, and that he had fought for his freedom as few other men could have fought, and that no-one dared to touch him or drive him away or hardly even speak to him; but at the same time – and of this he was at least equally convinced – it was as if there were nothing more senseless, nothing more desperate than this freedom, this waiting, this invulnerability. (S, 133)

Karl Roßmann, it will be recalled, was similarly unnerved by the experience of freedom (V, 133). Perhaps the deepest damage done to the personality by its education in a society oriented towards struggle and the achievement of goals is that it leaves the individual unable to ask what value or meaning life might contain once these constraints are removed. A similar experience of empty victory and ensuing isolation returns to K. in a dream as he sits half asleep, propped up on the official Bürgel's bed. In his dream he is fighting with one of the officials, a secretary who resembles the statue of a naked Greek god, but who is so concerned to cover up his nakedness that he is unable to fight, and who merely squeals like a girl being tickled when K. attacks him (S, 319). Suddenly, however, his opponent and the rest of the company are gone, leaving K. alone in an empty room. He then cuts his foot on a broken champagne glass, a detail which recalls the pain he once felt in his leg when the teacher made him jump down from the churchyard wall. Although K. likes to tell himself that the early victory over the wall remains a source of confidence in later life, it seems that his few victories over powerful opponents do not in fact bring the satisfaction he expects. Ironically, at the moment when he recalls his childhood triumph, he is actually clinging gratefully to the arm of another human being, without whose help he would be quite lost.

The episode in Bürgel's room complements that in the courtyard in another respect. After dreaming of his duel with the official-cum-statue, K. falls into a deep sleep. As he sleeps, Bürgel reveals things about the relationship between officials and petitioners which would be invaluable to K. if only he could hear them. The fact that K. is asleep by this stage could be regarded simply as an ironic twist of fate, were it not for the fact that K. *wants* very much to fall asleep, both because he has drunk some rum and because of a strong disinclination towards everything which has to do with him (S, 315). Bürgel thus describes to deaf ears what would happen in the quite unlikely, indeed virtually impossible circumstance of a petitioner entering an official's room at some unguarded moment (as K. has just done). The official, he says, would be seized by an irresistible desire to grant the petitioner's request and tell him all he wants to know, regardless of whether this might conflict with his duty as an official, or whether he has the authority to do so, and regardless even of the fact that his doing so will 'effectively tear the organisation of the bureaucracy apart' (S, 324). Just as the sweet smell of the brandy in Klamm's sledge makes K. think of praise and kind words from a loved person, so, it seems, the official would be unable to resist the desire to enter the poor life of the petitioner and to move about in it as if in his own 'property' (S, 324). The desire of the weak for closeness to the powerful, in other words, is matched by the desire of the powerful for intimacy with the weak.

It has been argued that this scene contains the key to the novel.[18] Here, after all, Kafka is imparting privileged information to the reader, since Bürgel's words are conveyed quite independently of any possible distortions produced by the subjective perspective of K. If only he were awake, it is argued, K. would learn that his combative approach to the castle is quite misdirected, as the officials actually harbour kind human impulses. If there is any such glimmer of comfort in Bürgel's account, it is hedged about by a tangle of ironies. Firstly, Bürgel speaks specifically of *un*official feelings towards petitioners, feelings which would rip the bureaucracy apart if acted upon. Thus benevolence is not to be expected from 'the castle' as such but, at best, from the human beings who serve it. Secondly, to assume that Bürgel is telling the truth, the whole truth and nothing but the truth, would be to assign to him a greater degree of reliability than any other character in the novel merits. Yet, if a telephone call allegedly from the head of a section confirming K.'s appointment as land surveyor can later be called into doubt (was it merely a joke by a bored official?), and if Frieda and Olga can accuse one another of untrustworthiness, why should Bürgel be believed implicitly? If Bürgel is not actually lying, he may be indulging in the kind of self-gratifying fantasy to which other characters (including K.) are prone. But even if one allows that Bürgel's account of the inner life of officialdom would be endorsed by all the other officials, his vision of happiness remains disturbing in a number of ways. When Bürgel speaks of entering the life of a petitioner as if it were the official's own property or possession ('Besitz'), he is thinking of another person as an object in just the same way as K. regards Frieda as a possession which he must first wrest from Klamm and then regain when she is taken away by Jeremias. Bürgel's waking dream, in other words, is eaten through by the worm of power. If the official were to grant the petitioner's request, Bürgel claims, he would suddenly be acquiring power far beyond his rank. Conversely, the petitioner would be in the role of a 'robber in the forest' (S, 324–5), able to 'control everything' ('alles beherrschen' – S, 325) by his mere helpless presence, and forcing the officials to make sacrifices of which they would normally be incapable. Like the thoughts inspired in K. by the smell of brandy in Klamm's carriage, Bürgel's dream expresses a desire for human closeness. Yet it appears that neither the 'son' nor the 'father' can conceive of such closeness without power playing a part, whether it be in the form of praise gratefully received or of a demand gladly granted. The experience of power, it seems, penetrates very deeply, even into men's dreams of liberation from it.

The brief fantasies of K. or Bürgel should therefore not be given undue weight in understanding K. or life as it is lived in village and castle. The structure of power is the given context in which everyone here operates. At some time or other the 'supposed castle' was constructed on top of the hill, apparently from the stones of village houses. At some time or other, presumably, people became either officials or peasants. The origins of these things are never mentioned, the facts simply taken for granted. Yet it may not be necessary to know how things began, for we are shown what maintains the structure of power in the present, namely the aspiration to rise in the hierarchy or to have contact with the powerful, pleasure in asserting power over others, and a self-enforced consensus amongst the ruled that whatever happens is, more or less, for the best.

REFLECTIONS

Kafka was fond of using metaphors of place to characterize the self. In an early letter to Oskar Pollak, for example, he wrote that some books were like a 'key to strange rooms in one's own castle' (B, 20). In his notebooks he described the self as a building containing a room where activity could be heard (GW 6, 44). On another occasion he described a character whose path is blocked by a long, white, curved wall which proves to be his own forehead (GW 6, 128). In many variants of such spatial imagery Kafka sought to convey the complexity of the self and the difficulties the mind experiences in relating to all the distant or secret recesses of the being to which it belongs. Although *The Castle* does not present a simple allegory of the self, K.'s ineffectual surveying of the village and castle brings to light numerous analogies between the challenger and the challenged.[19] In particular, each exhibits very similar internal contradictions.

There is a correspondence, for example, between the changing aspect of the castle and conflicting attitudes in K. The distant, unapproachable aspect of the castle corresponds to the awe K. occasionally admits to feeling towards the powerful. Conversely, his impression that the 'supposed' castle is little more than an assemblage of village houses suggests that he also entertains doubts about whether the powerful are truly higher beings worthy of challenge. There may be some connection between this doubt in K.'s mind and occasional signs of reluctance to enter the castle despite all his protested determination to enter it. Once, for example, he pretends to be his own assistant Josef and telephones the castle to ask when his master may be admitted. To the curt answer 'Never', he replies 'Good'

(S, 34). This might simply mean he is happy to learn that the castle will continue resisting his efforts to enter it, but it could equally well mean just what it says, namely that he is content never to be admitted. This possibility is strengthened by an equally curious response on another occasion. While walking back from the castle in the gathering gloom with Barnabas, he hears the peal of a great bell from the receding castle:

> As if some sign were to be given him to mark his temporary departure, however, the sound of a bell rang out, merry and exuberant, a bell which made the heart reverberate for a moment at least, as if it were threatened – for the sound was painful too – with the fulfilment of its uncertain longings. (S, 25–6)

A mixture of joy and pain inspired by the *threatened* fulfilment of one's uncertain longings are paradoxical, ambivalent feelings indeed in a man supposedly bent on making his way to the castle by the quickest route. Is he actually afraid of reaching his supposed goal, perhaps because of what he might find there, or perhaps because he is attached to his travelling and striving as ends in themselves? Although K. may cherish the memory of the unhesitating, pointed church spire of home, it appears that the 'uncertain, irregular and broken' outlines of the castle's tower are actually a truer reflection of his contradictory feelings. It may be, indeed, that he likes to identify with the image of the church spire precisely in order *not* to recognize his likeness in the ramshackle tower he finds here.

The variable aspect of the castle is matched by contradictory statements from villagers and officials alike as to the possibility of gaining access to it. While one official says on the telephone that K. may 'never' hope to enter, and the landlady and Momus insist that the only route of communication is the slow, official one, Bürgel claims that a petitioner only needs to approach an official at an unguarded moment to have any request granted. Like the bureaucracy as a whole, individuals in village and castle seem to be divided between openness to social contact and aversion to it. Klamm seems to be closed off like the castle as he sits over his beer, his eyes protected from any intrusive gaze by the light reflecting from his pince-nez. One of the symbolic overtones of Klamm's strange name has to do with narrowness or closure and hence with secrecy (as in 'klammheim-lich').[20] On the other hand, he calls for female company frequently. Klamm's female counterpart is the teacher Gisa who, despite her great need for solitude, entertains the devoted attentions of Schwarzer. Even Sortini, one of the most reserved of officials, can be overcome by urgent passion for the village girl Amalia. Despite the fact that officials are said generally to be extremely 'sensitive' and in need of protection from any intrusion, Bürgel seems to be quite delighted to have the opportunity to chatter the night away with K.

Again, the contradictions observable in these figures reflect much the same mixture of traits in K. His tendency to solitude, already suggested by his unaccompanied journey to the castle, is made explicit by his desire to avoid all conversation with the peasants when he first arrives at the Bridge Inn. Repeatedly K. can be seen to avoid contact with others, particularly if they seem to be of inferior status or in some way threatening (as he perceives the assistants sent by Erlanger to be). Conversely, K. seeks contact with those he thinks will serve his purposes, such as Frieda, Pepi, Frau Brunswick or Barnabas. There are times, however, when K. simply feels a need for company, even if there is no particular purpose to be served by it. It is he who strikes up a conversation with the landlord at the inn over breakfast; it is he who seeks friendship with the teacher because he feels he belongs neither to the peasants nor to the castle. While walking arm in arm with Olga he acknowledges reluctantly the feeling of well-being it gives him (S, 44–5). To an extent K. seems surprised by his sociable impulses, since he finds dealing with people a strain: 'He felt irresistibly drawn to seek new acquaintances, but every new acquaintance increased his tiredness' (S, 19). It is this sociable impulse in K. which colours his first reaction to the assistants as they come prancing through the snow: 'He had a great desire to be taken along by these two; although it did not seem to him that their acquaintance would yield very much, they were clearly good travelling companions who would lift his spirits' (S, 23). According to the assistants, Erlanger's intention in assigning them this role is indeed to amuse K. and cheer him up. Only when K. discovers that they have been sent by the castle (to spy on him, as he assumes) does K. insist on keeping them at a distance, a clear illustration of the way his narrowing self-definition as a challenger leads him to suppress a more carefree, aimless or childlike side of his nature.[21] As he becomes more hostile to the assistants, they become more of a threat to him and, in particular, to his relationship with Frieda. Thus 'the castle' (or its officials) is just as capable of making sociable gestures to match K.'s social impulses as it is of becoming closed off, defensive and even aggressive in response to similar behaviour from him. The symmetries resemble those of shadow-boxing.

One of the tactics often used by K. to keep others at bay is pretence or deception. When Schwarzer accuses him of being in the village without permission from the castle, K. feigns confusion and ignorance: ' "What village have I strayed into? Is there a castle here, then?"' (S, 10). The reader knows that K. must be lying, because the first thing he had looked for in the dark was the castle on the hill. Having changed his story completely by claiming to be the land surveyor summoned by the Count himself, K. then turns to the wall and pretends to go back to sleep, until, that is, he recognizes that 'it made no sense to play the sleeping man' (S, 11), since to do so would prevent Schwarzer reaching the telephone to call the castle. One could list very many examples of K. play-acting in one way or another, some of the most unpalatable being his attempts to control Frieda and manipulate her for his own purposes by pretending to be devoted to her. One of the most satisfying scenes in the novel is the one where Frieda, having observed K.'s attempted manipulation of Hans Brunswick, exposes K. for the self-centred hypocrite he is. This is not quite the whole story, admittedly, but it is a fair part of it.

K. does not, however, have a monopoly on deception. His initial impression that Schwarzer has the 'face of an actor' (S, 9) might simply indicate that K. projects onto others his own readiness to deceive, but there are many in both village and castle who dissimulate just as much as he does. If the village superintendent is to be believed, the telephone call confirming K.'s appointment was merely a 'joke' on the part of some stray official. Is the 'supposed' castle on the hill itself perhaps nothing more than a village pretending to be a castle? The reports of the variable appearance of Klamm may, as Olga says, be partly attributable to the subjective state of different observers, but even the different stories about him may not match up to the real changeability of his appearance. Perhaps Klamm is a master of disguise, or perhaps this one name is shared by several officials. At any rate, the general inscrutability of Klamm ('"Who knows his intentions?"', asks the landlady – S, 64) and of the castle hierarchy as a whole corresponds to K.'s own secretiveness and perhaps even confusion about his goals. Characteristically, however, K. is just as reluctant to admit to uncertainty on his part as on that of the castle. Although he finds contradictions in a letter from Klamm, for example, he dismisses the thought that these could stem from indecision: 'He barely considered the thought, a crazy one in relation to such an authority, that indecision might have played a part here' (S, 34).

If K. is frustrated in his efforts to penetrate the bureaucracy, those he meets are no less irritated by the lack of transparency in this stranger 'whose intentions are unknown' (S, 63). Conversely, K.'s tendency to distrust people (which coexists with gullibility about things he *wants* to believe) is matched by the endless 'Kontrollämter' (offices responsible for checking and control) in the castle; the official Sordini in particular is said to 'trust no-one' (S, 81). That K.'s suspicions are sometimes justified is shown by the case of Barnabas, for whom Olga has made close-fitting clothes of silky appearance precisely in order to create the illusion that he is a messenger from the castle, an illusion to which K.'s preconceptions admittedly make him susceptible. Olga had wanted K. to believe that her brother could help him communicate with the castle because she in turn needed to have a mission for Barnabas, an excuse for him to visit the castle, and hence a means of reviving the family's flagging hopes. K. the deceiver, in other words, was deceived, the exploiter exploited.

The contradictions in K. are perhaps most pronounced in his relationship with Frieda. He is first attracted to her by the confident, 'victorious' look he detects in her eyes, an attraction which is increased by the discovery that she is Klamm's mistress. K.'s purpose in getting to know her is to use her in his struggle. Yet when they lie together for the first time amidst the dirt and beer-puddles on the tap-room floor he undergoes a disconcerting experience:

> Hours went past there, hours of shared breathing, shared heartbeat, hours in which K. constantly felt he was losing his way or that he was far away in some strange place, further away than anyone else before him, a strange place where even the air had not the slightest trace of the air at home, where one felt one must suffocate from strangeness, a place of senseless temptations where one could do no other than keep going on, losing one's way more and more. (S, 55)

The passage shows K. to be a man deeply divided, attracted and threatened in equal measure by the experience of intimacy with Frieda. Whereas the challenger and quester in him feels that he is losing his way in a place not of his seeking, some other part of him so welcomes the aberration that he is drawn ever further into it. The fact that the 'air' in this inward place seems utterly different from the air of home suggests that home was not a place where K. knew such closeness to another person. In this detail lies a further indication that his obsessively will-directed approach to life has been moulded by a society with competitive or even combative values.

The moment of intimacy is a unique one for both K. and Frieda. When they next lie together, they are unable to recover the same degree of closeness. In their efforts to do so they are likened to two dogs scraping the ground in search of something: 'There they lay, but not with such abandon as on that first night. She was looking for something and he was looking for something, furiously, grimacing, boring their heads into the breast of the other [...] like dogs scraping desperately on the ground, they scraped at each other's bodies' (S, 59–60). Somehow K. and Frieda have become closed off from one another again, rather as the castle or Klamm seem closed off to the questing K. This may be because each is using the other for his or her own purpose, seeking the satisfaction of some individual need in the other rather than giving up control over any sense of direction, as the earlier experience of real intimacy had required K. to do. In K.'s case the narrative perspective repeatedly allows the reader to see him producing an objectified and alienated picture of Frieda in his mind as he casts her in the role of the attentive housewife or bait with which to entice Klamm into conflict or negotiation. Thus he forces himself to praise Frieda's efforts at making their schoolroom habitable with the barest minimum of resources, although he is actually thinking about his walk with Barnabas and his message to Klamm (S, 154). In so short a time K. has become the stereotype of the condescending man of the house who, because he is grateful for his coffee, tolerates the 'inevitable white table-cloth' and the flower-patterned cup on the improvised table (S, 154). Even such condescension becomes less easy as Frieda's attractions fade in step with her dwindling value as a prize to be gained or traded. Yet the fault is not his alone, for Frieda has interests of her own which she sees K. as serving. There is a possessiveness about her which would rather keep K. in the deep, narrow bed of the grave than allow him the freedom to pursue his goals (S, 170). Buried under the rubble of selfishness, each of them appears to have a need for the other. Given the strength of each individual's will, however, moments of genuine closeness prove to be exceptional. In conversation with Pepi, K. later regrets his neglect of Frieda and confesses to the emptiness of a life spent chasing elusive goals (S, 369), but this insight does not lead him to abandon his quest or struggle. Although K. is shown to be deluded in his pursuit of power, Kafka offers no sustainable alternative. In contrast to many of his Expressionist contemporaries, who had called out for a 'New Human Being' ('der neue Mensch') to emerge, Kafka was sceptical about whether such a transformation, however desirable in principle, could be achieved in practice.

AN UNINTENDED DESTINATION

Like Kafka's other novels, *The Castle* was left unfinished. According to Max Brod, Kafka had conceived of an ending in which K. would receive on his death-bed exceptional permission from the castle to stay and work in the village.[22] Given the contrasting endings he considered for *The Missing Person*, one cannot be sure that Kafka would have stuck to this plan. However, Brod's report has a plausible ring about it, in that the image of K. on his death-bed would fit in well with the contrasting motifs of movement and stasis which run through the novel. During the first four days of K.'s stay in the village he meets four figures in a lying or half-lying position: the overweight and sickly landlady who pines for her long-lost affair with Klamm; Frau Brunswick, a woman from the castle whose eyes ignore the child at her breast as she stares up into empty space; the village superintendent, and the official Bürgel. Like Josef K.'s first meeting with representatives of the court, K.'s introduction to an official from the castle takes place as he lies in bed. By the end of his very first morning in the village K. feels unusually tired; by the time he enters Bürgel's room his greatest wish is simply to lie down, go to sleep and hear nothing more concerning himself. A final scene at his death-bed would have rounded off this pattern neatly.

For K. to die in the village would be appropriate for several other reasons. Firstly, the action of the novel would then have the form of an incomplete journey. As Friedrich Beißner pointed out many years ago, 'the failure to arrive' is a central theme or situation in Kafka's writing.[23] In one of his late jottings (written at about the same time as *The Castle*) Kafka took Moses's failure to reach the Promised Land to be a paradigm of human life:

> The essence of the journey through the desert. A human being who makes this journey as the tribal leader of his organism with a residue (more is inconceivable) of awareness of what is happening. He has the scent of Canaan his whole life through; that he should not catch sight of the country until just before his death is implausible. The only sense this last prospect can have is to show what an incomplete moment human life is, incomplete because this kind of life could last for ever and yet the outcome would be nothing more than a moment. Moses fails to reach Canaan, not because his life was too short but because it was a human life. (GW 11, 190)

The particular incompleteness of K.'s life, which issues in his inability to pass through the village to reach the castle (his chosen, and false, Canaan), is entirely consistent with everything the novel reveals about his relationship to the world of village and castle.

What K. finds in this world is a confusing and contradictory society which mirrors his own confusions and contradictions. K. is divided, as we have seen, between the need for isolation and for sociability, so that he is sometimes drawn in awe to the images of the closed-off, self-absorbed castle or of the soaring 'eagle' Klamm, while at others he wants human company and warmth. The sharpest form of this conflict is the tension between his stubborn will to subordinate everything to his chosen goal and fleeting, but nonetheless important moments of intimacy with Frieda. His attitude to power is riven with inconsistencies as he is inclined variously to challenge it, fear it, contemplate the banality of it and feel respect or even tenderness for its representatives. Even victory or freedom are no longer simple, unambiguous values for him when he is left to stand alone in the courtyard of the Masters' Inn, or when he dreams of duelling with the statue of an embarrassed Greek god. Nowhere is K.'s inner division expressed more effectively, however, than in his response to the ringing of the castle's great bell, at which his heart feels both quickened and threatened by the thought that his desires might be fulfilled. Inevitably, such ambivalence engenders stasis. K. does not and cannot go further than the village at the foot of the castle mount because, in a sense, he has already arrived at his proper destination, a place which reflects back to eyes which cannot – or will not – see the very contradictions in his will which have brought him here and which hold him here.

The ringing of the castle's great bell is followed by the faint, monotonous chiming of a smaller bell, perhaps in the castle, perhaps in the village itself. This second bell, K. feels, is 'better suited to the slow journey and the wretched but unrelenting coachman' (S, 26). Although this journey takes place in the gathering dusk of K.'s first, brief day in the village, there is a quality of foreboding about it, the suggestion of a hearse and the tolling of the bell for the dead. There are other suggestions in the novel of the presence of death in village and castle. Klamm's name has overtones not just of secrecy and a narrow, enclosed space, but also, or indeed mainly, of being stiff with cold. With his black, long-tailed coat, it is as if one of the crows circling the castle has taken on human form. Although he meets its representatives in the village, K. never once detects the least sign of life up in the castle itself. If, as has been suggested, the castle in some sense houses death,[24] then, according to Kafka's view of things, it is right that K. should be unable to reach it by an effort of will. In another of Kafka's fragmentary fictions the hunter Gracchus dies only too gladly, leaping into the boat of death and looking forward eagerly to reaching the Beyond. Yet his fate is never to enter the world of the dead because he is still driven by the powerful will which governs the living. The children who lie down in the snow or the savages who lie down in the sand of the shore or the bachelor who lies drinking rainwater in the gutter – all these, by contrast, are figures of Kafka's who *relinquish* the will when 'death desires them'.

The most important moment in K.'s life before coming to the castle, it appears, was when he climbed the churchyard wall as a youngster. It was a moment of great pride, with some suggestion even of having triumphed over death as he looked down at the crosses 'sinking in the earth' (S, 40) below him. Not the castle where he seeks a second such triumph, but the village where he is gradually worn down by the unavailing struggle with a reflection of his own contradictory will is the appropriate place for K.'s journey to end. Just as the fate of the 'man from the country' was to die at the threshold of a door meant only for him,[25] K.'s unintended but proper destination is a place where the essential incompleteness of human life, which in his case is a life driven by a will obsessed with empty images of power and authority, is revealed, but not recognized.

6

Conclusion

The novel, Georg Lukács wrote in 1920, just two years before Kafka began *The Castle*, is a form which was developed in order to explore the troubled relationship of the problematic individual to itself, which is to say, to the social world and the world of ideas from which it emerged.[1] No doubt this definition is unnecessarily exclusive and ponderous, but it applies to many of the finest examples of the genre, including the novels of Kafka.

In all three of his novels, it has been argued here, Kafka imagines social life from the point of view of a personality moulded so powerfully and at such an early age by the values, expectations and practices of society, that it remains haunted by them for life, trapped, as it were, in a closed circuit. Kafka's novels are subjective in the sense that he lends his imagination – his 'dream-like inner life' – to his damaged protagonists. As a result the world they traverse deviates from our everyday world both in detail and in its structure, so that the same pattern of injury and ineffectual attempts to escape or compensate for it is repeated over and over again. Yet, though Kafka narrates from a point of view which overlaps considerably with that of the protagonist whose world he imagines, his consciousness is wider than, and critical of, that of his characters. In each novel it is clear that the protagonist's own will shares the responsibility for reproducing the damaging structures in which it is trapped. To borrow a vivid image from Kafka's notebooks, the wall encircling the lives of these characters reveals itself, on closer inspection, to be their own forehead: their inner world and the world 'outside' are continuous with one another. Equally, however, the emphasis changes from novel to novel. Whereas *The Missing Person* is inspired mainly by anger at the hurt done to a relatively (only relatively) innocent youngster by a harsh society, *The Trial* is imbued with the feelings of guilt, self-hatred and exhaustion of a man who has achieved outward success by pursuing a respectable and law-abiding career in the same kind of competitive, disciplinarian society. By the time he wrote *The Castle* Kafka had come to a more resigned, less tortured view of the dialectic between the damaged personality and its reflections in a deformed and deforming world.

Painful and frustrating though Kafka's analysis of social and psychological mechanisms often is, his vision is not unrelievedly bleak. In all three novels there are brief moments of sympathy or affection which throw the surrounding cruelty or indifference into relief, and suggest that relationships should not, possibly even need not, be like this. Unlike many of his younger Expressionist contemporaries, however, Kafka could not in good conscience proclaim the advent of a new world which they hoped would emerge from the purgatory of the First World War. His contribution, rather, was to help to define the reciprocally damaging relationship between society and the individual will. How that relationship might be changed, his novels do not say. But that it needs to be, they do.

Notes

---

1 A Writer's Life

1. For a biography in English see: Ronald Hayman, *K. A Biography of Kafka* (London, 1981). A mass of factual detail is contained in the *Kafka-Handbuch*, vol. 1, ed. H. Binder (Stuttgart, 1979). For visual illustrations of Kafka's world, see: Klaus Wagenbach, *Franz Kafka. Bilder aus seinem Leben* (Berlin, 1989).

2. *Franz Kafka. Der Dichter über sein Werk*, ed. Erich Heller and Joachim Beug (Munich, 1977), p. 151. As the most convenient collection of comments by Kafka on his writing, both in general and in relation to particular works, this will be cited frequently, with the reference given in the form DW followed by a page reference, directly after the quotation. Occasionally the text has to be modified to take account of the critical edition.

3. For a fascinating account of the ways in which Kafka's art anticipated his life, see: Jürg Amann, *Das Symbol Kafka* (Berne, 1974). A symbolic interpretation of features of Kafka's life, such as his bachelorhood, is to be found in: G. Kurz, *Traum-Schrecken. Kafkas literarische Existenzanalyse* (Stuttgart, 1980).

4. Kafka felt that only the first chapter of the novel, 'The Stoker', came from 'inner truth' (DW, 41).

5. He wrote to Felice Bauer: 'I only come awake amongst the inner figures' (DW, 137).

6. For an analysis of the process of writing and of its traces in Kafka's texts, see: Malcolm Pasley, *'Die Schrift ist unveränderlich ...'. Essays zu Kafka* (Frankfurt/M., 1995).

7. Letter to Oskar Pollak, 20 December 1902, *Briefe 1902–1924*, ed. Max Brod (Frankfurt/M., 1958), p.14. All further references will take the form (B, page no.).

8. See: Anthony Northey, 'Die Kafkas. Juden? Christen? Tschechen? Deutsche?', in: *Kafka und Prag*, ed. Kurt Krolop and Hans Dieter Zimmermann (Berlin and New York, 1994), pp. 11–32.

9. See: Wagenbach, *Franz Kafka. Bilder aus seinem Leben*, p.36.

10. Diary entry, 24 October 1911 (GW 9, 82). References to the new, critical edition of Kafka's writings will be in this abbreviated form. See the Bibliography for details.

11. *Briefe an Milena*, ed. J. Born and M. Müller (Frankfurt/M., 1983), p. 294; all further references will take the form (BM, page no.).

12. Recent studies of Kafka's relationship to Judaism include: R. Robertson, *Kafka. Judaism, Politics, and Literature* (Oxford, 1985); K.E. Grözinger, *Kafka and Kabbalah* (New York, 1994); *Kafka und das Judentum*, ed. K.E. Grözinger, S. Moses and H.D. Zimmermann (Frankfurt/M., 1987).

13. This can be found in the volume *Zur Frage der Gesetze* (GW 7, 10–66).

14. 'As you read it, understand all the tricks of the advocate, it is an advocate's letter. And at the same time never forget your great Nevertheless' (BM, 85).

15. 'They are in the hands of the most meagre power and their reason is not even calm enough to acknowledge this power with looks and bows and win its favour'; diary entry, 7 February 1912 (GW 10, 33).

16. In a sequence of entries in Kafka's diary from June 1910, fragments of a story about a 'little occupant of the ruins', Kafka thrusts the accusation that educators destroy the child's personality, 'like a dagger through society' (GW 9, 18).

17. The phrase was coined by Elias Canetti in: *Das Gewissen der Worte. Essays* (Munich and Vienna, 1983), p. 127.

18. Admittedly, the laughing Arab in the story 'Jackals and Arabs' (GW 1, 213) is an exception to this rule.

19. This much-quoted phrase is recorded in: Gustav Janouch, *Gespräche mit Kafka* (Frankfurt/M., 1968), p. 104. As Janouch is not considered a reliable source, the attribution must be treated with caution.

20. Such imagery is frequently found in mystical writings such as those of St John of the Cross, who may in turn have derived it from the language of the Bible. See, for example: P. Grant, *Literature of Mysticism in Western Tradition* (London, 1983).

21. Before the new, critical edition of the diaries this much-quoted passage contained a serious error, 'gewagt' ('dared') having been misread as 'gesagt' ('said'); cf. DW, 19.

22. The fear of self-loss through intimacy with another person is one Kafka shared with his character K. in *The Castle* (see below, p. 132).

23. This is another passage where the critical edition differs in two small but important details from the previous version of the text. In DW (and the editions on which it is based) the text runs: 'das Hinausspringen aus der Totschlägerreihe, Tat-Beobachtung, Tat-Beobachtung', whereas the critical edition deletes the first comma and replaces the hyphens with dashes, so that the text now reads: 'aus der Totschlägerreihe Tat – Beobachtung, Tat – Beobachtung' (GW 11, 210).

24. Letter to Oskar Baum, June 1918 (B, 242).

25. Kafka used the metaphor again in his diary (8 May 1922), referring to one of his last stories, possibly 'A Hunger Artist': 'The work closes itself as an unhealed wound can close itself' (GW 11, 230).

26. Diary entry, 15 September 1917 (GW 11, 161).

27. The execution machine used in 'In the Penal Colony' inscribes the text of a broken law into the flesh of condemned men by means of a 'harrow'. An otherwise obscure entry in Kafka's last diary (8 May 1922) concerning 'work with the plough' may also be a metaphorical reflection on writing (GW 11, 230).

28. Letter to Max Brod, October 1917 (B, 177).

29. Kafka repeatedly quoted a remark supposedly made by Flaubert when he
     saw a young married couple: 'Ils sont dans le vrai.' See: *Briefe an Felice und
     andere Korrespondenz aus der Verlobungszeit,* ed. E. Heller and J. Born (New York
     and Frankfurt/M., 1967), p. 637.
30. 'Why I am a Fate' is the title of the last section of Nietzsche's *Ecce Homo*; see:
     Basic Writings of Nietzsche, trans. Walter Kaufmann (New York, 1968). For a
     discussion of the ethic of strenuousness in modern German literature, of
     which many of Kafka's texts are classic examples, see: J.P. Stern, *The Dear
     Purchase. A Theme in German Modernism* (Cambridge, 1995).
31. 'One must be dead in order to be wholly a creator'; *Tonio Kröger. Mario und der
     Zauberer* (Frankfurt/M., 1973), p. 26. Cf. Kafka's letter to Felice: 'Writing in
     this sense is a deeper sleep, and thus death, and just as one cannot pull a dead
     man out of his grave, so one cannot pull me away from my desk during the
     night' (DW, 139).
32. 'Ein Brief' in: Hugo von Hofmannsthal, *Gesammelte Werke,* vol. 7 (Frankfurt/
     M., 1979), pp. 461–72. For a detailed analysis of the early literary influences
     on Kafka, see the *Kafka-Handbuch,* vol. 1, particularly pp. 309–23.

2 Reading Kafka

1. *Zu Franz Kafka,* ed. Günter Heintz (Stuttgart, 1979), p. 8. Even a recent critic
    of the critics uses this type of phrase just as freely as the commentators he
    criticizes, e.g.: 'There is no doubt that Kafka's irreducible ambiguity is
    ensconced in his paradoxes'; F.R. Kempf, *Everyone's Darling. Kafka and the
    Critics of his Short Fiction* (Columbia, 1994), p. 91.
2. Even stories generally well regarded by many readers, such as 'In the Penal
    Colony', contained passages which Kafka regarded as 'Machwerk'; see his
    letter to the publisher Kurt Wolff, 4 September 1917 (B, 159). Kafka also
    applied the term 'Konstruktion' disparagingly to his own personality, e.g.:
    'this unconnected construction that I am'; letter to Felice Bauer, 18–19
    February, 1913 (DW, 74).
3. This remark about 'music' refers specifically to 'The Judgement' but the
    importance of fear ('Angst') as a motive is more generally attested: 'Perhaps
    there are other kinds of writing, but I know only this: at night, when fear will
    not let me sleep, I know only this' (DW, 160).
4. This remark refers to his decision to re-start his diary in 1910, a form of
    writing to which he turned repeatedly when other forms failed him.
5. 'Art has more need of craft than craft has of art' (DW, 114).
6. The following discussion of different approaches makes no claim to inform
    the reader exhaustively about the number and range of interpretations
    already in existence. Instead it simply sketches some main lines of enquiry
    and briefly assesses their validity. For an analytic bibliography of secondary
    literature up to 1985, see: Maria Luise Caputo-Mayr and Julius M. Herz,
    Franz Kafka. Eine kommentierte Bibliographie der Sekundärliteratur (Berne and Stutt-
    gart, 1987). Other useful surveys and assessments of the literature (e.g. by
    Beicken, Binder, Dietz, Dodd, Kempf, Krusche and Robertson) are listed
    below in the Bibliography.

7. Notebook entry, 25 February 1918: 'Unlike Kierkegaard I was not led into life by the admittedly already heavily sinking hand of Christianity, nor have I, like the Zionists, seized the last corner of the Jewish prayer-shawl before it flew away. I am an end or a beginning' (GW 6, 215).

8. Ritchie Robertson, for example, has recently revived one of Buber's arguments about the angels as 'unjust judges' in a cautious effort to reconcile the agents of the court with the notion of divine justice: ' "Von den ungerechten Richtern" – Zum allegorischen Verfahren in Kafkas *Der Proceß*, in: *Nach erneuter Lektüre. Franz Kafkas 'Der Proceß*, ed. Hans Dieter Zimmermann (Würzburg, 1992), pp. 201–9.

9. Cf. Kafka's half serious, half comical description of the kind of Abraham (lacking all belief in his calling or that of his son) who might exist today; letter to Robert Klopstock, June 1921 (B, 333–4).

10. See: T.J. Reed, 'Kafka und Schopenhauer. Philosophisches Denken und dichterisches Bild', *Euphorion* 59 (1965), pp. 160–72; R. Robertson, *Kafka. Judaism, Politics, and Literature* (Oxford, 1985), pp. 185–217.

11. Arthur Schopenhauer, *The World as Will and Idea*, trans. R. Haldane and J. Kemp (London, 1906).

12. Erich Heller, *Franz Kafka* (Glasgow, 1974), p. 47.

13. See: *Franz Kafka. Kritik und Rezeption zu seinen Lebzeiten 1912–1924*, ed. Jürgen Born (Frankfurt/M., 1979).

14. See: Reed, 'Kafka und Schopenhauer'.

15. See: R. Robertson, 'In Search of the Historical Kafka. A Selective Review of Research, 1980–92', *The Modern Language Review* 89/1 (1994), pp. 116–19.

16. Wilhelm Emrich, *Franz Kafka. Das Baugesetz seiner Dichtung. Der mündige Mensch jenseits von Nihilismus und Tradition* (Frankfurt/M., 1958), trans. S. Zeben Buehne as: *Franz Kafka. A Critical Study of his Writings* (New York, 1984).

17. Prominent among the Lacanians is Charles Bernheimer, *Flaubert and Kafka. Studies in Psychopoetic Structure* (New Haven and London, 1982). For a synthesis of the arguments of Derrida, Foucault and Lacan, see: Hans Helmut Hiebel, *Die Zeichen des Gesetzes. Recht und Macht bei Franz Kafka* (Munich, 1983). For an 'anti-Oedipal' reading, see: G. Deleuze and F. Guattari, *Kafka. Toward a Minor Literature*, trans. D. Ponan (Minneapolis, 1986).

18. For an account of Kafka's views on psychoanalysis and a critique of psychoanalytic approaches to his work, see: Lawrence Ryan, ' "Zum letzten Mal Psychologie!" Zur psychologischen Deutbarkeit der Werke Franz Kafkas', in: *Psychologie in der Literaturwissenschaft*, ed. Wolfgang Paulsen (Heidelberg, 1971), pp.157–73.

19. Charles Neider, *The Frozen Sea. A Study of Franz Kafka* (New York, 1948).

20. Walter Sokel, *Franz Kafka. Tragik und Ironie. Zur Struktur seiner Kunst* (Munich and Vienna, 1964).

21. Now available in a single volume entitled *Der Erzähler Franz Kafka* (Frankfurt/M., 1983).

22. See, for example: Martin Walser, *Beschreibung einer Form* (Munich, 1961), and Jörgen Kobs, *Kafka. Untersuchungen zu Bewußtsein und Sprache seiner Gestalten* (Bad Homburg, 1970).

23. See, for example: Roy Pascal, *Kafka's Narrators. A Study of his Stories and Sketches* (Cambridge, 1982).

24. See, for example: Patrick O'Neill, 'The Comedy of Stasis. Narration and Knowledge in Kafka's *Prozeß*, in: *Franz Kafka (1883–1983). His Craft and Thought*, ed. Roman Struc and J.C.Yardley (Waterloo, Ontario, 1986), pp. 49–73.
25. See, for example, Gerhard Neumann, 'Der Zauber des Anfangs und das "Zögern vor der Geburt"', in: *Nach erneuter Lektüre. Franz Kafkas 'Der Proceß'*, ed. Hans Dieter Zimmermann (Würzburg, 1992), pp. 121–42.
26. Stanley Corngold, *The Commentators' Despair. The Interpretation of Kafka's 'Metamorphosis'* (Port Washington and London, 1973).
27. Stanley Corngold, 'Angst und Schreiben in einer frühen Aufzeichnung Kafkas', in: *Franz Kafka Symposium*, ed. Maria Luise Caputo-Mayr (Berlin, 1978), pp. 59–70.
28. *Zu Franz Kafka*, p. 15.

3 The Missing Person

1. *Der Verschollene*, the title adopted for the critical edition because it is the only one used by Kafka, cannot be rendered adequately in English. The adjective 'verschollen' refers to people or certain things (such as ships or manuscripts) which have gone missing or of which no report has been received. With reference to people it can have legal force (equivalent to the term 'prepositus' in English law), whereby a prescribed period of 'Verschollenheit' allows the presumption of death. Kafka's legal training may have suggested the title to him. 'Lost', 'missing' or 'disappeared' all convey just part of the sense.
2. On an earlier visit to the asbestos factory Kafka had already observed that 'one' (i.e. the management) did not greet the (female) workers (GW 10, 32).
3. See: *Der Verschollene. Apparatband*, ed. Jost Schillemeit (Frankfurt/M., 1983), pp. 59, 68. The hidden links between the travels of the hero and the process of narration may have suggested Karl's surname to Kafka ('Roß-mann' translates as 'horse-man'). In fact Kafka's writings abound with metaphorical links between writing and riding or horses: in the 'Description of a Struggle', for example, the narrator talks/rides his way through an imaginary landscape while supposedly mounted on the back of his acquaintance (GW 5, 61–2).
4. Karl later gives his age as sixteen in conversation with the head cook (V, 137). Kafka also changed Karl's age to sixteen for the publication of Chapter 1 as a separate story, but at the beginning of the manuscript he is seventeen years old.
5. Kafka's main sources of information about America were: Arthur Holitscher, *Amerika – heute und morgen* (Berlin, 1912); an illustrated lecture by Frantisek Soukup and his book, *America. A Series of Pictures from American Life* (in Czech); Johann Vilhelm Jensen, 'Der kleine Ahasverus', a novella published in the *Neue Rundschau*, June 1909. For further details, see: A. Wirkner, *Kafka und die Außenwelt. Quellenstudien zum 'Amerika'-Fragment* (Stuttgart, 1976).
6. The discrepancies between Kafka's fictional America and its real counterpart have been noted by many commentators. See, for example: Carl Steiner, 'Kafkas Amerika. Illusion oder Wirklichkeit?', in: *Franz Kafka Symposium*, ed. Maria Luise Caputo-Mayr (Berlin, 1978), pp. 46–58.

7. Cf. Wilhelm Emrich, *Franz Kafka. A Critical Study of his Writings* (New York, 1984), pp. 227–58. For a Marxist perspective, see: K. Hermsdorf, *Kafka. Weltbild und Roman* (Berlin, 1961).

8. See: J. Pütz, *Kafkas 'Verschollener', ein Bildungsroman?* (Frankfurt/M., 1983).

9. The improbable frequency of these coincidences is also noted by Urs Ruf who concludes that a 'hidden law' governs their occurrence. See: Urs Ruf, *Franz Kafka. Das Dilemma der Söhne* (Berlin, 1974), p. 72.

10. See: Romans 15:19; Acts 2:43.

11. As Walter Sokel observes, Kafka was concerned with 'the system of rule of which the situation in the family is just a part. He is concerned with the secret of power, and in the America-novel this secret is unmasked more plainly than in most of Kafka's other works.' Walter Sokel, 'Zwischen Drohung und Errettung. Zur Funktion Amerikas in Kafkas Roman *Der Verschollene*', in: *Amerika in der deutschen Literatur*, ed. S. Bauschinger et al. (Stuttgart, 1975), p. 261.

12. The illogicality and injustice of Karl's punishment for Johanna's seduction of him are discussed in: Hans Hiebel, 'Parabelform und Rechtsthematik in Franz Kafkas Romanfragment *Der Verschollene*', in: *Die Parabel*, ed. T. Elm and H.H. Hiebel (Frankfurt/M., 1986), pp. 219–54.

13. Kafka pointed this out in a letter to Milena (1920) who had translated 'arm' into Czech as 'indigent' (BM, 16).

14. 'The basic structure can be derived from a situation experienced in early childhood which, because it is repeated later, is felt to be typical': Heinz Hillmann, 'Kafkas *Amerika*. Literatur als Problemlösungsspiel', in: *Der deutsche Roman im 20. Jahrhundert*, vol. 1, ed. Manfred Brauneck (Bamberg, 1976), p. 139.

15. Similarly, in 'The Judgement' the adult Georg Bendemann still sees in his father the 'giant' he knew in childhood (GW 1, 44).

16. See: *Der Verschollene. Apparatband*, pp. 124–6. The muddling of names also occurs in the manuscript of 'The Metamorphosis', where Kafka sometimes wrote 'Karl' instead of 'Gregor'.

17. Kafka pointed out to Milena that her translation of this phrase into Czech did not quite convey the feeling of magnificence: ' "freie Lüfte" ist ein wenig großartiger aber da ist wohl kein Ausweg' (BM, 16).

18. 'Die ist aber grossartig'; see: *Der Verschollene. Apparatband*, p. 123.

19. See: Hiebel, 'Parabelform und Rechtsthematik', p. 230.

20. In what may well be a wry writerly joke about the imaginary nature of these places Kafka even has his protagonist pass through a room containing an abandoned writing desk (V, 10), the writer having disappeared, presumably, into the story.

21. See: *Der Verschollene. Apparatband*, p. 141.

22. Jörgen Kobs puts Karl's inaccurate perceptions and erroneous judgements at the centre of his interpretation of the novel. See: Jörgen Kobs, *Kafka. Untersuchungen zu Bewußtsein und Sprache seiner Gestalten*, ed. U. Brech (Bad Homburg, 1970), *passim*.

23. In a letter to Minze Eisner in 1921 (B, 310) Kafka refers to a passage in Schopenhauer where the view from a balcony serves to illustrate the mistakenly harmonious view of the world taken by anyone who is happy. As if to

confirm this warning, Karl, too, experiences the cruel difference between aesthetic impression and the reality awaiting him in the midst of life.

24. Cf. Friedrich Schiller, *On the Aesthetic Education of Man*, ed./trans. E.M. Wilkinson and L.A. Willoughby (Oxford, 1967), particularly letters 14 and 15.

25. Cf. Gerhard Neumann, 'Der Wanderer und der Verschollene. Zum Problem der Identität in Goethes *Wilhelm Meister* und in Kafkas *Amerika*-Roman', in: *Paths and Labyrinths*, ed. J.P. Stern and J.J. White (London, 1985), pp. 43–65.

26. J.W. Goethe, *Wilhelm Meisters Lehrjahre*, Berliner Ausgabe, vol. 10 (Berlin, 1976), pp. 20–1.

27. The baying dogs and the moonlight (V, 100) suggest the presence of the hunting goddess, Diana, who may wish to take revenge on Karl for resisting the charms of Klara. Diana's role as the avenger of women is developed more fully in *The Trial* (see below, p. 96).

28. J.W. Goethe, *Faust*, Part I, Sc. 1 ('Nacht'), lines 282–4, quoted from the edition by E. Trunz (Munich, 1963), p. 20.

29. See: Wolfgang Jahn, *Kafkas Roman 'Der Verschollene' ('Amerika')* (Stuttgart, 1965), p. 8.

30. Ulf Abraham defines Karl's guilt feelings as those of an 'undeserving favourite' in: *Der verhörte Held. Recht und Schuld im Werk Franz Kafkas* (Munich, 1985), p. 152.

31. The transformation of a sanctuary into a prison is a recurrent theme in Kafka's fiction, from Gregor Samsa's habit of locking his bedroom door to the labyrinthine burrow built by the unnamed creature in 'The Burrow' (GW 8, 165–208). The reversal has a counterpart in Kafka's own experience, where a 'repulsively successful' childhood game of making himself different from others led eventually to feelings of unbridgeable isolation (GW 11, 208).

32. The incident may derive from Kafka's own nocturnal banishment to the balcony by his irritated father. See: GW 7, 14–15.

33. Although Kafka mentions only *David Copperfield* as an influence on the novel, it is possible that *Oliver Twist*, *Great Expectations* and other works by Dickens may also have supplied character types and situations. The hints that the 'Theatre of Oklahoma' is a fraudulent undertaking, for example, may originate in the spurious Eden to which the gullible hero of *Martin Chuzzlewit* is lured.

34. Peter von Matt has tried to present the excessive Brunelda as the embodiment of matriarchal-Rabelaisian values and hence as 'the only power capable of opposing the dictatorship of a thoroughly rationalized civilization'. See 'Kafkas Venus', in: Peter von Matt, *Das Schicksal der Phantasie* (Munich, 1994), p. 295. Von Matt does not make it clear, however, how her self-indulgence differs, except perhaps in degree, from that of Mack. If Brunelda embodies alternative values, these are lost on the hygiene-loving Karl.

35. Holitscher, *Amerika – heute und morgen*, p. 367.

36. Just as 'Negro' may have been chosen because of a symbolic link with the blackness of the jackdaw ('kavka') (or possibly because Holitscher mentions the hanging of a black youth), 'Leo', the name Kafka first gave to Karl in this scene, was possibly a private allusion to the 'Löwy' side of his own family. Wolfgang Jahn also points to a passage in the diary where Kafka and Felice are called 'Leopold (or Leo) S.' and 'Felice S.'. See: Wolfgang Jahn, 'Kafkas

Handschrift zum *Verschollenen (Amerika)*. Ein vorläufiger Textbericht', *Jahrbuch der deutschen Schillergesellschaft* 9 (1965), p. 549.

37. Wolfgang Jahn puts the myth of the Fall from Paradise at the centre of his interpretation of the novel. See: Wolfgang Jahn, *Kafkas Roman 'Der Verschollene' ('Amerika')* (Stuttgart, 1965), p. 18 *et seq*. Ralf Nicolai does the same, but identifies 'The Fall' with human self-consciousness or 'Reflexion'. See: Ralf Nicolai, *Kafkas Amerika-Roman 'Der Verschollene'. Motive und Gestalten* (Würzburg, 1981), p. 11 and *passim*.

38. 'The desire for refuge required for work is already given to us by the general old miracle of the rib and the expulsion to which it gave rise'; letter to Felix Weltsch, December 1917 (B, 212).

39. In *The Castle* K. has a similar experience of 'empty' freedom (see below, pp. 124–5). Both characters are bound inwardly to an unjust society which has damaged them or against which they are struggling.

40. The active nature of Kafka's imaginary re-ordering of the world has been stressed by Peter von Matt: 'What Kafka enjoys while writing is supreme power, perfect power, dominion without limits.' Peter von Matt, ...*fertig ist das Angesicht. Zur Literaturgeschichte des menschlichen Gesichts* (Munich, 1983), p. 14.

41. In a letter to his publisher Wolff in 1916 (DW, 85) Kafka explained that 'das Peinliche' (painful and embarrassing character) of 'In the Penal Colony' reflected that of the times in general and of his own time in particular.

4 *The Trial*

1. The link between the beginning and end of the novel would have been even clearer if Kafka had not deleted from the manuscript K.'s thought that he might yet have to defend the 'gentlemen' ('Herren') from the court against the state. See: *Der Proceß. Apparatband*, ed. Malcolm Pasley (Frankfurt/M., 1990), p. 322.

2. For a discussion of the 'narrative situation', see: William J. Dodd, *Kafka. 'Der Prozeß'* (Glasgow, 1991), pp. 11–17.

3. Quoted from the translation by Willa and Edwin Muir published by Penguin Books (Harmondsworth, 1966). The translation by D. Scott and C. Waller published by Picador (London, 1977) correctly omits the word 'fine' but otherwise remains misleading.

4. Friedrich Beißner, *Der Erzähler Franz Kafka* (Frankfurt/M., 1983), p. 45.

5. For a discussion of body language in the novel, see: Klaus Jeziorkowski, ' "Bei dieser Sinnlosigkeit des Ganzen." Zu Franz Kafkas Roman *Der Proceß*', in: *Franz Kafka. Sonderband* (Munich, 1994), pp. 200–17.

6. See: Max Brod, *Über Franz Kafka* (Frankfurt/M., 1966), p. 156.

7. It is possible that Kafka left the unfinished chapters of the novel in that state because they hint at the opinions of the narrator more strongly than usual. In the chapter 'Journey to Mother', in particular, the account of K.'s spurious justifications for not visiting his nearly blind mother is closer to sarcasm than irony. For an interpretation which attaches particular importance to this fragment, see: Eric Marson, *Kafka's 'Trial'. The Case against Josef K.* (St Lucia, Queensland, 1975).

8. As we have seen (above, p. 48), hats and caps were equally important in *The Missing Person*. Such details indicate just how consistently Kafka's fictions deal with the same themes, an aspect often overlooked or underplayed by those who argue that they offer no positively identifiable meanings.

9. Here again *The Trial* intensifies a detail from *The Missing Person*; whereas Karl Roßmann feels ashamed to appear in public without a jacket, Josef K. is actually stripped to the waist. For an elaborate interpretation of the symbolism of dress in the novel, see: Mark Anderson, *Kafka's Clothes. Ornament and Aestheticism in the Habsburg 'Fin de Siècle'* (Oxford, 1992), pp. 145–73.

10. Kafka's own visits to prostitutes are documented in his diaries, e.g. GW 12, pp. 41, 70.

11. Cf. the schoolroom in *The Castle* (below, pp. 111–12), where K. and Frieda are subject to the same kind of inconvenience and humiliation.

12. In the manuscript Kafka suppressed an even crasser indication of their sexual behaviour: 'just that her unbuttoned blouse hung down around her waist and that a man was pressing her torso, which was dressed only in a shift, against himself', *Der Proceß. Apparatband*, p. 192.

13. Fräulein Bürstner's name may allude to the verb 'bürsten' which is obscene slang for 'sexual intercourse'.

14. In a letter to Max Brod in November 1917 Kafka describes his earlier thoughts of suicide and the arguments which held him back from this step: 'If you can kill yourself, in a sense you don't have to any more' (B, 195).

15. This is possibly another of K.'s allusions to the link between the fiction and its author, rather like the empty writing desk Karl Roßmann sees below decks. For an account of the links between the process of writing *The Trial* and the progress of K.'s trial, see: *Franz Kafka. 'Der Proceß'. Die Handschrift redet*, ed. Malcolm Pasley, *Marbacher Magazin*, Heft 52 (1990), pp. 22–4.

16. The motif also plays an important role in the opening chapters of both *The Missing Person* and *The Castle*.

17. There is perhaps a suggestion here that the executioners are so old that they have to be washed by someone else. Fear of ageing may be one of the factors underlying the crisis in Josef K.'s life, as it is in the case of Georg Bendemann in 'The Judgement'.

18. For an illuminating discussion of power in the novel, see: Karol Sauerland, 'Der ideale Machtapparat und das Individuum', in: *Nach erneuter Lektüre. Franz Kafkas 'Der Proceß'*, ed. H.D. Zimmermann (Würzburg, 1992), pp. 235–50; Ulf Abraham, 'Rechtsspruch und Machtwort. Zum Verhältnis von Rechtsordnung und Ordnungsmacht bei Kafka', and Christine Lubkoll, ' "Man muß nicht alles für wahr halten, man muß es nur für notwendig halten." Die Theorie der Macht in Franz Kafkas Roman *Der Proceß*, both in: *Franz Kafka: Schriftverkehr*, ed. Wolf Kittler and Gerhard Neumann (Freiburg, 1990), pp. 248–78 and 279–94.

19. Two books entirely devoted to the exegesis of this parable have been published in recent years: Hartmut Binder, *'Vor dem Gesetz'. Einführung in Kafkas Welt* (Stuttgart and Weimar, 1993), and Manfred Voigts (ed.), *Franz Kafka. 'Vor dem Gesetz'. Aufsätze und Materialien* (Würzburg, 1994).

20. Cf. the reflections on justice in Kafka's diary on 20 January 1922: 'Just as in the desperate hour of your death you cannot meditate about right and

wrong, so it is in the midst of desperate life. It is enough that the arrows fit exactly into the wounds which they have struck' (GW 11, 203).

21. Cf. Kafka's observation in his diary in February 1920: 'Original sin, the old injustice done by man, consists in the reproach man makes and from which he does not desist, that an injustice has been done to him, that the original sin was committed against him' (GW 11, 181).

22. The theme of 'Berechnung' or 'calculation' recurs persistently both in Kafka's fiction and in his judgements on his own failure to live life fully and trustingly.

23. The Greek (Nike) and Roman (Victoria) goddesses of victory are usually depicted with wings on their backs rather than at their heels.

24. This same dark red glow was seen by Karl Roßmann in the depths of the President's box in the Theatre of Oklahoma (see above, p. 61).

25. Cf. the merging of Liberty and Justice in the first chapter of *The Missing Person*.

26. Kafka's unnecessary repetition of the motif of deceptive portraiture may be a consequence of the novel's intermittent composition over a lengthy period.

27. By the end of his trial K. achieves at least intermittent glimpses of his condition, as when he resolves, sardonically, to try to enjoy 'the last semblance of life' (P, 238) on the way to the quarry. For a discussion of the themes of illusion and theatricality, see: James Rolleston, *Kafka's Narrative Theater* (University Park and London, 1974).

28. Karl Roßmann imagines similarly that the eyes of New York are all focused on him (V, 18).

29. The wall is one of Kafka's most widely used images, frequently symbolizing an insurmountable barrier, but sometimes its opposite, the vain attempt to create some impenetrable protective shield.

30. K.'s emotional distance from his mother is underscored by the physical distance between their homes.

31. The importance of distinguishing guilt feelings from objective guilt has been argued repeatedly by J.P. Stern. See, for example: 'The Law of *The Trial*', in: *On Kafka. Semi-Centenary Perspectives*, ed. F. Kuna (London, 1976), pp. 22–41. The distinction has been elaborated further by others, including: H.H. Hiebel, 'Schuld oder Scheinbarkeit der Schuld? Zu Kafkas Roman *Der Proceß*', in: *Das Schuldproblem bei Franz Kafka*, ed. Wolfgang Kraus and Norbert Winkler (Vienna, Cologne and Weimar, 1994), pp. 95–117.

32. 'Man cannot live without constant trust in something indestructible within him, although what is indestructible and his trust in it can remain constantly hidden from him' (GW 6, 236).

33. 'A first sign of the beginning of understanding is the wish to die' (GW 6, 230).

34. See: Patrick O'Neill, 'The Comedy of Stasis. Narration and Knowledge in Kafka's *Prozeß*', in: *Franz Kafka (1883–1983). His Craft and Thought*, ed. R. Struc and J.C. Yardley (Waterloo, Ontario, 1986), p. 53.

35. In the 'Letter to Father' Kafka recalls that, although he was seldom actually beaten by his father, the constant threat of it was even more intimidating (GW 7, 29).

36. K. later returned to the link between violence and socialization in the story of the self-educated ape Rotpeter in 'A Report for an Academy' (GW 1, 234), where the awakening of consciousness in the ape is attributed to the pain of two shots from a hunter's gun.

37. The case for reading *The Trial* as a 'metaphysical crime novel' is re-stated in: Ritchie Robertson, *Kafka. Judaism, Politics, and Literature* (Oxford, 1985), p. 90 *et seq.*

38. Cf. Kafka's aphorisms in: GW 6, 228–48.

39. Notoriously, Kafka described the dissolution of the engagement as the 'court in the hotel' (GW 11, 24).

40. On 7 October 1914, for example, he noted in his diary, 'I have taken a week's leave to drive the novel forwards' (DW, 79), and on 1 November, 'Yesterday after a long time advanced a good bit' (DW, 80). Such metaphors of forward progression (or the lack of it) pervade Kafka's reflections on his writing.

41. Although not quite so 'protected and crawled inside my work' (DW, 78) as he had been two years previously (at the time of 'The Judgement'), Kafka was delighted to find himself writing freely once more at the beginning of *The Trial*.

42. In the 'Letter to Father' Kafka described the 'terrible trial' going on between his father and the rest of the family, in which the father always claimed to be the judge but in which he was actually just as much of a weak and blind party as the others (GW 7, 38–9).

43. See above, p. 41.

5 *The Castle*

1. One of the small but significant editorial interventions made by Max Brod in his original edition, and corrected in the new critical edition, occurs in this opening paragraph. Brod changed *führt* ('leads') to *führte* ('led'), thereby eliminating a possible distinction at this point between the perspective of the narrator (whose consciousness is expressed in the present tense) and that of K. (whose consciousness is generally conveyed by the use of free indirect speech in the past tense). The present tense may, however, simply be a residue of the fact that Kafka originally wrote the novel as a first person narrative spoken by the protagonist, but then changed his mind, substituting 'K.' for 'I' and making other appropriate changes. See: D. Cohn, 'K. Enters *The Castle*. On the Change of Person in Kafka's Manuscript', *Euphorion* 62/1 (1968), pp. 28–45. As a first-person narrator K. would naturally use the present tense, since he is describing his encounter with a 'real' and still existent castle. Kafka may either simply have overlooked the tense of this verb when revising the text (as Brod clearly assumed), or he may have chosen to retain the present tense in order to lend narratorial authority to the castle's existence independently of K.'s encounter with it. Although this particular instance is ambiguous, there are many other signs of the narrator's distinct and frequently ironical presence in the text. The fullest account of the devices which permit criticism of K.'s thoughts and actions despite the use of free indirect style is to be found in: Richard Sheppard, *On Kafka's Castle. A Study* (London, 1973).

2. 'It is necessary to dive beneath the surface, so to speak, and to sink more quickly than that which is sinking before one's eyes' (DW, 147).

3. For a summary of the attempts to locate the physical or literary sources of Kafka's castle, see: H. Binder, *Kafka-Kommentar*, vol. 2 (Munich, 1976), pp 284–5.

4. See, for example: Marthe Robert, *L'Ancien et le nouveau. De Don Quichotte à Franz Kafka* (Paris, 1963).

5. Peter Beicken, *Franz Kafka. Eine kritische Einführung in die Forschung* (Frankfurt/ M., 1974), p. 331. For an analysis of the relation between temporal distortion and the consciousness of K., see: Winfried Kudszus, 'Erzählhaltung und Zeitverschiebung in Kafkas "Prozeß" und "Schloß"', in: *Franz Kafka*, ed. H. Politzer (Darmstadt, 1973), pp. 331–50.

6. This muddling of the signs of age is not uncommon in Kafka. The friend of Georg Bendemann in 'The Judgement', for example, is described as an 'old child' (GW 1, 40). The motif can be associated either with immaturity despite advancing years or, as in the case of Bürgel, with the retention of childlike hope.

7. For an account of restricted spaces in Kafka's fiction, see: Klaus Ramm, *Reduktion als Erzählprinzip bei Kafka* (Frankfurt/M., 1971).

8. For a discussion of the role of K.'s childhood in giving him a 'pre-formed' (and deformed) consciousness, see: K.P. Philippi, *Reflexion und Wirklichkeit. Untersuchungen zu Kafkas Roman 'Das Schloß'* (Tübingen, 1965), p. 200 *et seq.*

9. Various fragments of the story of 'Der Jäger Gracchus' are to be found in GW 6, pp. 40–5, 96–100.

10. GW 9, pp. 89–94, 98–9.

11. Critics who argue that the castle is fundamentally a benevolent institution which aims to make K. attend to neglected areas of his personality also tend to criticize Amalia's rejection of Sortini as an act of arrogance or of narcissistic frigidity which rejects 'a mythic experience of death and rebirth'. See: Sheppard, *On Kafka's Castle*, p. 207.

12. Cf. the aggressive quality of the official Josef K.'s embrace of Fräulein Bürstner in *The Trial* (see above, p. 76).

13. Peter Beicken characterizes this phenomenon aptly as a 'consensus between the powerful and the oppressed'; *Franz Kafka. Eine kritische Einführung in die Forschung*, p. 334.

14. This song is supposedly sung by a skivvy at an inn who dreams of taking revenge on her male customers by revealing herself to be a pirate chief with the power to order the bombardment of the town and the murder of all the men in it. See: Bertolt Brecht, *Große kommentierte Berliner und Frankfurter Ausgabe. Stücke 2* (Berlin, Weimar and Frankfurt/M., 1988), pp. 248–50.

15. See: Hinrich Siefken, *Kafka. Ungeduld und Lässigkeit. Zu den Romanen 'Der Prozeß' und 'Das Schloß'* (Munich, 1977), p. 48.

16. This might be another of Kafka's joking allusions to his presence in his own fiction, in that Klamm's dress is suggestive of the crow family which is a private cipher for Kafka; crows also circle the castle. Other possible masks for Kafka in the novel include the young man Schwarzer, dressed in 'city clothes' (S, 9) and with the face of an actor, and his girlfriend Gisa, who is content to tolerate Schwarzer's presence, provided he does not disturb her obsession with books.

17. Such attention-seeking was reflected back to K. in the image of the castle tower as a melancholy figure breaking through the roof to show himself to

the world. Kafka's (undelivered) confession to his father that his writing had to do with him (GW 7, 47) indicates that he recognized a similar ambivalence towards power in himself.

18. See, for example: Sheppard, *On Kafka's Castle*, pp. 182–3.
19. It has often been noted that K.'s alleged profession as a 'Landvermesser' hints at certain flaws in his character: his inaccurate estimates of the world he has entered ('vermessen' = 'to measure wrongly') and his arrogant overestimation of himself ('sich vermessen' = 'to overreach oneself').
20. The meaning of tightness or narrowness in Middle High German 'klam' is preserved in the verbs 'klemmen' and 'beklemmen', but also in the Austrian word 'Klamm', meaning a narrow mountain gorge, usually with a torrent running through it.
21. For a fuller account of the role of the assistants, see: Sheppard, *On Kafka's Castle*, pp. 48–53.
22. See Brod's first postscript to his edition, *Das Schloß* (New York and Frankfurt/M., 1951), p. 491.
23. See: Friedrich Beißner, *Der Erzähler Franz Kafka* (Frankfurt/M., 1983), p. 63.
24. See: Franz Kuna, *Franz Kafka. Literature as Corrective Punishment* (London, 1974), p. 136 *et seq.*
25. At one point K., too, imagines himself standing before Klamm's door and speaking to the 'doorkeeper' (S, 151).

6 Conclusion

1. See: Georg Lukács, *Die Theorie des Romans* (Darmstadt and Neuwied, 1963), p. 70.

Bibliography

A. PRIMARY SOURCES

1 Works by Kafka

In recent years a group of scholars have prepared a new, critical edition of Kafka's writings, based mainly on the manuscript versions of the texts. Now that these are available in paperback they are likely to become the versions most widely used in schools and universities by students of German. Given this and the fact that English translations are necessarily problematic (since puns rarely translate into puns and etymological links are often lost), all quotations in the present study take the form of *ad hoc* translations of the German text in the critical edition. References are mostly given in the form (GW volume no., page no.) in the body of the text. The paperback edition is published under the title: Franz Kafka, *Gesammelte Werke in zwölf Bänden*, edited by Hans-Gerd Koch (Frankfurt/M.: Fischer Taschenbuch Verlag, 1994). The volumes containing the novels are referred to in the body of the text by their own abbreviations, namely:

V = *Der Verschollene* = *The Missing Person*
P = *Der Proceß* = *The Trial*
S = *Das Schloß* = *The Castle*

In the hardback critical edition each volume is accompanied by a volume of critical apparatus. Reference is made here to the apparatus of the following volumes:

Der Verschollene, ed. Schillemeit, J. (Frankfurt/M.: S. Fischer, 1983)
Der Proceß, ed. Pasley, M. (Frankfurt/M.: S. Fischer, 1990)
Das Schloß, ed. Pasley, M. (Frankfurt/M.: S. Fischer, 1982)
Tagebücher, ed. Koch, H.-G., Müller, M. and Pasley, M., 2 vols (Frankfurt/M.: S. Fischer, 1990)
Nachgelassene Schriften und Fragmente, ed. Born, J., Neumann, G., Pasley, M. and Schillemeit, J., 4 vols (Frankfurt/M.: S. Fischer, 1992/93)

The numbers and titles of all the volumes in the paperback edition are as follows:

GW 1 = *Ein Landarzt und andere Drucke zu Lebzeiten*
GW 2 = *Der Verschollene*
GW 3 = *Der Proceß*
GW 4 = *Das Schloß*
GW 5 = *Beschreibung eines Kampfes und andere Schriften aus dem Nachlaß*

GW   6 =   *Beim Bau der chinesischen Mauer und andere Schriften aus dem Nachlaß*
GW   7 =   *Zur Frage der Gesetze und andere Schriften aus dem Nachlaß*
GW   8 =   *Das Ehepaar und andere Schriften aus dem Nachlaß*
GW   9 =   *Tagebücher. Band 1: 1909–1912*
GW 10 =   *Tagebücher. Band 2: 1912–1914*
GW 11 =   *Tagebücher. Band 3: 1914–1923*
GW 12 =   *Reisetagebücher*

Kafka's letters are cited from the following editions:
Briefe 1902–1924, ed. Brod, M. (Frankfurt/M.: S. Fischer, 1958), abbreviated to (B)
Briefe an Felice und andere Korrespondenz aus der Verlobungszeit, ed. Heller, E. and Born, J. (Frankfurt/M.: S. Fischer, 1967), abbreviated to (BF)
Briefe an Milena, ed. Born, J. and Müller, M. (Frankfurt/M.: S. Fischer, 1983), abbreviated to (BM)
Franz Kafka. Der Dichter über sein Werk, ed. Heller, E. and Beug, J. (Munich: Deutscher Taschenbuch Verlag, 1977), abbreviated to (DW); an anthology of Kafka's comments on writing.

2 Works by other authors

Brecht, Bertolt, *Große kommentierte Berliner und Frankfurter Ausgabe. Stücke 2* (Berlin, Weimar and Frankfurt/M.: Aufbau/Suhrkamp, 1988)
Goethe, Johann Wolfgang, *Faust*, ed. Trunz, E. (Munich: C.H. Beck, 1963)
—— *Wilhelm Meisters Lehrjahre*, Berliner Ausgabe, vol. 10 (Berlin: Aufbau, 1976)
Hofmannsthal, Hugo von, 'Ein Brief' in: *Gesammelte Werke*, vol. 7 (Frankfurt/M.: S. Fischer, 1979)
Mann, Thomas, *Tonio Kröger. Mario und der Zauberer* (Frankfurt/M.: Fischer Taschenbuch Verlag, 1973)
Nietzsche, Friedrich, 'Ecce Homo', in: *Basic Writings of Nietzsche*, trans. Kaufmann, Walter (New York: Vintage Books, 1968)
Schiller, Friedrich, *On the Aesthetic Education of Man*, ed./trans. Wilkinson, E.M. and Willoughby, L.A. (Oxford: Clarendon Press, 1967)
Schopenhauer, Arthur, *The World as Will and Idea*, trans. Haldane, R. and Kemp, J. (London: Keegan Paul and Trench, 1906)

B. CRITICAL AND BACKGROUND LITERATURE

1 Bibliography and surveys of critical literature

Beicken, P.U., *Franz Kafka. Eine kritische Einführung in die Forschung* (Frankfurt/M.: Athenäum, 1974)
Caputo-Mayr, M.L. and Herz, J., *Franz Kafka. Eine kommentierte Bibliographie der Sekundärliteratur* (Berne and Stuttgart: Francke, 1987)
Dietz, L., *Franz Kafka* (Stuttgart: Metzler, ²1990)
Dodd, W.J. (ed.), *Kafka. 'The Metamorphosis', 'The Trial', and 'The Castle'* (London and New York: Longman, 1995)

Heintz, G. (ed.), *Zu Franz Kafka* (Stuttgart: Klett, 1979)

Hughes, K., 'Kafka-Research 1974–79', in: *New German Critique* 22 (1981), pp. 163–83

Kempf, F.R., *Everyone's Darling. Kafka and the Critics of his Short Fiction* (Columbia: Camden House, 1994)

Krusche, D., *Kafka und Kafka-Deutung. Die problematisierte Interaktion* (Munich: Wilhelm Fink, 1974)

Robertson, R., 'In Search of the Historical Kafka. A Selective Review of Research 1980–92', *The Modern Language Review* 89/1 (1994), pp. 107–37

Rolleston, J., 'Kafka Criticism. A Typological Perspective in the Centenary Year', in: Udoff, A. (ed.), *Kafka and the Contemporary Critical Performance* (Bloomington: University of Indiana Press, 1987), pp. 1–32

2 Biographical, historical and religious background

Amann, J., *Das Symbol Kafka* (Berne: Francke, 1974)

Anderson, M. (ed.), *Reading Kafka. Prague, Politics and the Fin de Siècle* (New York: Schocken, 1989)

Anz, Th., *Franz Kafka* (Munich: C.H. Beck, 1989)

Beck, E.T., *Kafka and the Yiddish Theater. Its Impact on his Work* (Madison, Milwaukee and London: University of Wisconsin Press, 1971)

Beicken, P., *Franz Kafka. Leben und Werk* (Stuttgart: Klett, 1990)

Binder, H., *Franz Kafka. Leben und Persönlichkeit* (Stuttgart: Kröner, 1990)

—— *Kafka-Handbuch*, vol. 1 (Stuttgart: Kröner, 1979)

Born, J. (ed.), *Franz Kafka. Kritik und Rezeption zu seinen Lebzeiten 1912–1924* (Frankfurt/M.: S. Fischer, 1979)

Brod, M., *Franz Kafka. A Biography*, trans. Humphreys Roberts, G. and Winston, R. (New York: Schocken, 1963)

—— *Der Prager Kreis*, Nachwort von Peter Demetz (Frankfurt/M.: Suhrkamp, 1979)

—— *Über Franz Kafka* (Frankfurt/M.: Fischer Bücherei, 1966)

Canetti, E., *Das Gewissen der Worte. Essays* (Munich and Vienna: Hanser, 1983)

Gilman, S., *Franz Kafka. The Jewish Patient* (London: Routledge, 1996)

Grant, P., *Literature of Mysticism in Western Tradition* (London: Macmillan, 1983)

Grözinger, K.E., *Kafka and Kabbalah* (New York: Continuum, 1994)

Grözinger K.E., Moses, S. and Zimmermann, H.D. (eds), *Kafka und das Judentum* (Frankfurt/M.: Athenäum, 1987)

Hayman, R., *K. A Biography of Kafka* (London: Weidenfeld and Nicolson, 1981)

Holitscher, A., *Amerika – heute und morgen* (Berlin: S. Fischer, 1912)

Janouch, G., *Gespräche mit Kafka* (Frankfurt/M.: S. Fischer, 1968)

Mailloux, P., *A Hesitation before Birth. A Life of Franz Kafka* (London and Toronto: Associated University Presses, 1989)

Northey, A., *Kafka's Relatives. Their Lives and his Writing* (New Haven and London: Yale University Press, 1991)

—— 'Die Kafkas. Juden? Christen? Tschechen? Deutsche?', in: Krolop, K. and Zimmermann, H.D. (eds), *Kafka und Prag* (Berlin and New York: de Gruyter, 1994), pp. 11–32

Pawel, E., *The Nightmare of Reason. A Life of Franz Kafka* (New York: Giroux, 1984)

Stern, J.P. (ed.), *The World of Franz Kafka* (London: Weidenfeld and Nicolson, 1980)

Stölzl, C., *Kafkas böses Böhmen. Zur Sozialgeschichte eines Prager Juden* (Munich: edition text + kritik, 1975)

Unseld, J., *Franz Kafka. Ein Schriftstellerleben. Die Geschichte seiner Veröffentlichungen* (Frankfurt/M.: S. Fischer, 1984)

Wagenbach, K., *Franz Kafka. Eine Biographie seiner Jugend 1883–1912* (Berne: Francke, 1958)

—— *Franz Kafka. Bilder aus seinem Leben* (Berlin: Verlag Klaus Wagenbach, 1989)

3 General literary criticism

Adamzik, S., *Kafka. Topographie der Macht* (Basle and Frankfurt/M.: Stroemfeld/ Roter Stern, 1992)

Anders, G. *Franz Kafka* (London: Bowes and Bowes, 1960)

Anderson, M., *Kafka's Clothes. Ornament and Aestheticism in the Habsburg 'Fin de Siècle'* (Oxford: Clarendon Press, 1992)

Arnold, H.L. (ed.), *Franz Kafka. Sonderband* (Munich: edition text + kritik, 1994)

Baumgart, R., *Selbstvergessenheit. Drei Wege zum Werk. Thomas Mann, Franz Kafka, Bertolt Brecht* (Munich: Hanser, 1989)

Beißner, F., *Der Erzähler Franz Kafka*, intro. Keller, W. (Frankfurt/M.: Suhrkamp, 1983)

Bernheimer, C., *Flaubert and Kafka. Studies in Psychopoetic Structure* (New Haven and London: Yale University Press, 1982)

Binder, H., *Kafka-Handbuch*, vol. 2 (Stuttgart: Kröner, 1979)

—— *Kafka-Kommentar zu den Romanen, Rezensionen, Aphorismen und zum Brief an den Vater*, vol. 2 (Munich: Winkler, 1976)

—— *Kafka. Der Schaffensprozeß* (Frankfurt/M.: Suhrkamp, 1983)

Born, J., Dietz, L., Pasley, M., Raabe, P., Wagenbach, K. (eds), *Kafka-Symposion* (Berlin: Verlag Klaus Wagenbach, 1965)

Corngold, S., *The Commentators' Despair. The Interpretation of Kafka's 'Metamorphosis'* (Port Washington and London: The Kennikat Press, 1973)

—— 'Angst und Schreiben in einer frühen Aufzeichnung Kafkas', in: Caputo-Mayr, M.L. (ed.), *Franz Kafka Symposium* (Berlin: Agora, 1978), pp. 59–70.

—— *The Fate of the Self. German Writers and French Theory* (New York: Columbia University Press, 1986)

—— *Franz Kafka. The Necessity of Form* (Ithaca and London: Cornell University Press, 1988)

Deleuze, G. and Guattari, F., *Kafka. Toward a Minor Literature*, trans. Ponan, D. (Minneapolis: University of Minnesota Press, 1986)

Emrich, W., *Franz Kafka. A Critical Study of his Writings*, trans. Zeben Buehne, S. (New York: Frederick Ungar, 1984)

Flores, A. (ed.), *The Kafka Debate. New Perspectives for our Time* (New York: Gordian Press, 1977)

Foulkes, A.P., *The Reluctant Pessimist. A Study of Franz Kafka* (The Hague/Paris: Mouton, 1967)

Gray, R. (ed.), *Kafka. A Collection of Critical Essays* (Englewood Cliffs, N.J.: Prentice-Hall, 1962)

—— *Franz Kafka* (Cambridge: Cambridge University Press, 1973)

Heidsieck, A., *The Intellectual Contexts of Kafka's Fiction. Philosophy, Law, Religion* (Columbia: Camden House, 1994)

Heller, E., *Franz Kafka* (Glasgow: Fontana/Collins, 1974)

Hermsdorf, K., *Kafka. Weltbild und Roman* (Berlin: Rütten und Loening, 1961)

Hibberd, J., *Kafka in Context* (London: Studio Vista, 1975)

Kobs, J., *Kafka. Untersuchungen zu Bewußtsein und Sprache seiner Gestalten*, ed. Brech, U. (Bad Homburg: Athenäum, 1970)

Koelb, C., *Kafka's Rhetoric. The Passion of Reading* (Ithaca and London: Cornell University Press, 1989)

Kraft, H., *Mondheimat-Kafka* (Pfullingen: Verlag Günther Neske, 1983)

Kuna, F., *Franz Kafka. Literature as Corrective Punishment* (London: Paul Elek, 1974)

——(ed.) *On Kafka. Semi-Centenary Perspectives* (London: Paul Elek, 1976)

Kurz, G., *Traum-Schrecken. Kafkas literarische Existenzanalyse* (Stuttgart: Metzler, 1980)

Lukács, G., *Die Theorie des Romans* (Darmstadt and Neuwied: Luchterhand, 1963)

Matt, P. von, *... fertig ist das Angesicht. Zur Literaturgeschichte des menschlichen Gesichts* (Munich and Vienna: Hanser, 1983)

Müller-Seidel, W., 'Franz Kafkas *Brief an den Vater*. Ein literarischer Text der Moderne', *Orbis Litterarum* 42 (1987), pp. 353–74

Neider, C., *The Frozen Sea. A Study of Franz Kafka* (New York: Oxford University Press, 1948)

Pascal, R., *Kafka's Narrators. A Study of his Stories and Sketches* (Cambridge: Cambridge University Press, 1982)

Pasley, M., *'Die Schrift ist unveränderlich...'. Essays zu Kafka* (Frankfurt/M.: Fischer Taschenbuch Verlag, 1995)

Politzer, H., *Franz Kafka. Parable and Paradox* (Ithaca and New York: Cornell University Press, 1966)

——(ed.), *Franz Kafka* (Darmstadt: Wissenschaftliche Buchgesellschaft, 1973)

Ramm, K., *Reduktion als Erzählprinzip bei Kafka* (Frankfurt/M.: Athenäum, 1971)

Robert, M., *Franz Kafka's Loneliness*, trans. Manheim, R. (London: Faber and Faber, 1981)

Robertson, R., *Kafka. Judaism, Politics, and Literature* (Oxford: Clarendon Press, 1985)

Rolleston, J., *Kafka's Narrative Theater* (University Park and London: Pennsylvania State University Press, 1974)

Ryan, L., ' "Zum letzten Mal Psychologie!" Zur psychologischen Deutbarkeit der Werke Franz Kafkas', in: Paulsen, W. (ed.), *Psychologie in der Literaturwissenschaft* (Heidelberg: Lothar Stiehm, 1971), pp. 157–73

Sokel, W. R., *Franz Kafka. Tragik und Ironie. Zur Struktur seiner Kunst* (Munich and Vienna: Langen und Müller, 1964)

Spann, M., *Franz Kafka* (London: George Prior, 1976)

Stern, J.P., *The Dear Purchase. A Theme in German Modernism* (Cambridge: Cambridge University Press, 1995)

Stern J.P. and White, J.J. (eds), *Paths and Labyrinths* (London: Institute of Germanic Studies, 1985)

Thorlby, A., *A Student's Guide to Kafka* (London: Heinemann, 1972)

Udoff, A. (ed.), *Kafka and the Contemporary Critical Performance* (Bloomington: Indiana University Press, 1987)

Vogl, J., *Ort der Gewalt. Kafkas literarische Ethik* (Munich: Wilhelm Fink, 1990)

Walser, M., *Beschreibung einer Form* (Munich: Hanser, 1961)

4 Commentaries on the novels

The Missing Person

Abraham, U., *Der verhörte Held. Recht und Schuld im Werk Franz Kafkas* (Munich: Wilhelm Fink, 1985)

Hiebel, H.H., 'Parabelform und Rechtsthematik in Franz Kafkas Romanfragment *Der Verschollene*', in: Elm, T. and Hiebel, H.H. (eds), *Die Parabel. Parabolische Formen in der deutschen Dichtung des 20. Jahrhunderts* (Frankfurt/M.: Suhrkamp, 1986), pp. 219–54.

Hillmann, H., 'Kafkas *Amerika*. Literatur als Problemlösungsspiel', in: Brauneck, M. (ed.), *Der deutsche Roman im 20. Jahrhundert* (Bamberg: Buchner, 1976), vol. 1, pp. 135–58

Jahn, W., 'Kafkas Handschrift zum *Verschollenen (Amerika)*. Ein vorläufiger Textbericht', *Jahrbuch der deutschen Schillergesellschaft* 9 (1965), pp. 541–52

—— *Kafkas Roman 'Der Verschollene' ('Amerika')* (Stuttgart: Metzler, 1965)

von Matt, P., 'Kafkas Venus', in: von Matt, P., *Das Schicksal der Phantasie* (Munich: Hanser, 1994), pp. 292–6

Neumann, G., 'Der Wanderer und der Verschollene. Zum Problem der Identität in Goethes *Wilhelm Meister* und in Kafkas *Amerika*-Roman', in: Stern, J.P. and White, J.J. (eds), *Paths and Labyrinths* (London: Institute of Germanic Studies, 1985), pp. 43–65

Nicolai, R.R., *Kafkas Amerika-Roman 'Der Verschollene'. Motive und Gestalten* (Würzburg: Königshausen und Neumann, 1981)

Plachta, B., '*Der Verschollene*', in: *Franz Kafka. Romane und Erzählungen*, ed. Müller, M. (Stuttgart: Reclam, 1994), pp. 75–97

Pütz, J., *Kafkas 'Verschollener', ein Bildungsroman?* (Frankfurt/M.: Peter Lang, 1983)

Ruf, U., *Franz Kafka. Das Dilemma der Söhne* (Berlin: Erich Schmidt, 1974)

Sokel, W., 'Zwischen Drohung und Errettung. Zur Funktion Amerikas in Kafkas Roman *Der Verschollene*', in: Bauschinger S., Denkler H. and Malsch W. (eds), *Amerika in der deutschen Literatur* (Stuttgart: Reclam, 1975), pp. 246–71

Spilka, M., *Dickens and Kafka. A Mutual Interpretation* (Bloomington: Indiana University Press, 1963)

Steiner, C., 'Kafkas Amerika. Illusion oder Wirklichkeit?', in: Caputo-Mayr, M.L. (ed.), *Franz Kafka Symposium* (Berlin: Agora, 1978), pp. 46–58

Thalmann, J., *Wege zu Kafka. Eine Interpretation des Amerika-Romans* (Stuttgart: Frauenfeld, 1966)

Wirkner, A., *Kafka und die Außenwelt. Quellenstudien zum 'Amerika'-Fragment* (Stuttgart: Klett, 1976)

The Trial

Abraham, U., 'Rechtsspruch und Machtwort. Zum Verhältnis von Rechtsordnung und Ordnungsmacht bei Kafka', in: Kittler, W. and Neumann, G. (eds), *Franz Kafka. Schriftverkehr* (Freiburg: Rombach, 1990), pp. 248–78

Binder, H., '*Vor dem Gesetz'. Einführung in Kafkas Welt* (Stuttgart and Weimar: Metzler, 1993)

Dodd, W.J., *Kafka. 'Der Prozeß'* (Glasgow: University of Glasgow French and German Publications, 1991)

Engelmann, P. (ed.), *Préjugés. 'Vor dem Gesetz'* (Vienna: Passagen Verlag, 1992)

Fingerhut, K., 'Franz Kafka. *Der Prozeß'*, in: Lehmann, J. (ed.), *Deutsche Romane von Grimmelshausen bis Walser* (Kronberg/Ts.: Scriptor, 1982), pp. 143–76

Hiebel, H.H., *Die Zeichen des Gesetzes. Recht und Macht bei Franz Kafka* (Munich: Wilhelm Fink, 1983)

——'Schuld oder Scheinbarkeit der Schuld? Zu Kafkas Roman *Der Proceß'*, in: Kraus, W. and Winkler, N. (eds), *Das Schuldproblem bei Franz Kafka* (Vienna, Cologne and Weimar: Böhlau, 1994), pp. 95–117

Jeziorkowski, K., ' "Bei dieser Sinnlosigkeit des Ganzen." Zu Franz Kafkas Roman *Der Proceß'*, in: *Franz Kafka. Sonderband* (Munich: edition text + kritik, 1994), pp. 200–17

Kudszus, W., 'Changing Perspectives in *The Trial* and *The Castle'*, in: Flores, A. (ed.), *The Kafka Debate. New Perspectives for our Time* (New York: Gordian Press, 1977), pp. 385–95

Lubkoll, C., ' "Man muß nicht alles für wahr halten, man muß es nur für notwendig halten." Die Theorie der Macht in Franz Kafkas Roman *Der Proceß'*, in: Kittler, W. and Neumann, G. (eds), *Franz Kafka. Schriftverkehr* (Freiburg: Rombach, 1990), pp. 279–94

Marson, E., *Kafka's 'Trial'. The Case against Josef K.* (St Lucia, Queensland: University of Queensland Press, 1975)

Müller, M., *'Der Proceß'*, in: *Romane des 20. Jahrhunderts*, vol. 1 (Stuttgart: Reclam, 1993), pp. 101–27

——(ed.), *Franz Kafka, 'Der Proceß'. Erläuterungen und Dokumente* (Stuttgart: Reclam, 1993)

O'Neill, P., 'The Comedy of Stasis. Narration and Knowledge in Kafka's *Prozeß'*, in: Struc, R. and Yardley, J.C. (eds), *Franz Kafka (1883–1983). His Craft and Thought* (Waterloo, Ontario: Wilfred Laurier University Press, 1986), pp. 49–73

Pasley, M. (ed.), *Franz Kafka. 'Der Proceß'. Die Handschrift redet*, in: *Marbacher Magazin*, Heft 52 (1990), pp. 5–40

Robertson, R., *'Der Proceß'*, in: *Franz Kafka. Romane und Erzählungen*, ed. Müller, M. (Stuttgart: Reclam, 1994), pp. 98–145

Rolleston, J. (ed.), *Twentieth-Century Interpretations of 'The Trial'. A Collection of Critical Essays* (Englewood Cliffs, N.J.: Prentice Hall, 1976)

Sauerland, K., 'Der ideale Machtapparat und das Individuum', in: Zimmermann, H.D. (ed.), *Nach erneuter Lektüre. Franz Kafkas 'Der Proceß'* (Würzburg: Königshausen und Neumann, 1992), pp. 235–50

Sheppard, R., *'The Trial, The Castle*. Towards an Analytical Comparison', in: Flores, A. (ed.), *The Kafka Debate. New Perspectives for our Time* (New York: Gordian Press, 1977), pp. 396–417

Siefken, H., *Kafka. Ungeduld und Lässigkeit. Zu den Romanen 'Der Prozeß' und 'Das Schloß'* (Munich: Wilhelm Fink, 1977)

Sokel, W., 'The Programme of K.'s Court. Oedipal and Existential Meanings of *The Trial'*, in: Kuna, F. (ed.), *On Kafka. Semi-Centenary Perspectives* (London: Paul Elek, 1976), pp. 1–21

Speidel, W., *A Complete Contextual Concordance to Franz Kafka 'Der Prozeß'* (Leeds: W.S. Maney, 1978)

Stern, J.P., 'The Law of *The Trial'*, in: Kuna, F. (ed.), *On Kafka. Semi-Centenary Perspectives* (London: Paul Elek, 1976), pp. 22–41

Voigts, M. (ed.), *Franz Kafka. 'Vor dem Gesetz'. Aufsätze und Materialien* (Würzburg: Königshausen und Neumann, 1994)

Zimmermann, H.D. (ed.), *Nach erneuter Lektüre. Franz Kafkas 'Der Proceß'* (Würzburg: Königshausen und Neumann, 1992)

The Castle

Cohn, D., 'K. Enters *The Castle*. On the Change of Person in Kafka's Manuscript', *Euphorion* 62/1 (1968), pp. 28–45

Dowden, Stephen, *Kafka's Castle and the Critical Imagination* (Columbia: Camden House, 1995)

Gray, R., *Kafka's Castle* (Cambridge: Cambridge University Press, 1956)

Keller, K., *Gesellschaft in mythischem Bann* (Wiesbaden: Akademischer Verlag Athenaion, 1977)

Kudszus, W., 'Erzählhaltung und Zeitverschiebung in Kafkas "Prozeß" und "Schloß"', in: Politzer, H. (ed.), *Franz Kafka* (Darmstadt: Wissenschaftliche Buchgesellschaft, 1973), pp. 331–50

Moníková, L., '*Das Schloß* als Diskurs. Die Entstehung der Macht aus Projektionen', *Sprache im technischen Zeitalter* 85 (1983), pp. 98–106

Müller, M., '*Das Schloß*', in: *Franz Kafka. Romane und Erzählungen*, ed. Müller, M. (Stuttgart: Reclam, 1994), pp. 253–84

Neumeyer, P.F. (ed.), *Twentieth-Century Interpretations of 'The Castle'* (Englewood Cliffs, N.J.: Prentice Hall, 1969)

Nicolai, R., *Ende oder Anfang. Zur Einheit der Gegensätze in Kafkas 'Schloß'* (Munich: Wilhelm Fink, 1977)

Philippi, K.P., *Reflexion und Wirklichkeit. Untersuchungen zu Kafkas Roman 'Das Schloß'* (Tübingen: Niemeyer, 1965)

Reed, T.J., 'Kafka und Schopenhauer. Philosophisches Denken und dichterisches Bild', *Euphorion* 59 (1965), pp. 160–72

Robert, M., *L'Ancien et le nouveau. De Don Quichotte à Franz Kafka* (Paris: Grasset, 1963)

Sheppard, R., *On Kafka's Castle. A Study* (London: Croom Helm, 1973)

Index

Page numbers in brackets indicate an implicit reference to the item concerned.

159